A Budget of Christmas Tales

Charles Dickens and others

[ZHINGOORA BOOKS]

~ 1 ~

TABLE OF CONTENTS.

CHRISTMAS TALES.

A CHRISTMAS CAROL.

BY CHARLES DICKENS.

Stave One.

MARLEY'S GHOST.

Marley was dead, to begin with. There is no doubt whatever about that. The register of his burial was signed by the clergyman, the clerk, the undertaker, and the chief mourner. Scrooge signed it. And Scrooge's name was good upon 'Change, for anything he chose to put his hand to.

Old Marley was dead as a door-nail.

Scrooge knew he was dead? Of course he did. How could it be otherwise? Scrooge and he were partners for I don't know how many years. Scrooge was his sole executor, his sole administrator, his sole assign, his sole residuary legatee, his sole friend, and sole mourner. And even Scrooge was not so dreadfully cut up by the sad event, but that he was an excellent man of business on the very day of the funeral, and solemnized it with an undoubted bargain.

The mention of Marley's funeral brings me back to the point I started from. There is no doubt that Marley was dead. This must be distinctly understood, or nothing wonderful can come of the story I am going to relate.

Scrooge never painted out Old Marley's name. There it stood, years afterward, above the warehouse door: Scrooge and Marley. The firm was known as Scrooge and Marley. Sometimes people new to the business called Scrooge Scrooge, and sometimes Marley, but he answered to both names. It was all the same to him.

Oh! But he was a tight-fisted hand at the grindstone, Scrooge! a squeezing, wrenching, grasping, scraping, clutching, covetous, old sinner! Hard and sharp as flint, from which no steel had ever struck out generous fire; secret and self-contained, and solitary as an oyster. The cold within him froze his old features, nipped his pointed nose, shriveled his cheek, stiffened his gait; made his eyes red, his thin lips blue; and spoke out shrewdly in his grating voice. A frosty rime on his head, and on his eyebrows, and his wiry chin.

External heat and cold had little influence on Scrooge. No warmth could warm, no wintry weather chill him. No wind that blew was bitterer than he, no falling snow was more intent upon its purpose, no pelting rain less open to entreaty. Foul weather didn't know where to have him. The heaviest rain, and snow, and hail, and sleet, could boast of the advantage over him in only one respect. They often "came down" handsomely, and Scrooge never did.

Nobody ever stopped him in the street to say, with gladsome looks, "My dear Scrooge, how are you? When will you come to see me?" No beggars implored him to bestow a trifle, no children asked him what it was o'clock, no man or woman ever once in all his life inquired the way to such and such a place, of Scrooge.

But what did Scrooge care? It was the very thing he liked. To edge his way along the crowded paths of life, warning all human sympathy to keep its distance, was what the knowing ones call "nuts" to Scrooge.

[Pg 15]

Once upon a time—of all the good days in the year, on Christmas Eve—old Scrooge sat busy in his counting-house. It was cold, bleak, biting weather: foggy withal: and he could hear the people in the court outside, go wheezing up and down, beating their hands upon their breasts, and stamping their feet upon the pavement stones to warm them. The city clocks had only just gone three, but it was quite dark already—it had not been light all day—and candles were flaring in the windows of the neighboring offices, like ruddy smears upon the palpable brown air.

The door of Scrooge's counting-house was open, that he might keep his eye upon his clerk, who in a dismal little cell beyond, a sort of tank, was copying letters. Scrooge had a very small fire, but the clerk's fire was so very much smaller that it looked like one coal. But he couldn't replenish it, for Scrooge kept the coal-box in his own room; and so surely as the clerk came in with the shovel, the master predicted that it would be necessary for them to part. Wherefore the clerk put on his white comforter, and tried to warm himself at the candle; in which effort, not being a man of strong imagination, he failed.

"A merry Christmas, uncle! God save you!" cried a cheerful voice. It was the voice of Scrooge's nephew, who came upon him so quickly that this was the first intimation he had of his approach.

"Bah!" said Scrooge. "Humbug!"

He had so heated himself with rapid walking in the fog and frost, this nephew of Scrooge's, that he was all in a glow; his face was ruddy and handsome; his eyes sparkled, and his breath smoked again.

"Christmas a humbug, uncle!" said Scrooge's nephew. "You don't mean that, I am sure?"

"I do," said Scrooge. "Merry Christmas! What right have you to be merry? What reason have you to be merry? You're poor enough."

"Come then," returned the nephew gaily. "What right have you to be dismal? What reason have you to be morose? You're rich enough."

Scrooge having no better answer ready on the spur of the moment, said, "Bah!" again; and followed it up with, "Keep Christmas in your own way, and let me keep it in mine."

"Keep it!" repeated Scrooge's nephew. "But you don't keep it."

"Let me leave it alone, then," said Scrooge. "Much good may it do you! Much good it has ever done you!"

"There are many things from which I might have derived good, by which I have not profited, I dare say," returned the nephew, "Christmas among the rest. But I am sure I have always thought of Christmas time, when it has come round—apart from the veneration due to its sacred name and origin, if anything belonging to it can be apart from that—as a good time; a kind, forgiving, charitable, pleasant time; the only time I know of, in the long calendar of the year, when men and women seem by one consent to open their shut-up hearts freely, and to think of people below them as if they really were fellow-passengers to the grave, and not another race of creatures bound on other journeys. And therefore, uncle, though it has never put a scrap of gold or silver in my pocket, I believe that it *has* done me good, and *will* do me good; and I say, God bless it!"

The clerk in the tank involuntarily applauded. Becoming immediately sensible of the impropriety, he poked the fire, and extinguished the last frail spark for ever.

"Let me hear another sound from *you*," said Scrooge, "and you'll keep your Christmas by losing your situation. You're quite a powerful speaker, sir," he added, turning to his nephew. "I wonder you don't go into Parliament."

"Don't be angry, uncle. Come! Dine with us to-morrow."

Scrooge said that he would see him—yes, indeed he did. He went the whole length of the expression, and said that he would see him in that extremity first.

"But why?" cried Scrooge's nephew, "Why?"

"Why did you get married?" said Scrooge.

"Because I fell in love."

"Because you fell in love!" growled Scrooge, as if that were the only one thing in the world more ridiculous than a merry Christmas. "Good afternoon!"

"Nay, uncle, but you never came to see me before that happened. Why give it as a reason for not coming now?"

"Good afternoon," said Scrooge.

"I want nothing from you; I ask nothing of you; why cannot we be friends?"

"Good afternoon," said Scrooge.

"I am sorry, with all my heart, to find you so resolute. We have never had any quarrel, to which I have been a party. But I have made the trial in homage to Christmas, and I'll keep my Christmas humor to the last. So a Merry Christmas, uncle!"

"Good afternoon!" said Scrooge.

"And a Happy New Year!"

"Good afternoon!" said Scrooge.

His nephew left the room without an angry word, notwithstanding. He stopped at the outer door to bestow the greetings of the season on the clerk, who, cold as he was, was warmer than Scrooge; for he returned them cordially.

"There's another fellow," muttered Scrooge; who overheard him: "my clerk, with fifteen shillings a week, and a wife and family, talking about a merry Christmas. I'll retire to Bedlam."

This lunatic, in letting Scrooge's nephew out, had let two other people in. They were portly gentlemen, pleasant to behold, and now stood, with their hats off, in Scrooge's office. They had books and papers in their hands, and bowed to him.

"Scrooge and Marley's, I believe," said one of the gentlemen, referring to his list. "Have I the pleasure of addressing Mr. Scrooge, or Mr. Marley?"

"Mr. Marley has been dead these seven years," Scrooge replied. "He died seven years ago, this very night."

"We have no doubt his liberality is well represented by his surviving partner," said the gentleman, presenting his credentials.

It certainly was; for they had been two kindred spirits. At the ominous word "liberality," Scrooge frowned, and shook his head, and handed the credentials back.

"At this festive season of the year, Mr. Scrooge," said the gentleman, taking up a pen, "it is more than usually desirable that we should make some slight provision for the poor and destitute, who suffer greatly at the present time. Many thousands are in want of common necessaries; hundreds of thousands are in want of common comforts, sir."

"Are there no prisons?" asked Scrooge.

"Plenty of prisons," said the gentleman, laying down the pen again.

"And the Union workhouses?" demanded Scrooge. "Are they still in operation?"

"They are. Still," returned the gentleman, "I wish I could say they were not. Under the impression that they scarcely furnish Christian cheer of mind or body to the multitude, a few of us are endeavoring to raise a fund to buy the poor some meat and drink, and means of warmth. We choose this time, because it is a time, of all others, when Want is keenly felt, and Abundance rejoices. What shall I put you down for?"

"Nothing!" Scrooge replied.

"You wish to be anonymous?"

"I wish to be left alone," said Scrooge. "Since you ask me what I wish, gentlemen, that is my answer. I don't make merry myself at Christmas, and I can't afford to make idle people merry. I help to support the establishments I have mentioned—they cost enough; and those who are badly off must go there."

"Many can't go there; and many would rather die."

"If they would rather die," said Scrooge, "they had better do it, and decrease the surplus population. Besides—excuse me—I don't know that."

"But you might know it," observed the gentleman.

"It's not my business," Scrooge returned. "It's enough for a man to understand his own business, and not to interfere with other people's. Mine occupies me constantly. Good afternoon, gentlemen!"

Seeing clearly that it would be useless to pursue their point, the gentlemen withdrew. Scrooge resumed his labors with an improved opinion of himself, and in a more facetious temper than was usual with him.

At length the hour of shutting up the counting-house arrived. With an ill-will Scrooge dismounted from his stool, and tacitly admitted the fact to the expectant clerk in the tank, who instantly snuffed his candle out, and put on his hat.

"You'll want all day to-morrow, I suppose?" said Scrooge.

"If quite convenient, sir."

"It's not convenient," said Scrooge, "and it's not fair. If I was to stop half-a-crown for it, you'd think yourself ill-used, I'll be bound?"

The clerk smiled faintly.

"And yet," said Scrooge, "you don't think me ill-used, when I pay a day's wages for no work."

The clerk observed that it was only once a year.

"A poor excuse for picking a man's pocket every twenty-fifth of December!" said Scrooge, buttoning his great coat to the chin. "But I suppose you must have the whole day. Be here all the earlier next morning."

The clerk promised that he would; and Scrooge walked out with a growl. The office was closed in a twinkling, and the clerk, with the long ends of his white comforter dangling below his waist (for he boasted no great coat), went down a slide on Cornhill, at the end of a lane of boys, twenty times, in honor of its being Christmas-eve, and then ran home to Camden Town as hard as he could pelt, to play at blindman's buff.

Scrooge took his melancholy dinner in his usual melancholy tavern; and having read all the newspapers, and beguiled the rest of the evening with his banker's-book, went home to bed. He lived in chambers which had once belonged to his deceased partner. They were a gloomy suite of rooms, in a lowering pile of building up a yard, where it had so little business to be, that one could scarcely help fancying it must have run there when it was a young house, playing at hide-and-seek with other houses, and have forgotten the way out again. It was old enough now, and dreary enough; for nobody lived in it but Scrooge, the other rooms being all let out as offices.

Every room above, and every cask in the wine-merchant's cellars below, appeared to have a separate peal of echoes of its own. Scrooge was not a man to be frightened by echoes. He fastened the door, and walked across the hall, and up the stairs; slowly too: trimming his candle as he went. Half a dozen gas-lamps out of the street wouldn't have lighted the entry too well, so you may suppose that it was pretty dark with Scrooge's dip.

Up Scrooge went, not caring a button for that. Darkness is cheap, and Scrooge liked it. But before he shut his heavy door, he walked through his rooms to see that all was right.

Quite satisfied, he closed his door, and locked himself in; double-locked himself in, which was not his custom. Thus secured against surprise, he, took off his cravat; put on his dressing gown and slippers, and his night-cap; and sat down before the fire to take his gruel. As he threw his head back in the chair, his glance happened to rest upon a bell, a disused bell, that hung in the room, and communicated for some purpose now forgotten with a chamber in the highest story of the building. It was with great astonishment, and with a strange, inexplicable dread, that as he looked, he saw this bell begin to swing. It swung so softly in the outset that it scarcely made a sound; but soon it rang out loudly, and so did every bell in the house.

This might have lasted half a minute, or a minute, but it seemed an hour. The bells ceased as they had begun, together. They were succeeded by a clanking noise deep down below, as if some person were dragging a heavy chain over the casks in the wine-merchant's cellar. Scrooge then remembered to have heard that ghosts in haunted houses were described as dragging chains.

The cellar-door flew open with a booming sound, and then he heard the noise much louder, on the floors below; then coming up the stairs; then coming straight toward his door.

"It's humbug still!" said Scrooge. "I won't believe it."

His color changed though, when, without a pause, it came on through the heavy door, and passed into the room before his eyes. Upon its coming in, the dying flame leaped up, as though it cried "I know him! Marley's ghost!" and fell again.

The same face: the very same. The chain he drew was clasped about his middle. It was long and wound about him like a tail; and it was made (for Scrooge observed it closely) of cash-boxes, keys, padlocks, ledgers, deeds, and heavy purses wrought in steel.

"How now" said Scrooge, caustic and cold as ever. "What do you want with me?"

"Much!"—Marley's voice, no doubt about it.

"Who are you?"

"Ask me who I was."

"Who were you then?" said Scrooge, raising his voice. "You're particular, for a shade." He was going to say "to a shade," but substituted this, as more appropriate.

"In life I was your partner, Jacob Marley."

"Can you—can you sit down?" asked Scrooge, looking doubtfully at him.

"I can."

"Do it, then."

Scrooge asked the question, because he didn't know whether a ghost so transparent might find himself in a condition to take a chair; and felt that in the event of its being impossible, it might involve the necessity of an embarrassing explanation. But the Ghost sat down on the opposite side of the fireplace, as if he were quite used to it.

Scrooge fell upon his knees, and clasped his hands before his face.

"Mercy!" he said, "Dreadful apparition, why do you trouble me?"

"Man of the worldly mind!" replied the Ghost, "do you believe in me or not?"

"I do," said Scrooge. "I must. But why do spirits walk the earth, and why do they come to me?"

"It is required of every man," the Ghost returned, "that the spirit within him should walk abroad among his fellow-men, and travel far and wide; and if that spirit goes not forth in life, it is condemned to do so after death. It is doomed to wander through the world—oh, woe is me!—and witness what it cannot share, but might have shared on earth, and turned to happiness!"

The spectre raised a cry, and shook its chain and wrung its shadowy hands.

"You are fettered," said Scrooge, trembling. "Tell me why?"

"I wear the chain I forged in life," replied the Ghost. "I made it link by link, and yard by yard; I girded it on of my own free will, and of my own free will I wore it. Is its pattern strange to *you*?"

Scrooge trembled more and more.

"Or would you know," pursued the Ghost, "the weight and length of the strong coil you bear yourself? It was full as heavy and as long as this, seven Christmas Eves ago. You have labored on it since. It is a ponderous chain!"

Scrooge glanced about him on the floor, in the expectation of finding himself surrounded by some fifty or sixty fathoms of iron cable; but he could see nothing.

"Jacob," he said imploringly. "Old Jacob Marley, tell me more. Speak comfort to me, Jacob!"

"I have none to give," the Ghost replied. "It comes from other regions, Ebenezer Scrooge, and is conveyed by other ministers, to other kinds of men. Nor can I tell you what I would. A very little more, is all permitted to me. I cannot rest, I cannot stay, I cannot linger anywhere. My spirit never walked beyond our counting-house—mark me!—in life my spirit never roved beyond the narrow limits of our money-changing hole; and weary journeys lie before me!"

It was a habit with Scrooge, whenever he became thoughtful, to put his hands in his breeches' pockets. Pondering on what the Ghost had said, he did so now, but without lifting up his eyes, or getting off his knees.

"You must have been very slow about it, Jacob," Scrooge observed, in a business-like manner, though with humility and deference.

"Slow!" the Ghost repeated.

"Seven years dead," mused Scrooge. "And traveling all the time?"

"The whole time," said the Ghost. "No rest, no peace. Incessant torture of remorse."

"You travel fast?" said Scrooge.

"On the wings of the wind," replied the Ghost.

"You might have got over a great quantity of ground in seven years," said Scrooge.

The Ghost, on hearing this set up another cry, and clanked its chain hideously.

"Oh! captive, bound, and double-ironed," cried the Phantom, "not to know that ages of incessant labor, by immortal creatures, for this earth must pass into eternity before the good of which it is susceptible is all developed. Not to know that any Christian spirit working kindly in its little sphere, whatever it may be, will find its mortal life too short for its vast means of usefulness. Not to know that no space of regret can make amends for one life's opportunities misused! Yet such was I! Oh! such was I!"

"But you were always a good man of business, Jacob," faltered Scrooge, who now began to apply this to himself.

"Business!" cried the Ghost, wringing its hands again. "Mankind was my business. The common welfare was my business; charity, mercy, forbearance, and benevolence, were, all my business. The dealings of my trade were but a drop of water in the comprehensive ocean of my business!"

It held up its chain at arm's length, as if that were the cause of all its unavailing grief, and flung it heavily upon the ground again.

"At this time of the rolling year," the Spectre said, "I suffer most. Why did I walk through crowds of fellow-beings with my eyes turned down, and never raise them to that blessed Star which led the Wise Men to a poor abode? Were there no poor homes to which its light would have conducted me?"

Scrooge was very much dismayed to hear the Spectre going on at this rate, and began to quake exceedingly.

"Hear me!" cried the Ghost. "My time is nearly gone."

"I will," said Scrooge. "But don't be hard upon me! Don't be flowery, Jacob! Pray!"

"How it is that I appear before you in a shape that you can see, I may not tell. I have sat invisible beside you many and many a day."

It was not an agreeable idea. Scrooge shivered, and wiped the perspiration from his brow.

"That is no light part of my penance," pursued the Ghost. "I am here to-night to warn you, that you have yet a chance and hope of escaping my fate. A chance and hope of my procuring, Ebenezer."

"You were always a good friend to me," said Scrooge. "Thank'ee!"

"You will be haunted," resumed the Ghost, "by Three Spirits."

Scrooge's countenance fell.

"Is that the chance and hope you mentioned. Jacob?" he demanded, in a faltering voice.

"It is."

"I—I think I'd rather not," said Scrooge.

~ 19 ~

"Without their visits," said the Ghost, "you cannot hope to shun the path I tread. Expect the first to-morrow, when the bell tolls One."

"Couldn't I take 'em all at once, and have it over, Jacob?" hinted Scrooge.

"Expect the second on the next night at the same hour. The third, upon the next night when the last stroke of Twelve has ceased to vibrate. Look to see me no more; and look that, for your own sake, you remember what has passed between us!"

The apparition walked backward from him toward the window, and floated out upon the bleak, dark night.

Scrooge followed to the window; desperate in his curiosity. He looked out.

The air was filled with phantoms, wandering hither and thither in restless haste, and moaning as they went. Every one of them wore chains like Marley's ghost; some few (they might be guilty governments) were linked together; none were free. Many had been personally known to Scrooge in their lives. He had been quite familiar with one old ghost, in a white waistcoat, with a monstrous iron safe attached to its ankle, who cried piteously at being unable to assist a wretched woman with an infant, whom it saw below upon a door-step. The misery with them all was, clearly, that they sought to interfere, for good, in human matters and had lost the power for ever.

Whether these creatures faded into mist, or mist enshrouded them, he could not tell. But they and their spirit voices faded together; and the night became as it had been when he walked home.

Scrooge closed the window, and examined the door by which the Ghost had entered. It was double-locked, as he had locked it with his own hands, and the bolts were undisturbed. He tried to say "Humbug!" but stopped at the first syllable. And being, from the emotion he had undergone, or the fatigues of the day, or his glimpse of the Invisible World, or the dull conversation of the Ghost, or the lateness of the hour, much in need of repose, went straight to bed, without undressing, and fell asleep upon the instant.

Stave Two.

THE FIRST OF THE THREE SPIRITS.

When Scrooge awoke, it was so dark, that, looking out of bed, he could scarcely distinguish the transparent window from the opaque walls of his chamber. He was endeavoring to pierce the darkness with his ferret eyes, when the chimes of a neighboring church clock struck twelve.

"Why it isn't possible," said Scrooge, "that I can have slept through a whole day and far into another night!"

Scrooge lay and thought and thought it over and over, and could make nothing of it. The more he thought, the more perplexed he was, and the more he endeavored not to think, the more he thought. Marley's ghost bothered him exceedingly. "Was it a dream or not?"

Scrooge lay in this state until he remembered, on a sudden, that the Ghost had warned him of a visitation when the bell tolled One. He resolved to lie awake until the hour was passed; and considering that he could not go to sleep, this was perhaps the wisest resolution in his power.

He was more than once convinced he must have sunk into a doze unconsciously, and missed the clock. At length it broke upon his listening ear.

"The hour itself," said Scrooge, triumphantly, "nothing else!"

He spoke before the hour bell sounded, which it now did with a deep, dull, hollow, melancholy One. Light flashed up in the room upon the instant, and the curtains of his bed were drawn.

The curtains of his bed were drawn aside, I tell you, by a hand. Not the curtains at his feet, nor the curtains at his back, but those to which his face was addressed. The curtains of his bed were drawn aside; and Scrooge, starting up into a half-recumbent attitude, found himself face to face with the visitor who drew them.

It was a strange figure—like a child: yet not so like a child as like an old man, viewed through some supernatural medium, which gave him the appearance of having receded from the view, and being diminished to a child's proportions. Its hair, which hung about its neck and down its back, was white as if with age; and yet the face had not a wrinkle in it, and the tenderest bloom was on the skin. The arms were very long and muscular; the hands the same, as if its hold were of uncommon strength. Its legs and feet, most delicately formed, were, like those upper members, bare. It wore a tunic of the purest white; and round its waist was bound a lustrous belt, the sheen of which was beautiful. It held a branch of fresh green holly in its hand; and, in singular contradiction of that wintry emblem, had its dress trimmed with summer flowers. But the strangest thing about it was, that from the crown of its head there sprung a bright clear jet of light, by which all this was visible; and which was doubtless the occasion of its using, in its duller moments, a great extinguisher for a cap, which it now held under its arm.

"Are you the Spirit, sir, whose coming was foretold to me?" asked Scrooge.

"I am!"

The voice was soft and gentle. Singularly low, as if instead of being so close beside him, it were at a distance.

"Who, and what are you?" Scrooge demanded.

"I am the Ghost of Christmas Past."

"Long Past?" inquired Scrooge; observant of its dwarfish stature.

"No. Your past."

Scrooge then made bold to inquire what business brought him there.

"Your welfare!" said the Ghost.

Scrooge expressed himself much obliged, but could not help thinking that a night of unbroken rest would have been more conducive to that end. The Spirit must have heard him thinking, for it said immediately:

"Your reclamation, then. Take heed!"

It put out its strong hand as it spoke, and clasped him gently by the arm.

"Rise! and walk with me!"

It would have been in vain for Scrooge to plead that the weather and the hour were not adapted to pedestrian purposes; that bed was warm and the thermometer a long way below freezing; that he was clad but lightly in his slippers, dressing-gown, and night-cap; and that he had a cold upon him at the time. The grasp, though gentle as a woman's hand, was not to be resisted. He rose: but finding that the Spirit made toward the window, clasped its robe in supplication.

"I am a mortal," Scrooge remonstrated, "and liable to fall."

"Bear but a touch of my hand *there*," said the Spirit, laying it upon his heart, "and you shall be upheld in more than this!"

As the words were spoken, they passed out, and stood upon an open country road, with fields on either hand. The city had entirely vanished. Not a vestige of it was to be seen. The darkness and the mist had vanished with it, for it was a clear, cold, winter day, with snow upon the ground.

"Good Spirit!" said Scrooge, clasping his hands together, as he looked about him. "I was bred in this place. I was a boy here!"

The Spirit gazed upon him mildly. Its gentle touch, though it had been light and instantaneous, appeared still present to the old man's sense of feeling. He was conscious of a thousand odors floating in the air, each one connected with a thousand thoughts, and hopes, and joys, and cares long, long, forgotten!

"Your lip is trembling," said the Ghost. "And what is that upon your cheek?"

Scrooge muttered, with an unusual catching in his voice, that it was a pimple; and begged the Ghost to lead him where he would.

"You recollect the way?" inquired the Spirit.

"Remember it!" cried Scrooge with fervor; "I could walk it blindfold."

"Strange to have forgotten it for so many years!" observed the Ghost. "Let us go on."

They walked along the road, Scrooge recognizing every gate, and post, and tree; until a little market-town appeared in the distance, with its bridge, its church, and winding river. Some shaggy ponies now were seen trotting toward them with boys upon their backs, who called to other boys in country gigs and carts, driven by farmers. All these boys were in great spirits, and shouted to each other, until the broad fields were so full of merry music, that the crisp air laughed to hear it.

"These are but shadows of the things that have been," said the Ghost. "They have no consciousness of us."

The jocund travelers came on; and as they came, Scrooge knew and named them every one. Why was he rejoiced beyond all bounds to see them? Why did his cold eye glisten, and his heart leap up as they went past? Why was he filled with gladness when he heard them give each other Merry Christmas, as they parted at cross-roads and bye-ways, for their several homes? What was Merry Christmas to Scrooge? Out upon Merry Christmas! What good had it ever done to him?

"The school is not quite deserted," said the Ghost. "A solitary child, neglected by his friends, is left there still."

Scrooge said he knew it. And he sobbed.

They left the high-road, by a well remembered lane, and soon approached a mansion of dull red brick, with a little weathercock-surmounted cupola, on the roof, and a bell hanging in it. It was a large house, but one of broken fortunes; for the spacious offices were little used, their walls were damp and mossy, their windows broken, and their gates decayed. Fowls clucked and strutted in the stables; and the coach-houses and sheds were overrun with grass. Nor was it more retentive of its ancient state within; for entering the dreary hall, and glancing through the open doors of many rooms, they found them poorly furnished, cold, and vast. There was an earthy savor in the air, a chilly bareness in the place, which associated itself somehow with too much getting up by candle-light, and not too much to eat.

They went, the Ghost and Scrooge, across the hall, to a door at the back of the house. It opened before them, and disclosed a long, bare, melancholy room, made barer still by lines of plain deal forms and desks. At one of these a lonely boy was reading near a feeble fire; and Scrooge sat down upon a form, and wept to see his poor forgotten self as he had used to be.

"I wish," Scrooge muttered, putting his hand in his pocket, and looking about him, after drying his eyes with his cuff: "but it's too late now."

"What is the matter?" asked the Spirit.

"Nothing," said Scrooge. "Nothing. There was a boy singing a Christmas Carol at my door last night. I should like to have given him something: that's all."

The Ghost smiled thoughtfully, and waved its hand: saying as it did so, "Let us see another Christmas!"

Scrooge's former self grew larger at the words, and the room became a little darker and more dirty. The panels shrunk, the windows cracked; fragments of plaster fell out of the ceiling, and the naked laths were shown instead; but how all this was brought about, Scrooge knew no more than you do. He only knew that it was quite correct: that everything had happened so: that there he was, alone again, when all the other boys had gone home for the jolly holidays.

He was not reading now, but walking up and down despairingly. Scrooge looked at the Ghost, and with a mournful shaking of his head, glanced anxiously toward the door.

It opened; and a little girl much younger than the boy, came darting in, and putting her arms about his neck, and often kissing him, addressed him as her "Dear, dear brother."

"I have come to bring you home, dear brother!" said the child, clapping her tiny hands, and bending down to laugh. "To bring you home, home, home!"

"Home, little Fan?" returned the boy.

"Yes," said the child, brimful of glee. "Home, for good and all. Home, for ever and ever. Father is so much kinder than he used to be, that home's like Heaven! He spoke so gently to me one dear night when I was going to bed, that I was not afraid to ask him once more if you might come home; and he said Yes, you should; and sent me in a coach to bring you. And you're to be a man!" said the child, opening her eyes; "and are never to come back here: but first, we're to be together all the Christmas long, and have the merriest time in all the world."

"You are quite a woman, little Fan!" exclaimed the boy.

She clapped her hands and laughed, and tried to touch his head; but being too little, laughed again, and stood on tiptoe to embrace him. Then she began to drag him, in her childish eagerness, toward the door; and he, nothing loth to go, accompanied her.

A terrible voice in the hall cried, "Bring down Master Scrooge's box, there!" and in the hall appeared the schoolmaster himself, who glared on Master Scrooge with a ferocious condescension, and threw him into a dreadful state of mind by shaking hands with him. Master Scrooge's trunk being tied on to the top of the chaise, the children bade the schoolmaster good-bye right willingly; and getting into it, drove gaily down the garden-sweep: the quick wheels dashing the hoar-frost and snow from off the dark leaves of the evergreens like spray.

"Always a delicate creature, whom a breath might have withered," said the Ghost. "But she had a large heart!"

"So she had," cried Scrooge. "You're right. I will not gainsay it Spirit. God forbid!"

"She died a woman," said the Ghost, "and had, as I think, children."

"One child," Scrooge returned.

"True," said the Ghost. "Your nephew!"

Scrooge seemed uneasy in his mind; and answered briefly, "Yes."

Although they had but that moment left the school behind them, they were now in the busy thoroughfares of a city, where shadowy passengers passed and repassed; where shadowy carts and coaches battled for the way, and all the strife and tumult of a real city were. It was made plain enough, by the dressing of the shops, that here too it was Christmas time again; but it was evening, and the streets were lighted up.

The Ghost stopped at a certain warehouse door, and asked Scrooge if he knew it.

"Know it!" said Scrooge. "Was not I apprenticed here!"

They went in. At sight of an old gentleman in a Welsh wig, sitting behind such a high desk, that if he had been two inches taller he must have knocked his head against the ceiling, Scrooge cried in great excitement:

"Why, it's old Fezziwig! Bless his heart; it's Fezziwig alive again!"

Old Fezziwig laid down his pen, and looked up at the clock, which pointed to the hour of seven. He rubbed his hands; adjusted his capacious waistcoat; laughed all over himself, from his shoes to his organ of benevolence; and called out in a comfortable, oily, rich, fat, jovial voice:

"Yo ho, there! Ebenezer! Dick!"

Scrooge's former self, now grown a young man, came briskly in, accompanied by his fellow-'prentice.

"Dick Wilkins, to be sure!" said Scrooge to the Ghost. "Bless me, yes. There he is. He was very much attached to me, was Dick. Poor Dick! Dear, dear!"

"Yo ho, my boys!" said Fezziwig, "No more work to-night. Christmas Eve, Dick, Christmas, Ebenezer. Let's have the shutters up," cried old Fezziwig, with a sharp clap of his hands, "before a man can say Jack Robinson!"

You wouldn't believe how those two fellows went at it! They charged into the street with the shutters—one, two, three—had 'em up in their places—four, five, six—barred 'em and pinned 'em—seven, eight, nine—and came back before you could have got to twelve, panting like race-horses.

"Hilli-ho!" cried old Fezziwig, skipping down from the high desk, with wonderful agility. "Clear away, my lads, and let's have lots of room here!"

Clear away! There was nothing they wouldn't have cleared away, or couldn't have cleared away, with old Fezziwig looking on. It was done in a minute. Every movable was packed off, as if it were dismissed from public life for evermore; the floor was swept and watered, the lamps were trimmed, fuel was heaped upon the fire; and the warehouse was as snug, and warm, and dry, and bright a play-room as you would desire to see upon a winter's night.

In came a fiddler with a music-book, and went up to the lofty desk, and made an orchestra of it, and tuned like fifty stomach-aches. In came Mrs. Fezziwig, one vast substantial smile. In came the three Miss Fezziwigs, beaming and lovable. In came all the young men and women employed in the business. In came the housemaid, with her cousin, the baker. In came the cook, with her brother's particular friend, the milkman. In they all came, one after another; some shyly, some boldly, some gracefully, some awkwardly, some pushing, some pulling; in they all came, anyhow and everyhow.

There were dances, and there were forfeits, and more dances, and there was cake, and there was a great piece of Cold Roast, and there was a great piece of Cold Boiled, and there were mince-pies.

When the clock struck eleven, this domestic ball broke up. Mr. and Mrs. Fezziwig took their stations, one on either side the door, and shaking hands with every person individually as he or she went out, wished him or her a Merry Christmas. When everybody had retired but the two 'prentices they did the same to them; and thus the cheerful voices died away, and the lads were left to their beds; which were under a counter in the back-shop.

During the whole of this time, Scrooge had acted like a man out of his wits. His heart and soul were in the scene, and with his former self. He corroborated everything, remembered everything, enjoyed everything, and underwent the strangest agitation. It was not until now, when the bright faces of his former self and Dick were turned from them, that he remembered the Ghost, and became conscious that it was looking full upon him, while the light upon its head burnt very clear.

"A small matter," said the Ghost, "to make these silly folks so full of gratitude."

"Small!" echoed Scrooge.

The spirit signed to him to listen to the two apprentices, who were pouring out their hearts in praise of Fezziwig; and when he had done so said,

"Why! Is it not? He has spent but a few pounds of your mortal money: three or four, perhaps. Is that so much that he deserves this praise?"

"It isn't that," said Scrooge, heated by the remark, and speaking unconsciously like his former, not his latter self. "It isn't that, Spirit. He has the power to render us happy or unhappy; to make our service light or burdensome; a pleasure or a toil. Say that his power lies in words and looks; in things so slight and insignificant that it is impossible to add and count 'em up; what then? The happiness he gives, is quite as great as if it cost a fortune."

He felt the Spirit's glance, and stopped.

"What is the matter?" asked the Ghost.

"Nothing particular," said Scrooge.

"Something, I think?" the Ghost insisted.

"No," said Scrooge, "No. I should like to be able to say a word or two to my clerk just now. That's all."

His former self turned down the lamps as he gave utterance to the wish: and Scrooge and the Ghost again stood side by side in the open air.

"My time grows short," observed the Spirit. "Quick!"

This was not addressed to Scrooge, or to any one whom he could see, but it produced an immediate effect. For again Scrooge saw himself. He was older now; a man in the prime of life. His face had not the harsh and rigid lines of later years; but it had begun to wear the signs of care and avarice. There was an eager, greedy, restless motion in the eye, which showed the passion that had taken root, and where the shadow of the growing tree would fall.

He was not alone, but sat by the side of a fair young girl in a mourning-dress: in whose eyes there were tears, which sparkled in the light that shone out of the Ghost of Christmas Past.

"It matters little," she said, softly. "To you, very little. Another idol has displaced me; and if it can cheer and comfort you in time to come, as I would have tried to do, I have no just cause to grieve."

"What idol has displaced you?" he rejoined.

"A golden one."

"This is the even-handed dealing of the world!" he said. "There is nothing on which it is so hard as poverty; and there is nothing it professes to condemn with such severity as the pursuit of wealth!"

"You fear the world too much," she answered, gently. "All your other hopes have merged into the hope of being beyond the chance of its sordid reproach. I have seen your nobler aspirations fall off one by one, until the master-passion, Gain, engrosses you. Have I not?"

~ 33 ~

"What then?" he retorted. "Even if I have grown so much wiser, what then? I am not changed toward you."

She shook her head.

"Am I?"

"Our contract is an old one. It was made when we were both poor and content to be so, until, in good season, we could improve our worldly fortune by our patient industry. You *are* changed. When it was made, you were another man."

"I was a boy," he said impatiently.

"Your own feeling tells you that you were not what you are," she returned. "I am. That which promised happiness when we were one in heart, is fraught with misery now that we are two. How often and how keenly I have thought of this, I will not say. It is enough that I *have* thought of it, and can release you."

"Have I ever sought release?"

"In words. No. Never."

"In what, then?"

"In a changed nature; in an altered spirit; in another atmosphere of life; another Hope as its great end. In everything that made my love of any worth or value in your sight. If this had never been between us," said the girl, looking mildly, but with steadiness, upon him; "can even I believe that you would choose a dowerless girl: or, choosing her, do I not know that your repentance and regret would surely follow? I do; and I release you. With a full heart, for the love of him you once were."

~ 34 ~

He was about to speak; but she left him and they parted.

"Spirit!" said Scrooge, "show me no more! Conduct me home. Why do you delight to torture me?"

"I told you these were shadows of the things that have been," said the Ghost. "That they are what they are, do not blame me!"

"Remove me!" Scrooge exclaimed. "I cannot bear it!"

He turned upon the Ghost, and seeing that it looked upon him with a face, in which some strange way there were fragments of all the faces it had shown him, wrestled with it.

"Leave me! Take me back. Haunt me no longer!"

In the struggle—if that can be called a struggle in which the Ghost, with no visible resistance on its own part was undisturbed by any effort of its adversary—Scrooge was conscious of being exhausted, and overcome by an irresistible drowsiness; and, further, of being in his own bed-room. He had barely time to reel to bed, before he sank into a heavy sleep.

Stave Three.

THE SECOND OF THE THREE SPIRITS.

Awaking in the middle of a prodigiously tough snore, and sitting up in bed to get his thoughts together, Scrooge had no occasion to be told that the bell was again upon the stroke of One. He felt that he was restored to consciousness in the right nick of time, for the especial purpose of holding a conference with the second messenger despatched to him through Jacob Marley's intervention. But, finding that he turned uncomfortably cold when he began to wonder which of his curtains this new spectre would draw back, he put them every one aside with his own hands, and lying down again, established a sharp look-out all round the bed. For he wished to challenge the Spirit on the moment of its appearance, and did not wish to be taken by surprise and made nervous.

Now, being prepared for almost anything, he was not by any means prepared for nothing; and, consequently, when the bell struck One, and no shape appeared, he was taken with a violent fit of trembling. Five minutes, ten minutes a quarter of an hour went by, yet nothing came. All this time, he lay upon his bed, the very core and centre of a blaze of ruddy light, which streamed upon it when the clock proclaimed the hour; and which, being only light, was more alarming than a dozen ghosts, as he was powerless to make out what it meant. At last, however, he began to think that the source and secret of this ghostly light might be in the adjoining room, from whence, on further tracing it, it seemed to shine. This idea taking full possession of his mind, he got up softly and shuffled in his slippers to the door.

The moment Scrooge's hand was on the lock, a strange voice called him by his name, and bade him enter. He obeyed.

It was his own room. There was no doubt about that. But it had undergone a surprising transformation. The walls and ceiling were so hung with living green, that it looked a perfect grove; from every part of which, bright gleaming berries glistened. The crisp leaves of holly, mistletoe, and ivy reflected back the light, as if so many little mirrors had been scattered there; and such a mighty blaze went roaring up the chimney, as that dull petrifaction of a hearth had never known in Scrooge's time, or Marley's, or for many and many a winter season gone. Heaped up on the floor, to form a kind of throne, were turkeys, geese, game, poultry, brawn, great joints of meat, sucking-pigs, long wreaths of sausages, mince-pies, plum-puddings, barrels of oysters, red hot chestnuts, cherry-cheeked apples, juicy oranges, luscious pears and immense twelfth-cakes, that made the chamber dim with their delicious steam. In easy state upon this couch there sat a jolly Giant, glorious to see; who bore a glowing torch, in shape not unlike horn, and held it up, high up, to shed its light on Scrooge, as he came peeping round the door.

"Come in!" exclaimed the Ghost "Come in! and know me better, man!"

Scrooge entered timidly, and hung his head before this Spirit. He was not the dogged Scrooge he had been; and though the Spirit's eyes were clear and kind, he did not like to meet them.

"I am the Ghost of Christmas Present," said the Spirit: "Look upon me! You have never seen the like of me before!" exclaimed the Spirit.

"Never," Scrooge made answer to it.

"Have never walked forth with the younger members of my family; meaning (for I am very young) my elder brothers born in these later years?" pursued the Phantom.

~ 37 ~

"I don't think I have," said Scrooge. "I am afraid I have not. Have you had many brothers, Spirit?"

"More than eighteen hundred," said the Ghost.

"A tremendous family to provide for," muttered Scrooge.

The Ghost of Christmas Present rose.

"Spirit," said Scrooge, submissively, "conduct me where you will. I went forth last night on compulsion, and I learnt a lesson which is working now. To-night, if you have aught to teach me, let me profit by it."

"Touch my robe!"

Scrooge did as he was told, and held it fast.

The whole scene vanished instantly and they stood in the city streets on Christmas morning, where (for the weather was severe) the people made a rough, but brisk and not unpleasant kind of music, in scraping the snow from the pavement in front of their dwellings, and from the tops of their houses, whence it was mad delight to the boys to see it come plumping down into the roadbelow, and splitting into artificial little snowstorms.

Perhaps it was the pleasure the good Spirit had in showing his sympathy with all poor men, that led him straight to Scrooge's clerk's; for there he went, and took Scrooge with him, holding to his robe; and on the threshold of the door the spirit smiled, and stopped to bless Bob Cratchit's dwelling with the sprinklings of his torch.

Then up rose Mrs. Cratchit, Cratchit's wife, dressed out but poorly in a twice-turned gown, but brave in ribbons, which are cheap and make a goodly show; and she laid the cloth, assisted by Belinda Cratchit, second of her daughters, also brave in ribbons; while Master Peter Cratchit plunged a fork into the saucepan of potatoes. And now two smaller Cratchits, boy and girl, came tearing in, screaming that outside the baker's they had smelt the goose, and known it for their own.

"What has ever got your precious father, then?" said Mrs. Cratchit. "And your brother, Tiny Tim! And Martha warn't as late last Christmas Day by half-an-hour!"

"Here's Martha, mother," said a girl appearing as she spoke.

"Here's Martha, mother," cried the two young Cratchits. "Hurrah! There's such a goose, Martha!"

"Why, bless your heart alive, my dear, how late you are!" said Mrs. Cratchit, kissing her a dozen times, and taking off her shawl and bonnet for her with officious zeal.

"We'd a deal of work to finish up last night," replied the girl, "and had to clear away this morning, mother!"

"Well! never mind so long as you are come," said Mrs. Cratchit. "Sit ye down before the fire, my dear, and have a warm, Lord bless ye!"

"No no! There's father coming," cried the two young Cratchits, who were everywhere at once. "Hide, Martha, hide!"

So Martha hid herself, and in came little Bob, the father, with at least three feet of comforter exclusive of the fringe hanging down before him; and his threadbare clothes darned up and brushed, to look seasonable; and Tiny Tim upon his shoulder. Alas for Tiny

Tim, he bore a little crutch, and had his limbs supported by an iron frame!

"Why, Where's our Martha?" cried Bob Cratchit looking round.

"Not coming," said Mrs. Cratchit.

"Not coming!" said Bob, with a sudden declension in his high spirits; for he had been Tim's blood horse all the way from church, and had come home rampant. "Not coming upon Christmas Day!"

Martha didn't like to see him disappointed, if it were only in joke; so she came out prematurely from behind the closet door, and ran into his arms, while the two young Cratchits hustled Tiny Tim, and bore him off into the wash-house, that he might hear the pudding singing in the copper.

"And how did little Tim behave?" asked Mrs. Cratchit, when she had rallied Bob on his credulity, and Bob had hugged his daughter to his heart's content.

"As good as gold," said Bob, "and better. Somehow he gets thoughtful, sitting by himself so much, and thinks the strangest things you ever heard. He told me, coming home, that he hoped the people saw him in the church, because he was a cripple, and it might be pleasant to them to remember upon Christmas Day, who made lame beggars walk and blind men see."

Bob's voice was tremulous when he told them this, and trembled more when he said that Tiny Tim was growing strong and hearty.

His active little crutch was heard upon the floor, and back came Tiny Tim before another word was spoken, escorted by his brother and sister to his stool beside the fire; and Master Peter and the two ubiquitous young Cratchits went to fetch the goose, with which they soon returned in high procession.

Mrs. Cratchit made the gravy (ready beforehand in a little saucepan) hissing hot; Master Peter mashed the potatoes with incredible vigor; Miss Belinda sweetened up the apple sauce; Martha dusted the hot-plates; Bob took Tiny Tim beside him in a tiny corner at the table; the two young Cratchits set chairs for everybody, not forgetting themselves, and mounting guard upon their posts, crammed spoons into their mouths, lest they should shriek for goose before their turn came to be helped. At last the dishes were set on, and grace was said. It was succeeded by a breathless pause, as Mrs. Cratchit, looking slowly all along the carving-knife, prepared to plunge it in the breast; but when she did, and when the long-expected gush of stuffing issued forth, one murmur of delight arose all round the board, and even Tiny Tim, excited by the two young Cratchits, beat on the table with the handle of his knife, and feebly cried Hurrah!

There never was such a goose. Bob said he didn't believe there ever was such a goose cooked. Its tenderness and flavor, size and cheapness, were the themes of universal admiration. Eked out by apple sauce and mashed potatoes, it was a sufficient dinner for the whole family; indeed, as Mrs. Cratchit said with great delight (surveying one small atom of a bone upon the dish), they hadn't ate it all at last! Yet every one had had enough. But now the plates being changed by Miss Belinda, Mrs. Cratchit left the room alone—too nervous to bear witnesses—to take the pudding up, and bring it in.

Oh, a wonderful pudding! Bob Cratchit said, and calmly too, that he regarded it as the greatest success achieved by Mrs. Cratchit since their marriage. Mrs. Cratchit said that now the weight was off her mind, she would confess she had her doubts about the quantity of flour. Everybody had something to say about it, but nobody said or thought it was at all a small pudding for a large family. It would have been flat heresy to do so. Any Cratchit would have blushed to hint at such a thing.

At last the dinner was all done, the cloth was cleared, the hearth swept, and the fire made up. Apples and oranges were put upon the table and a shovelful of chestnuts on the fire. Then all the Cratchit family drew round the hearth, in what Bob Cratchit called a circle, meaning half a one. Then Bob proposed: "A Merry Christmas to all, my dears. God bless us!"

Which all the family re-echoed.

"God bless us, every one!" said Tiny Tim, the last of all.

He sat very close to his father's side, upon his little stool. Bob held his withered little hand in his, as if he loved the child and wished to keep him by his side, and dreaded that he might be taken from him.

"Spirit," said Scrooge, with an interest he had never felt before, "tell me if Tiny Tim will live."

"I see a vacant seat," replied the Ghost, "in the poor chimney corner, and a crutch without an owner, carefully preserved. If these shadows remain unaltered by the Future the child will die."

"No, no," said Scrooge. "Oh, no, kind Spirit! say he will be spared."

"If these shadows remain unaltered by the Future none other of my race," returned the Ghost, "will find him here. What then? If he be like to die, he had better do it, and decrease the surplus population."

Scrooge hung his head to hear his own words quoted by the Spirit, and was overcome with penitence and grief.

"Man," said the Ghost, "if man you be in heart, not adamant, forbear that wicked cant until you have discovered what the surplus is and where it is. Will you decide what men shall live, what men shall die? It may be that in the sight of Heaven you are more worthless and less fit to live than millions like this poor man's child. Oh, God! to hear the insect on the leaf pronouncing on the too much life among his hungry brothers in the dust!"

Scrooge bent before the Ghost's rebuke, and trembling cast his eyes upon the ground. But he raised them speedily on hearing his own name.

"Mr. Scrooge!" said Bob; "I'll give you Mr. Scrooge, the Founder of the Feast!"

"The Founder of the Feast indeed!" cried Mrs. Cratchit, reddening. "I wish I had him here. I'd give him a piece of my mind to feast upon, and I hope he'd have a good appetite for it."

"My dear," said Bob, "the children! Christmas day."

Scrooge was the Ogre of the family. The mention of his name cast a dark shadow on the party, which was not dispelled for full five minutes.

After it had passed away, they were ten times merrier than before, from the mere relief of Scrooge the Baleful being done with. Bob Cratchit told them how he had a situation in his eye for Master Peter. The two young Cratchits laughed tremendously at the idea of Peter's being a man of business; and Peter himself looked thoughtfully at the fire from between his collars, as if he were deliberating what particular investments he should favor when he came into receipt of the bewildering income. Martha, who was a poor apprentice at a milliner's, then told them what kind of work she had to do, and how many hours she worked at a stretch, and how she meant to be abed to-morrow morning for a good long rest, to-morrow being a holiday she passed at home. Also how she had seen a countess and a lord some days before, and how the lord "was much about as tall as Peter," at which Peter pulled up his collars so high that you couldn't have seen his head if you had been there. By and by they had a song, about a lost child traveling in the snow, from Tiny Tim, who had a plaintive little voice, and sang it very well indeed.

There was nothing of high mark in this. They were not a handsome family; they were not well dressed; their shoes were far from being waterproof; their clothes were scanty; and Peter might have known, and very likely did, the inside of a pawnbroker's. But they were happy, grateful, pleased with one another, and contented with the time; and when they faded, and looked happier yet in the bright sprinklings of the Spirit's torch at parting, Scrooge had his eye upon them, and especially on Tiny Tim, until the last.

By this time it was getting dark and snowing pretty heavily; and as Scrooge and the Spirit went along the streets, the brightness of the roaring fires in kitchens, parlors, and all sorts of rooms, was wonderful. Here, the flickering of the blaze showed preparations for a cosy dinner, with hot plates baking through and through before the fire, and deep red curtains, ready to be drawn to shut out cold and darkness. There, all the children of the house were running out into the snow to meet their married sisters, brothers, cousins, uncles, aunts, and be the first to greet them.

It was a great surprise to Scrooge, as he meditated on these scenes, to hear a hearty laugh. It was a much greater surprise to Scrooge to recognize it as his own nephew's, and to find himself in a bright, dry, gleaming room, with the Spirit standing smiling by his side, and looking at that same nephew with approving affability!

"Ha! ha!" laughed Scrooge's nephew. "Ha! ha! ha!"

If you should happen, by any unlikely chance, to know a man more blessed in a laugh than Scrooge's nephew, all I can say is, I should like to know him too. Introduce him to me, and I'll cultivate his acquaintance.

It is a fair, even-handed, noble adjustment of things that while there is infection in disease and sorrow, there is nothing in the world so irresistibly contagious as laughter and good-humor. When Scrooge's nephew laughed in this way, holding his sides, rolling his head, and twisting his face into the most extravagant contortions, Scrooge's niece, by marriage, laughed as heartily as he. And their assembled friends being not a bit behindhand, roared out lustily.

"Ha, ha! Ha, ha, ha, ha!"

"He said that Christmas was a humbug, as I live!" cried Scrooge's nephew. "He believed it, too."

"More shame for him, Fred!" said Scrooge's niece, indignantly. Bless those women! they never do anything by halves. They are always in earnest.

She was very pretty; exceedingly pretty. With a dimpled, surprised-looking, capital face; a ripe little mouth that seemed made to be kissed—as no doubt it was; all kinds of good little dots about her chin, that melted into one another when she laughed; and the sunniest pair of eyes you ever saw in any little creature's head. Altogether she was what you would have called provoking, you know; but satisfactory, too. Oh, perfectly satisfactory.

"He's a comical old fellow," said Scrooge's nephew, "that's the truth: and not so pleasant as he might be. However, his offences carry their own punishment, and I have nothing to say against him."

"I have no patience with him," observed Scrooge's niece. Scrooge's niece's sisters, and all the other ladies, expressed the same opinion.

"Oh, I have!" said Scrooge's nephew. "I am sorry for him; I couldn't be angry with him if I tried. Who suffers by his ill whims! Himself, always. Here, he takes it into his head to dislike us, and he won't come and dine with us. What's the consequence? He don't lose much of a dinner."

"Indeed, I think he loses a very good dinner," interrupted Scrooge's niece. Everybody else said the same, and they must be allowed to have been competent judges, because they had just had dinner; and with the dessert upon the table, were clustered round the fire, by lamp-light.

"Well! I am very glad to hear it," said Scrooge's nephew, "because I haven't any great faith in these young housekeepers. What do *you* say, Topper?"

Topper had clearly got his eye upon one of Scrooge's niece's sisters, for he answered that a bachelor was a wretched outcast, who had no right to express an opinion on the subject. Whereat Scrooge's niece's sister—the plump one with the lace tucker: not the one with the roses—blushed.

"Do go on, Fred," said Scrooge's niece, clapping her hands. "He never finishes what he begins to say! He is such a ridiculous fellow!"

"I was only going to say," said Scrooge's nephew, "that the consequence of his taking a dislike to us, and not making merry with us, is, as I think, that he loses some pleasant moments, which could do him no harm. I am sure he loses pleasanter companions than he can find in his own thoughts, either in his mouldy old office, or his dusty chambers. I mean to give him the same chance every year, whether he likes it or not, for I pity him. He may rail at Christmas till he dies, but he can't help thinking better of it—I defy him—if he finds me going there, in good temper, year after year, and saying, 'Uncle Scrooge, how are you?' If it only puts him in the vein to leave his poor clerk fifty pounds, *that's* something; and I think I shook him yesterday."

It was their turn to laugh now, at the notion of his shaking Scrooge. But being thoroughly goodnatured, and not much caring what they laughed at, so that they laughed at any rate, he encouraged them in their merriment.

After tea they had some music. Scrooge's niece played well; and played among other tunes a simple little air (a mere nothing: you might learn to whistle it in two minutes), which had been familiar to the child who fetched Scrooge from the boarding-school, as he had been reminded by the Ghost of Christmas Past. When this strain of music sounded, all the things that the Ghost had shown him, came upon his mind; he softened more and more; and thought that if he could have listened to it often, years ago, he might have cultivated the kindnesses of life for his own happiness with his own hands, without resorting to the sexton's spade that buried Jacob Marley.

But they didn't devote the whole evening to music. After awhile they played at forfeits; for it is good to be children sometimes, and never better than at Christmas, when its mighty founder was a child himself.

Stop! There was first a glorious game at blindman's buff. Of course there was. And I no more believe Topper was really blind than I believe he had eyes in his boots. My opinion is, that it was a done thing between him and Scrooge's nephew; and that the Ghost of Christmas Present knew it. The way he went after that plump sister in the lace tucker, was an outrage on the credulity of human nature. Knocking down the fire-irons, tumbling over the chairs, bumping up against the piano, smothering himself amongst the curtains, wherever she went, there went he! He always knew where the plump sister was. He wouldn't catch anybody else. If you had fallen up against him, (as some of them did) on purpose, he would have made a feint of endeavoring to seize you, which would have been an affront to your understanding, and would instantly have sidled off in the direction of the plump sister. She often cried out that it wasn't fair; and it really was not. But when at last, he caught her; when, in spite of all her silken rustlings, and her rapid flutterings past him, he got her into a corner whence there was no escape; then his conduct was the most execrable. For his pretending not to know her; his pretending that it was necessary to touch her head-dress, and further to assure himself of her identity by pressing a certain ring upon her finger, and a certain chain about her neck; was vile, monstrous! No doubt she told him her opinion of it when, another blind-man being in office, they were so very confidential together, behind the curtains.

Scrooge's niece was not one of the blind-man's buff party, but was made comfortable with a large chair and a footstool, in a snug corner where the Ghost and Scrooge were close behind her. But she joined in the forfeits, and loved her love to admiration with all the letters of the alphabet. Likewise at the game of How, When, and Where, she was very great, and, to the secret joy of Scrooge's nephew, beat her sisters hollow: though they were sharp girls too, as Topper could have told you. There might have been twenty people there, young and old, but they all played, and so did Scrooge; for, wholly forgetting in the interest he had in what was going on, that his voice made no sound in their ears, he sometimes came out with his guess quite loud, and very often guessed right, too; for the sharpest needle, warranted not to cut in the eye, was not sharper than Scrooge; blunt as he took it in his head to be.

The Ghost was greatly pleased to find him in this mood, and looked upon him with such favor, that he begged like a boy to be allowed to stay until the guests departed. But this the Spirit said could not be done. The whole scene passed off; and he and the Spirit were again upon their travels.

Much they saw, and far they went, and many homes they visited, but always with a happy end. The Spirit stood beside sick beds, and they were cheerful; on foreign lands, and they were close at home; by struggling men, and they were patient in their greater hope; by poverty, and it was rich. In almshouse, hospital, and jail, in misery's every refuge, where vain man in his little brief authority had not made fast the door, and barred the Spirit out, he left his blessing, and taught Scrooge his precepts.

It was a long night, if it were only a night; but Scrooge had his doubts of this, because the Christmas Holidays appeared to be condensed into the space of time they passed together. It was strange, too, that while Scrooge remained unaltered in his outward form, the Ghost grew older, clearly older!

"Forgive me if I am not justified in what I ask," said Scrooge, looking intently at the Spirit's robe, "but I see something strange, and not belonging to yourself, protruding from your skirts. Is it a foot or a claw?"

"It might be a claw, for the flesh there is upon it," was the Spirit's sorrowful reply. "Look here."

From the foldings of its robe, it brought two children; wretched, abject, frightful, hideous, miserable. They knelt down at its feet, and clung upon the outside of its garment.

They were a boy and girl. Yellow, meagre, ragged, scowling, wolfish; but prostrate, too, in their humility. Where graceful youth should have filled their features out, and touched them with its freshest tints, a stale and shriveled hand, like that of age, had pinched, and twisted them, and pulled them into shreds. Where angels might have sat enthroned, devils lurked, and glared out menacing. No change, no degradation, no perversion of humanity, in any grade, through all the mysteries of wonderful creation, has monsters half so horrible and dread.

Scrooge started back, appalled. Having them shown to him in this way, he tried to say they were fine children, but the words choked themselves, rather than be parties to a lie of such enormous magnitude.

"Spirit, are they yours?" Scrooge could say no more.

"They are Man's," said the Spirit, looking down upon them. "And they cling to me, appealing from their fathers. This boy is Ignorance. This girl is Want. Beware of them both, and all of their degree, but most of all beware of this boy."

"Have they no refuge or resource?" cried Scrooge.

"Are there no prisons?" said the Spirit, turning on him for the last time with his own words. "Are there no work-houses?"

The bell struck twelve.

Scrooge looked about him for the Ghost, and saw it not. As the last stroke ceased to vibrate, he remembered the prediction of old

Jacob Marley, and lifting up his eyes, beheld a solemn Phantom, draped and hooded, coming like a mist along the ground toward him.

Stave Four.

THE LAST OF THE SPIRITS.

The Phantom slowly, gravely, silently, approached. When it came near him, Scrooge bent down upon his knee; for in the very air through which this Spirit moved it seemed to scatter gloom and mystery.

It was shrouded in a deep black garment, which concealed its head, its face, its form, and left nothing of it visible, save one outstretched hand. But for this it would have been difficult to detach its figure from the night, and separate it from the darkness by which it was surrounded.

He felt that it was tall and stately when it came beside him, and that its mysterious presence filled him with a solemn dread. He knew no more, for the Spirit neither spoke nor moved.

"I am in the presence of the Ghost of Christmas Yet To Come?" said Scrooge.

The Spirit answered not, but pointed onward with its hand.

"You are about to show me shadows of the things that have not happened, but will happen in the time before us," Scrooge pursued. "Is that so, Spirit?"

The upper portion of the garment was contracted for an instant in its folds, as if the Spirit had inclined its head. That was the only answer he received.

Although well used to ghostly company by this time, Scrooge feared the silent shape so much that his legs trembled beneath him, and he found that he could hardly stand when he prepared to follow it. The Spirit paused a moment, as observing his condition, and giving him time to recover.

But Scrooge was all the worse for this. It thrilled him with a vague uncertain horror, to know that behind the dusky shroud, there were ghostly eyes intently fixed upon him, while he, though he stretched his own to the utmost, could see nothing but a spectral hand and one great heap of black.

"Ghost of the Future!" he exclaimed, "I fear you more than any spectre I have seen. But as I know your purpose is to do me good and as I hope to live to be another man from what I was, I am prepared to bear you company, and do it with a thankful heart. Will you not speak to me?"

It gave him no reply. The hand was pointed straight before them.

"Lead on!" said Scrooge. "Lead on! The night is waning fast, and it is precious time to me, I know. Lead on, Spirit!"

The Phantom moved away as it had come toward him. Scrooge followed in the shadow of its dress, which bore him up, he thought, and carried him along.

They scarcely seemed to enter the city; for the city rather seemed to spring up about them, and encompass them of its own act. But there they were in the heart of it; on 'Change, amongst the merchants; who hurried up and down, and chinked the money in their pockets, and conversed in groups, and looked at their watches, and trifled thoughtfully with their great gold seals; and so forth, as Scrooge had seen them often.

The Spirit stopped beside one little knot of business men. Observing that the hand was pointed to them, Scrooge advanced to listen to their talk.

"No," said a great fat man with a monstrous chin, "I don't know much about it either way. I only know he's dead."

"When did he die?" inquired another.

"Last night, I believe."

"What has he done with his money?" asked a red-faced gentleman with a pendulous excrescence on the end of his nose, that shook like the gills of a turkey-cock.

"I haven't heard," said the man with the large chin, yawning again. "Left it to his company, perhaps. He hasn't left it to me. That's all I know."

This pleasantry was received with a general laugh.

"It's likely to be a very cheap funeral," said the same speaker; "for upon my life I don't know of anybody to go to it. Suppose we make up a party and volunteer?"

"I don't mind going if a lunch is provided," observed the gentleman with the excrescence on his nose. "But I must be fed, if I make one."

Another laugh.

"Well, I am the most disinterested among you, after all," said the first speaker, "for I never wear black gloves, and I never eat lunch. But I'll offer to go, if anybody else will. When I come to think of it, I'm not at all sure that I wasn't his most particular friend; for we used to stop and speak whenever we met. Bye, bye!"

Speakers and listeners strolled away, and mixed with other groups. Scrooge knew the men, and looked toward the Spirit for explanation. He was at first inclined to be surprised that the Spirit should attach importance to conversations apparently so trivial; but feeling assured that they must have some hidden purpose, he set himself to consider what it was likely to be. They could scarcely be supposed to have any bearing on the death of Jacob, his old partner, for that was past, and this Ghost's province was the future. Nor could he think of any one immediately connected with himself, to whom he could apply them.

They left the busy scene, and went into an obscure part of the town, where Scrooge had never penetrated before, although he recognized its situation and its bad repute. The ways were foul and narrow; the shops and houses wretched; the people half-naked, drunken, slipshod, ugly. Alleys and archways, like so many cesspools, disgorged their offences of smell, and dirt, and life, upon the straggling streets; and the whole quarter reeked with crime, with filth and misery.

Far in this den of infamous resort, there was a low-browed, beetling shop, below a pent-house roof, where iron, old rags, bottles, bones, and greasy offal were bought. Upon the floor within, were piled up heaps of rusty keys, nails, chains, hinges, files, scales, weights, and refuse iron of all kinds. Secrets that few would like to scrutinize were bred and hidden in mountains of unseemly rags, masses of corrupted fat, and sepulchres of bones. Sitting in among the wares he dealt in, by a charcoal stove, made of old bricks, was a grey-haired rascal, nearly seventy years of age; who had screened himself from the cold air without, by a frowsy curtaining of miscellaneous tatters hung upon a line; and smoked his pipe in all the luxury of calm retirement.

Scrooge and the Phantom came into the presence of this man, just as a woman with a heavy bundle slunk into the shop. But she had scarcely entered, when another woman, similarly laden, came in too; and she was closely followed by a man in faded black, who was no less startled by the sight of them, than they had been upon the recognition of each other. After a short period of blank astonishment, in which the old man with a pipe had joined them, they all three burst into a laugh.

"Let the charwoman alone to be the first!" cried she who had entered first. "Let the laundress alone to be the second; and let the undertaker's man alone to be the third. Look here, old Joe, here's a chance! If we haven't all three met here without meaning it!"

"You couldn't have met in a better place," said old Joe, removing his pipe from his mouth. "Come into the parlor."

The parlor was the space behind the screen of rags. The old man raked the fire together with an old stair-rod, and having trimmed his smoky lamp (for it was night), with the stem of his pipe, put it into his mouth again.

While he did this, the woman who had already spoken threw her bundle on the floor and sat down in a flaunting manner on a stool; crossing her elbows on her knees, and looking with a bold defiance at the other two. "Now, then!" cried the woman. "Who's the worse for the loss of a few things like these? Not a dead man, I suppose."

"No, indeed," said Mrs. Dilber, laughing.

"If he wanted to keep 'em after he was dead, a wicked old screw," pursued the woman, "why wasn't he natural in his lifetime? If he had been, he'd have had somebody to look after him when he was struck with Death, instead of lying gasping out his last there, alone by himself."

"It's the truest word that ever was spoke," said Mrs. Dilber. "It's a judgment on him."

"I wish it was a little heavier judgment," replied the woman; "and it should have been, you may depend upon it, if I could have laid my hands on anything else. Open that bundle, old Joe, and let me know the value of it. Speak out plain. I'm not afraid to be the first, nor afraid for them to see it. We knew pretty well that we were helping ourselves, before we met here, I believe. Open the bundle, Joe."

But the gallantry of her friends would not allow of this; and the man in faded black, mounting the breach first, produced *his* plunder. It was not extensive. A seal or two, a pencil-case, a pair of sleeve buttons, and a brooch of no great value, were all. They were severally examined and appraised by old Joe, who chalked the sums he was disposed to give for each, upon the wall, and added them up into a total when he found that there was nothing more to come.

"That's your account," said Joe, "and I wouldn't give another sixpence, if I was to be boiled for not doing it. Who's next?"

Mrs. Dilber was next. Sheets and towels, a little wearing apparel, two old-fashioned silver teaspoons, a pair of sugar-tongs, and a few boots. Her account was stated on the wall in the same manner.

"I always give too much to ladies. It's a weakness of mine, and that's the way I ruin myself," said old Joe. "That's your account. If you asked me for another penny, and made it an open question, I'd repent of being so liberal, and knock off half-a-crown."

"And now undo *my* bundle, Joe," said the first woman.

Joe went down on his knees for the greater convenience of opening it, and having unfastened a great many knots, dragged out a large heavy roll of some dark stuff.

"What do you call this?" said Joe. "Bed curtains!"

"Ah!" returned the woman, laughing and leaning forward on her crossed arms. "Bed curtains!"

"You don't mean to say you took 'em down rings and all, with him lying there?" said Joe.

"Yes, I do," replied the woman. "Why not?"

"You were born to make your fortune," said Joe, "and you'll certainly do it."

"I certainly shan't hold my hand, when I can get anything in it by reaching it out, for the sake of such a man as he was, I promise you, Joe," returned the woman coolly. "Don't drop that oil upon the blankets, now."

"His blankets?" asked Joe.

"Whose else's do you think?" replied the woman. "He isn't likely to take cold without 'em, I dare say."

"I hope he didn't die of anything catching? Eh?" said old Joe, stopping in his work, and looking up.

"Don't you be afraid of that," returned the woman. "I an't so fond of his company that I'd loiter about him for such things, if he did. Ah! you may look through that shirt till your eyes ache; but you won't find a hole in it, nor a threadbare place. It's the best he had, and a fine one too. They'd have wasted it, if it hadn't been for me."

"What do you call wasting of it?" asked old Joe.

"Putting it on him to be buried in, to be sure," replied the woman with a laugh. "Somebody was fool enough to do it, but I took it off again. If calico ain't good enough for such a purpose, it isn't good enough for anything. It's quite as becoming to the body. He can't look uglier than he did in that one."

Scrooge listened to this dialogue in horror. As they sat grouped about their spoil, in the scanty light afforded by the old man's lamp, he viewed them with a detestation and disgust, which could hardly have been greater, though they had been obscene demons, marketing the corpse itself.

"Ha, ha!" laughed the same woman, when old Joe, producing a flannel bag with money in it, told out their several gains upon the ground. "This is the end of it, you see? He frightened everyone away from him when he was alive, to profit us when he was dead! Ha! ha! ha!"

"Spirit!" said Scrooge, shuddering from head to foot, "I see, I see. The case of this unhappy man might be my own. My life tends that way, now. Merciful Heaven, what is this?"

He recoiled in terror, for the scene had changed, and now he almost touched a bed: a bare, uncurtained bed: on which, beneath a ragged sheet, there lay a something covered up which, though it was dumb, announced itself in awful language.

The room was very dark, too dark to be observed with any accuracy, though Scrooge glanced round it in obedience to a secret impulse, anxious to know what kind of room it was. A pale light rising in the outer air, fell straight upon the bed: and on it, plundered and bereft, unwatched, unwept, uncared for, was the body of this man.

Scrooge glanced toward the Phantom. Its steady hand was pointed to the head. The cover was so carelessly adjusted that the slightest raising of it, the motion of a finger upon Scrooge's part, would have disclosed the face. He thought of it, felt how easy it would be to do, and longed to do it; but had no more power to withdraw the veil than to dismiss the spectre at his side.

"Spirit!" he said, "this is a fearful place. In leaving it, I shall not leave its lesson, trust me. Let us go!"

Still the Ghost pointed with an unmoved finger to the head.

"I understand you," Scrooge returned, "and I would do it if I could. But I have not the power, Spirit. I have not the power."

Again it seemed to look upon him.

"If there is any person in the town, who feels emotion caused by this man's death," said Scrooge, quite agonized, "show that person to me, Spirit, I beseech you!"

The phantom spread its dark robe before him for a moment, like a wing; and withdrawing it, revealed a room by daylight, where a mother and her children were.

She was expecting some one, and with anxious eagerness; for she walked up and down the room; started at every sound; looked out from the window; glanced at the clock; tried, but in vain, to work with her needle; and could hardly bear the voices of her children in their play.

At length the long-expected knock was heard. She hurried to the door and met her husband; a man whose face was care-worn and depressed, though he was young. There was a remarkable expression in it now; a kind of serious delight of which he felt ashamed, and which he struggled to repress.

He sat down to the dinner that had been hoarding for him by the fire, and when she asked him faintly what news (which was not until after a long silence), he appeared embarrassed how to answer.

"Is it good," she said, "or bad?"—to help him.

"Bad," he answered.

"We are quite ruined?"

"No. There is hope yet, Caroline."

"If he relents," she said, amazed, "there is! Nothing is past hope, if such a miracle has happened."

"He is past relenting," said her husband. "He is dead."

She was a mild and patient creature, if her face spoke truth; but she was thankful in her soul to hear it, and she said so, with clasped hands. She prayed forgiveness the next moment, and was sorry: but the first was the emotion of her heart.

"What the half-drunken woman, whom I told you of last night, said to me, when I tried to see him and obtain a week's delay: and what I thought was a mere excuse to avoid me, turns out to have been quite true. He was not only very ill, but dying, then."

"To whom will our debt be transferred?"

"I don't know. But before that time we shall be ready with the money; and even though we were not, it would be bad fortune indeed to find so merciless a creditor in his successor. We may sleep to-night with light hearts, Caroline!"

Yes. Soften it as they would, their hearts were lighter. The children's faces, hushed and clustered round to hear what they so little understood, were brighter; and it was a happier house for this man's death! The only emotion that the Ghost could show him, caused by the event, was one of pleasure.

"Let me see some tenderness connected with the death," said Scrooge; "or that dark chamber, Spirit, which we left just now, will be for ever present to me."

The Ghost conducted him through several streets to poor Bob Cratchit's house; the dwelling he had visited before: and found the mother and the children seated round the fire.

Quiet. Very quiet. The noisy little Cratchits were as still as statues in one corner, and sat looking up at Peter, who had a book before him. The mother and her daughters were sewing. But surely they were very quiet!

"'And He took a child, and set him in the midst of them.'"

Where had Scrooge heard those words? He had not dreamed them. The boy must have read them out, as he and the Spirit crossed the threshold. Why did he not go on?

The mother laid her work upon the table, and put her hand up to her face.

"The color hurts my eyes," she said.

The color? Ah, poor Tiny Tim!

"They're better now again," said Cratchit's wife. "It makes them weak by candle-light; and I wouldn't show weak eyes to your father when he comes home, for the world. It must be near his time."

"Past it rather," Peter answered, shutting up his book. "But I think he has walked a little slower than he used, these few last evenings, mother."

They were very quiet again. At last she said, and in a steady, cheerful voice, that only faltered once:

"I have known him walk with—I have known him walk with Tiny Tim upon his shoulder, very fast indeed."

"And so have I," cried Peter. "Often."

"And so have I," exclaimed another. So had all.

"But he was very light to carry," she resumed, intent upon her work, "and his father loved him so, that it was no trouble: no trouble. And there is your father at the door!"

She hurried out to meet him; and little Bob in his comforter—he had need of it, poor fellow—came in. His tea was ready for him, and they all tried who should help him to it most. Then the two young Cratchits got upon his knees and laid, each child, a little cheek against his face, as if they said, "Don't mind it, father. Don't be grieved!"

Bob was very cheerful with them, and spoke pleasantly to all the family. He looked at the work upon the table, and praised the industry and speed of Mrs. Cratchit and the girls. They would be done long before Sunday, he said.

"Sunday! You went to-day, then, Robert?" said his wife.

"Yes, my dear," returned Bob. "I wish you could have gone. It would have done you good to see how green a place it is. But you'll see it often. I promised him that I would walk there on a Sunday. My little, little child!" cried Bob. "My little child!"

He broke down all at once. He couldn't help it. If he could have helped it, he and his child would have been farther apart perhaps than they were.

"Spectre," said Scrooge, "something informs me that our parting moment is at hand. I know it, but I know not how. Tell me what man that was whom we saw lying dead?"

The Ghost of Christmas Yet to Come conveyed him as before into the resorts of business men, but showed him not himself. Indeed, the Spirit did not stay for anything, but went straight on, as to the end just now desired, until besought by Scrooge to tarry for a moment.

"This court," said Scrooge, "through which we hurry now, is where my place of occupation is, and has been for a length of time. I see the house. Let me behold what I shall be, in days to come."

The Spirit stopped; the hand was pointed elsewhere.

"The house is yonder" Scrooge exclaimed. "Why do you point away?"

The inexorable finger underwent no change.

Scrooge hastened to the window of his office, and looked in. It was an office still, but not his. The furniture was not the same, and the figure in the chair was not himself. The Phantom pointed as before.

He joined it once again, and wondering why and whither he had gone, accompanied it until they reached an iron gate. He paused to look round before entering.

A churchyard. Here, then, the wretched man whose name he had now to learn, lay underneath the ground. It was a worthy place. Walled in by houses; overrun by grass and weeds, the growth of vegetation's death, not life; choked up with too much burying; fat with repleted appetite. A worthy place!

The Spirit stood among the graves, and pointed down to one. He advanced toward it trembling. The Phantom was exactly as it had been, but he dreaded that he saw new meaning in its solemn shape.

"Before I draw nearer to that stone to which you point," said Scrooge, "answer me one question. Are these the shadows of the things that will be, or are they shadows of the things that may be, only?"

Still the Ghost pointed downward to the grave by which it stood.

"Men's courses will foreshadow certain ends, to which, if persevered in, they must lead," said Scrooge, "But if the courses be departed from, the ends will change. Say it is thus with what you show me!"

The Spirit was immovable as ever.

Scrooge crept toward it, trembling as he went; and following the finger, read upon the stone of the neglected grave his own name, Ebenezer Scrooge.

"Am I that man who lay upon the bed?" he cried, upon his knees.

The finger pointed from the grave to him, and back again.

"No, Spirit! Oh, no, no!"

The finger still was there.

Holding up his hands in a last prayer to have his fate reversed, he saw an alteration in the Phantom's hood and dress. It shrunk, collapsed, and dwindled down into a bedpost.

Stave Five.

THE END OF IT.

Yes! and the bedpost was his own. The bed was his own, and the room was his own. Best and happiest of all, the time before him was his own, to make amends in!

He was so fluttered and so glowing with his good intentions, that his broken voice would scarcely answer to his call. He had been sobbing violently in his conflict with the Spirit, and his face was wet with tears.

"They are not torn down," cried Scrooge, folding one of his bed curtains in his arms, "they are not torn down, rings and all. They are here—I am here—the shadows of the things that would have been, may be dispelled. They will be. I know they will!"

He had frisked into the sitting-room, and was now standing there: perfectly winded.

"There's the saucepan that the gruel was in!" cried Scrooge, starting off again, and going round the fire-place. "There's the door by which the Ghost of Jacob Marley entered! There's the corner where the Ghost of Christmas Present sat! There's the window where I saw the wandering Spirits! It's all right, it's all true, it all happened. Ha, ha, ha!"

Really, for a man who had been out of practice for so many years, it was a splendid laugh, a most illustrious laugh. The father of a long, long line of brilliant laughs!

"I don't know what day of the month it is," said Scrooge. "I don't know how long I have been among the Spirits. I don't know anything. I'm quite a baby. Never mind. I don't care. I'd rather be a baby. Hallo! Whoop! Hallo here!"

He was checked in his transports by the churches ringing out the lustiest peals he had ever heard. Clash, clash, hammer; ding, dong, bell. Bell, dong, ding; hammer, clang, clash! Oh, glorious, glorious!

Running to the window, he opened it and put out his head.

"What's to-day?" cried Scrooge, calling downward to a boy in Sunday clothes, who perhaps had loitered in to look about him.

"Eh?" returned the boy, with all his might of wonder.

"What's to-day, my fine fellow?" said Scrooge.

"To-day!" replied the boy. "Why, Christmas Day."

"It's Christmas Day!" said Scrooge to himself. "I haven't missed it. The Spirits have done it all in one night. Hallo, my fine fellow!"

"Hallo!" returned the boy.

"Do you know the Poulterer's, in the next street but one, at the corner?" Scrooge inquired.

"I should hope I did," replied the lad.

"An intelligent boy!" said Scrooge. "A remarkable boy! Do you know whether they've sold the prize turkey that was hanging up there?"

"It's hanging there now," replied the boy.

"Is it?" said Scrooge. "Go and buy it."

"Walk-ER!" exclaimed the boy.

"No, no," said Scrooge, "I am in earnest. Go and buy it, and tell 'em to bring it here, that I may give them the directions where to take it. Come back with the man, and I'll give you a shilling."

The boy was off like a shot.

"I'll send it to Bob Cratchit's," whispered Scrooge, rubbing his hands, and splitting with a laugh. "He shan't know who sends it. It's twice the size of Tiny Tim."

The hand in which he wrote the address was not a steady one; but write it he did, somehow, and went down-stairs to open the street door, ready for the coming of the poulterer's man.

The chuckle with which he paid for the Turkey, and the chuckle with which he recompensed the boy, were only to be exceeded by the chuckle with which he sat down breathless in his chair again, and chuckled till he cried.

He dressed himself "all in his best," and got out into the streets. The people were by this time pouring forth, as he had seen them with the Ghost of Christmas Present; and walking with his hands behind him, Scrooge regarded every one with a delighted smile. He looked so irresistibly pleasant, in a word, that three or four good-humored fellows said "Good morning, sir! A Merry Christmas to you!" And Scrooge said often afterward, that of all the blithe sounds he ever heard, those were the blithest in his ears.

He had not gone far, when coming on toward him he beheld the portly gentleman, who had walked into his counting-house the day before, and said "Scrooge and Marley's, I believe?" It sent a pang across his heart to think how this old gentleman would look upon him when they met; but he knew what path lay straight before him, and he took it.

"My dear sir," said Scrooge, quickening his pace, and taking the old gentleman by both his hands, "how do you do? I hope you succeeded yesterday. It was very kind of you. A Merry Christmas to you, sir!"

"Mr. Scrooge?"

"Yes," said Scrooge. "That is my name, and I fear it may not be pleasant to you. Allow me to ask your pardon. And will you have the goodness"—here Scrooge whispered in his ear.

"Lord bless me!" cried the gentleman, as if his breath were taken away. "My dear Mr. Scrooge, are you serious?"

"If you please," said Scrooge. "Not a farthing less. A great many back payments are included in it, I assure you. Will you do me that favor?"

"My dear sir," said the other, shaking hands with him, "I don't know what to say to such munifi—"

"Don't say anything, please," retorted Scrooge. "Come and see me. Will you come and see me?"

"I will!" cried the old gentleman. And it was clear he meant to do it.

"Thank'ee," said Scrooge. "I am much obliged to you. I thank you fifty times. Bless you!"

He went to church, and walked about the streets and watched the people hurrying to and fro, and patted the children on the head, and looked down into the kitchens of houses, and up to the windows; and found everything could yield him pleasure. He had never dreamed that any walk—that any thing—could give him so much happiness. In the afternoon, he turned his steps toward his nephew's house.

He passed the door a dozen times, before he had the courage to go up and knock. But he made a dash, and did it.

"Is your master at home, my dear?" said Scrooge to the girl. Nice girl! Very.

"Yes, sir."

"Where is he?" said Scrooge.

"He's in the dining-room, sir, along with mistress. I'll show you up-stairs, if you please."

"Thank'ee. He knows me," said Scrooge, with his hand already on the dining-room lock. "I'll go in here, my dear."

He turned it gently, and sidled his face in, round the door. They were looking at the table (which was spread out in great array); for these young housekeepers are always nervous on such points, and like to see that everything is right.

"Fred!" said Scrooge.

"Why, bless my soul!" cried Fred, "who's that?"

"It's I. Your Uncle Scrooge. I have come to dinner. Will you let me in, Fred?"

Let him in! It is a mercy he didn't shake his arm off. He was at home in five minutes. Nothing could be heartier.

But he was early at the office next morning. Oh, he was early there. If he could only be there first, and catch Bob Cratchit coming late! That was the thing he had set his heart upon.

And he did it; yes, he did! The clock struck nine. No Bob. A quarter past. No Bob. He was full eighteen minutes and a half behind his time. Scrooge sat with his door wide open, that he might see him come into the tank.

His hat was off, before he opened the door; his comforter too. He was on his stool in a jiffy; driving away with his pen, as if he were trying to overtake nine o'clock.

"Hallo!" growled Scrooge, in his accustomed voice as near as he could feign it. "What do you mean by coming here at this time of day?"

"I am very sorry, sir," said Bob. "I *am* behind my time."

"You are!" repeated Scrooge. "Yes. I think you are. Step this way, sir, if you please."

"It's only once a year, sir," pleaded Bob, appearing from the tank. "It shall not be repeated. I was making rather merry yesterday, sir."

"Now, I'll tell you what, my friend," said Scrooge. "I am not going to stand this sort of thing any longer. And therefore I am about to raise your salary!"

"A Merry Christmas, Bob!" said Scrooge, with an earnestness that could not be mistaken, as he clapped him on the back, "A Merrier

Christmas, Bob, my good fellow, than I have given you for many a year! I'll raise your salary, and endeavor to assist your struggling family, and we will discuss your affairs this very afternoon. Make up the fires, and buy another coal scuttle before you dot another i, Bob Cratchit!"

Scrooge was better than his word. He did it all, and infinitely more; and to Tiny Tim, who did NOT die, he was a second father. He became as good a friend, as good a master, and as good a man, as the good old city knew, or any other good old city, town, or borough, in the good old world. Some people laughed to see the alteration in him, but he let them laugh, and little heeded them; for he was wise enough to know that nothing ever happened on this globe, for good, at which some people did not have their fill of laughter in the outset; and knowing that such as these would be blind anyway, he thought it quite as well that they should wrinkle up their eyes in grins, as have the malady in less attractive forms. His own heart laughed: and that was quite enough for him.

He had no further intercourse with Spirits, but lived upon the Total Abstinence Principle, ever afterward; and it was always said of him, that he knew how to keep Christmas well, if any man alive possessed the knowledge. May that be truly said of us, and all of us! And so, as Tiny Tim observed, God bless Us, Every One!

THE CHRISTMAS BABE.

BY MARGARET E. SANGSTER.

We love to think of Bethlehem,

That little mountain town,

To which, on earth's first Christmas Day,

Our blessed Lord came down.

A lowly manger for His bed,

The cattle near in stall,

There, cradled close in Mary's arms,

He slept, the Lord of all.

If we had been in Bethlehem,

We too had hasted fain

To see the Babe whose little face

Knew neither care nor pain.

Like any little child of ours,

He came unto His own,

Through Cross and shame before Him stretched,—

His pathway to His Throne.

If we had dwelt in Bethlehem,

We would have followed fast,

And where the Star had led our feet

Have knelt ere dawn was past.

Our gifts, our songs, our prayers had been

An offering, as He lay,

The blessed Babe of Bethlehem,

In Mary's arms that day.

Now breaks the latest Christmas Morn!

Again the angels sing,

And far and near the children throng

Their happy hymns to bring.

All heaven is stirred! All earth is glad!

For down the shining way,

The Lord who came to Bethlehem,

Comes yet, on Christmas Day.

A WESTERN CHRISTMAS IN THE OLD DAYS.

BY MRS. W. H. CORNING.

Christmas week there was no school, but such a succession of dining days, and visiting days, and day parties, and night parties, that Fanny, who looked forward to the week as a season of rest, thought that the regular routine of school duties would be less fatiguing.

Christmas at La Belle Prairie was the one jubilee of the year, something to be talked about for six months beforehand, and to be remembered as long after. It was a time of feasting and recreation for both master and servant. Days before, preparations commenced in the kitchen. Various smells issued from thence—savory smells of boiled, baked, and roasted meats; and sweet delicious smells of warm pastry and steaming cakes. Aunt Tibby was rolling pie-crust or stirring cake all day long, and the chopping of sausage-meat, the pounding of spices, and the beating of eggs were constantly heard. Everything was carried on with the greatest secrecy. The children were all kept out of the kitchen, and when "somefin' good" was to be transferred therefrom to Miss Car'line's store-room, Aunt Tibby came sailing in, holding it high above the reach of the curious little heads.

"I don't care," said Cal. "There's six pound-cakes all in a row on the store-room shelf. I see 'em when ma opened the door; and Marthy says one of 'em got currants in it, and there's a little shoat thar roasted whole. O! how I wish Christmas was come."

Coming suddenly upon Maud one day, Fanny found her with her apron half full of bran, while her fingers were busily at work upon a few pieces of faded silk. Maud tried to hide them at first, but finding by Fanny's question of "What is it, Maud?" that it was too late, she had looked up with a tired, flushed face and said:

"Miss Fanny, don't you tell now! will you? I'm makin' a pin-cushion for Aunt Phœbe, but it won't come square, all I can do. It acts awfully."

"Let me see what the trouble is," said Fanny, and sitting down, she examined the poor cushion; which, indeed, under Maud's hands, was not soon likely to come into shape.

"You see," said Maud, "I want to give aunty a Christmas gift, and I thought a cushion would be so nice, 'cause her old one that she wears pinned to her waist, you know, has burst a great hole, and the bran keeps tumbling out. I'm going to make her a right nice one, only I wish 'twas brighter, 'cause aunty likes red, and yellow, and all them, so bad."

Fanny searched her piece bag and brought forth bits of gay ribbon, the sight of which threw Maud into ecstasies of delight, then giving up the morning to the job, she cut and planned, and fitted and basted together, getting all in order, so that Maud could do the sewing herself.

"Aunty wouldn't think half so much of it if I didn't," said the child.

Well and faithfully Maud performed her labor of love, giving up her much-prized runs on the prairie, and resisting all the children's entreaties to play with them, till the Christmas gift was finished. It was no small task, for Maud most heartily hated to sew, and her fingers were anything but nimble in the operation. "I always did despise to sew, Miss Fanny," she said, "but I'm going to make this cushion for aunty anyhow."

It was finished at last, and, as Maud expressed it, "was just as beautiful as it could be." There never was a prouder, happier child. She did not thank Fanny in words for her assistance, but that night she came softly behind her, and putting her arms around her neck, gave her an earnest kiss, a proceeding which called forth an exclamation of surprise from Mrs. Catlett, for Maud was very chary of her caresses.

Christmas morning came, and long before daylight, every child upon the place, both black and white, was up ready to "march in Christmas." There had been mysterious preparations the night before, such as the hiding of tin pans and glass bottles under the bed, and the faint tooting of an old horn, heard down at the quarters, as though some one was rehearsing a part. Fanny was also astonished by an application from little "darky Tom" for permission to use her school-bell, the said cow-tinkler not being remarkable for sweetness of sound.

"O, yes, Tom, you may take it; but what can you want of it?"

"Couldn't tell no ways, Miss Fanny," said Tom, with a grin. "Mebbe Miss Fanny know in de mornin'."

Morning did indeed bring an explanation of the mystery. Assembling in the yard, the children marshaled themselves into marching order; Maud, of course, being captain, and taking the lead, bearing an old tin horn, while little black Tom brought up the rear with Fanny's unfortunate cow-bell.

In this order they commenced "marching in Christmas" to the music of the horn, the beating of tin pans, the rattling of bits of iron and pieces of wood, the jingling of bells, and the clapping of hands. Into the house, and up-stairs to the very doors of the sleeping-rooms, they all marched with their horrid din. It was received with tolerable good-humor by all but Nanny, who, deprived of her morning nap by the tumult, raved at the juvenile disturbers of the peace, and finally threw her shoes at them as they stood on the stairway. These were directly seized upon as trophies, and carried off in triumph to the quarters, where the young performers went through with the same operations.

"Christmas gift! Christmas gift!" was the first salutation from the servants this morning, and it was well worth while to give them some trifling present, were it only to hear their extravagant expressions of gratitude and delight. It was impossible to forget for a moment that it was Christmas. One could see it in the faces of the servants, released for a whole week from their daily tasks, and rejoicing in the prospect of dances, and parties, and visits to friends and kindred on distant plantations. The children, too, with their boisterous merriment and constant talk about the holidays, seemed determined to bear it in mind, and the great dinner—the one dinner of the year—in the preparation of which Aunt Tibby had exercised all her skill; this, in itself, seemed to proclaim that it was Christmas.

"Oh, Miss Fanny," said little Joy, "don't you wish Christmas lasted the whole year round?"

The short December day was fast drawing to a close, as a party of four rode leisurely along the road crossing La Belle Prairie. The ladies, though scarcely recognizable in their close hoods, long blue cotton riding skirts, and thick gloves, were none other than Miss Nancy Catlett and our friend Fanny, while their attendants were Mr. Chester, the town gentleman, and Massa Dave Catlett, who had come over from his new home in Kansas, on purpose to enjoy the Christmas festivities on the prairie. One of those night parties, of which Nanny had talked so much, was to come off at Col. Turner's, and this was the place of their destination. In accordance with the customs of society in these parts, they were to remain until the next day, and, accordingly, black Viny rode a little in the rear, mounted upon old "Poke Neck," and bearing sundry carpet-bags and valises, containing the ladies' party-dresses.

Just at dusk, our party reached their journey's end, and dismounting one by one from the horse-block in front of the house, they walked up the road, and were met in the porch by Miss Bell Turner, Nanny's particular friend. This young lady, with long curls and a very slender waist, performed the duties of hostess in a free and easy manner, ushering the gentlemen into the parlor, where a fire was blazing on the hearth, while the ladies, with their attendants, were conducted up-stairs to the dressing-room.

Here a dozen or more were engaged in the mysteries of the toilet, braiding, twisting, and curling, while as many servants were flying about, stumbling over each other, and creating the most dire confusion in their efforts to supply the wants of their respective mistresses. The beds and chairs were covered with dresses, capes, ribbons, curling-irons, flowers, combs, and brushes, and all the paraphernalia of the toilet, while the ladies themselves kept up a continual stream of conversation with each other and their attendants.

Into this scene Nanny entered with great spirit. Shaking hands all round, and introducing Fanny, she hastily threw off her bonnet and shawl, and bidding Viny unpack the things, she set about dressing in good earnest.

"How nice to get here so early," she said. "Now we can have a chance at the glass, and plenty of room to move about in."

Fanny wondered what she called plenty of room, but had yet to learn the signification of the term when applied to the dressing-room of a western party. Thicker and faster came the arrivals, and it being necessary that each lady should undergo a thorough transformation in dress, before making her appearance down-stairs, the labor and confusion necessary to bring this about can be imagined. Such hurryings to and fro, such knockings down and pickings up, such scolding and laughing, in short such a Babel of sounds as filled the room for an hour or two, Fanny had never heard before. Completing her own toilet as soon as possible, she seated herself upon one of the beds, and watched the proceedings with great interest.

"You Suke, bring me some more pins, directly." "O please, Miss Ellen, mind my wreath!" "Jule, how much longer are you goin' to keep the wash-bowl?" "Dar now, Miss Eveline done get her coat all wet." "Did you know Tom Walton was here? I see him in the passage." "Miss Belle, that's *my* starch-bag." "There, now! don't them slippers fit beautiful?" "Why don't that girl come back?" "O, Liza, just fasten up my dress, that's a dear girl!" "Come, girls, do hurry, we shan't be dressed to-night."

How it was all brought about, Fanny could not tell, but at last the ladies were dressed, the last sash pinned, and the last curl adjusted. Dresses of thin material, cut low in the neck, with short sleeves, seemed to be the order of the night, which with wreaths, and bunches of artificial flowers in the hair, gave the ladies a handsome appearance. With Miss Belle at the head, they all descended to the parlor, and found the gentlemen strolling about, employing themselves as they could, till the night's amusements commenced; and, indeed, both ladies and gentlemen manifested such eagerness to adjourn to the play-room, that the signal was soon given, and they proceeded forthwith to a log building in the yard, formerly used as a school-room.

Games soon commenced, and were carried on with great vigor, the young people making up in activity what was lacking in gracefulness of motion. Game after game was made out, the ladies vying with each other to see who should laugh the most, while those who were left chatted gayly together in groups, or tried their powers of fascination upon some long-limbed specimen of humanity.

"What calls the gentlemen up-stairs so frequently?" inquired Fanny, innocently, as groups of two and three disappeared up the steps leading to the room above.

"You are not aware, then, what a formidable rival the ladies have up in the loft?" said Mr. Chester, gravely, though there was a comical expression about the corners of his mouth.

"No, indeed."

"Well, I only hope you may not witness the overpowering influence sometimes exerted by this same rival," said Mr. Chester; "but honestly, Miss Hunter, there is serious danger that some of these light-footed young gentlemen may, ere long, be obliged to relinquish their places in our party, all through the attractions presented to them up yonder."

"I don't in the least know what you mean."

"In plain words, then, they are talking about horses up there; men are crazy over horses you know."

"Are you in earnest, Mr. Chester?"

"Certainly I am. It would not answer, I suppose, for ladies to intrude upon their modest retirement, or I could convince you in a moment."

"How can you joke about it, Mr. Chester? I think it is perfectly scandalous."

"Well, it is bad enough," said her companion, more gravely. "One living at the west becomes accustomed to such things."

"I never will," said Fanny. "If I had known these Christmas parties countenanced such impoliteness, I would have stayed at home."

"A set supper," Nanny had several times expressed a hope that Mrs. Turner would provide, and she was not disappointed. The long table was bountifully spread with the substantials of this life, and though not in the style of an entertainment in Fifth Avenue, it was admirably suited to the guests who partook of it. A roasted "shoat" graced each end of the board, a side of bacon the centre, while salted beef, cut in thin slices, with pickles and cheese, constituted the side-dishes. Hot coffee, corn bread and biscuit were passed to each guest, and a piece of pound-cake and a little preserved fruit for dessert.

There was plenty of laughter and hearty joking at the table, and the flushed faces and increased volubility of the gentlemen gave too certain evidence of the truth of Mr. Chester's assertions.

"The langest day maun hae an end," says the old Scotch proverb, audit was with a sigh of relief that Fanny at last saw Uncle Jake lay down the tortured fiddle, and the guests with lingering steps and wishful eyes retire to seek the few hours of repose that were left of the night. "Confusion worse confounded" reigned for a time in the apartment appropriated to the ladies' use, and the numerous couches spread upon the floor increased the difficulty of navigation. At last, when quiet seemed restored, and Fanny was sinking into a peaceful sleep, she was aroused by her neighbors in an adjoining bed, three young ladies who declared that they were "all but starved, and must have something to eat before they could go to sleep." One of the black women was despatched to the store-room for some slices of cold bacon, and sitting up in bed, with the candle before them, they made a hearty repast.

"Of course, you can't eat half as much as you want at table," said one of the young ladies, apologetically; "one always wants to appear delicate-like before the gentlemen."

"What in goodness' name, Nan, made breakfast so late?" said Dave the next morning, or rather noon, as they were returning home; "I thought one while we wasn't goin' to get any." "Why, you see, they hadn't any wheat flour in the house for the biscuit," said Nanny, "and they had to send three miles over the prairie to Mr. John Turner's to borrow some."

"Twenty people invited to stay over night, and no flour in the house?" said Fanny, in amazement.

"It rather shocks your Yankee ideas of looking out ahead, Miss Hunter," said Mr. Chester, laughing. "We are used to such things out this way."

"Oh! Miss Fanny, people can't remember everything, you know," said Nanny; "Belle says they never thought a word about it till this morning."

JOE'S SEARCH FOR SANTA CLAUS.

BY IRVING BACHELLER

A story, my child? Well, there's none that I know

As good as the story about little Joe.

He lived with his mother, just under the eaves

Of a tenement high, where the telegraph weaves

Its highway of wire, that everywhere goes,

And makes the night musical when the wind blows.

Their home had no father—the two were bereft

Of all but their appetites—those never left!

Joe's grew with his thought; a day never passed

He spent not in hunger to make the food last;

And days when his mother silently went

And stood by the windows—Joe knew what it meant.

They'd nothing for supper! The words were so sad

That somehow they drowned all the hunger he had.

And surely God's miracles never have ceased—

Joe's hunger grew less when his sorrows increased.

When the coal ran out in winter's worst storm,

The fire burnt the harder that kept their hearts warm.

Their windows revealed many wonderful sights,

Long acres of roofing and high-flying kites;

At sunset, the great vault of heaven aglow,

The lining of gold on the clouds hanging low,

The cross on the top of St. Mary's high tower

Ablaze with the light of that magical hour;

And still, as the arrows of light slanted higher,

The last thing in sight was the great cross of fire.

Each day, as it vanished, the history old

Of Christ's crucifixion was reverently told;

To Him the boy learned to confide all his woes,

But oftenest prayed for a new suit of clothes,

Since those that he wore didn't fit him at all—

The coat was too large and the trousers too small,

And Joe looked so queer, from his head to his feet,

It grieved his proud soul to be seen in the street.

And sometimes he cherished a secret desire

To own a hand-sled, or to build a bonfire;

But reached one conclusion by various routes—

He could have better fun with a new pair of boots.

He thought how the old pair, when shiny and whole,

Had squeaked in a way that delighted his soul,

And remembrance grew sad as he strutted around

And tried hard, but vainly, to waken that sound.

The day before Christmas brought trouble for Joe,

A thousand times worse. 'Twas a terrible blow

To hear that old Santa Claus, god of his dreams,

Would not come that year with his fleet-footed teams.

He'd seen them. Why, once, of a night's witching hour

He saw them jump over the cross on the tower

And scamper away o'er the snow-covered roofs,

His heart beating time to the sound of their hoofs.

Not coming this year? Santa Claus must be dead,

He thought, as with sad tears he crept into bed.

And, as he lay thinking, the long strings of wire

Sang low in the wind like a deep-sounding lyre,

And Joe caught the notes of this solemn refrain—

"He'll not come again! no, he'll not come again!"

And oh! how the depths of his spirit were stirred

By thoughts that were born of the music he heard!

How cold were the winds, and they sang in their strife,

Of storms yet to come in the winters of life.

They mocked him, but mark how the faith of the child

Stood firm as a fortress, its hope undefiled;

For still the boy thought that, if Santa Claus knew

How great were their needs and their comforts how few,

He would come; and at length, when the first rays of light

Had fathomed the infinite depths of the night,

And brightened the windows, Joe cautiously crept

Out of bed: and he dressed while his mother still slept,

And down the long stairways on tiptoe he ran;

Then out in the snow, with the will of a man,

He went, looking hither and thither, because,

Poor boy! he was trying to find Santa Claus.

He hurried along through the snow-burdened street

As if the good angels were guiding his feet;

And as the sun rose in the heavens apace,

A radiance fell on his uplifted face

That came from the cross gleaming far overhead—

A symbol of hope for the living and dead.

A moment he looked at the great house of prayer,

Then slyly peeked in to see what was there;

And entering softly he wandered at will

Through pathways of velvet, deserted and still,

And saw the light grow on a wonderful scene

Of ivy-twined columns and arches of green,

And back of the rail, where the clergyman knelt,

He sat on the cushions to see how they felt.

How soft was that velvet he stroked with his hand!

But when he lay down, oh, the feeling was grand!

And while he was musing the walls seemed to sway,

And slowly the windows went moving away.

What, ho! there he comes! with his big pack and all,

Down the sunbeams that slope from the high-windowed wall,

And Joe tried to speak, but could not, if he died,

When Santa Claus came and sat down by his side.

"A tenement boy! humph! he probably swears."

(Joe trembled, and tried hard to think of his prayers.)

He lifted Joe's eyelids, he patted his brow,

And said. "He is not a bad boy, anyhow."

But hark! there is music; a deep-swelling sound

Is sweeping on high as if heavenward bound.

And suddenly waking, Joe saw kneeling there

The rector, long-robed, who was reading a prayer.

"Provide for the fatherless children," said he

"The widowed, the helpless, the bond and the free."

The rector stops praying—his face wears a frown;

A ragged young gamin is pulling his gown.

"I knowed you would come," said the boy, half in fright—

"I knowed you would come—I was watchin' all night.

Say! what are ye goin' t'give mother an' me?

Le'me see what 'tis, Santa Claus—please le'me see!"

The rector looked down into Joe's honest face,

And a great wave of feeling swept over the place;

And tenderly laying his hand on Joe's head,

He turned to the people and solemnly said:

"We pray that the poor may be sheltered and fed,

And we leave it to Heaven to furnish the bread.

Ye know, while He feedeth the fowls in the air.

The children of mankind He leaves to man's care;"

And kissing Joe's face the preacher said then;

"Of such is the kingdom of Heaven. Amen!"

That day Santa Claus came to many a door

He'd forgotten to call at the evening before.

Was little Joe lucky? Well, now, you are right.

And the wires sang merrily all the next night.

ANGELA'S CHRISTMAS.

BY JULIA SCHAYER.

"Then it is 'yes,' father dear?" said Angela, looking across the breakfast table with a smile. It was her mother's smile, and the girl had filled her mother's vacant chair for more than a year.

The eyes of the father and daughter met, and Angela knew, before a word was said, that she had conquered.

"I hate to see you at your age, beginning to worry over these things," Ephraim Frazier said, regretfully. "Let the *old* women take care of the charities, dear. You keep on dancing in the sunshine a while longer, daughter."

Angela's smile grew graver, but not less sweet.

"I am twenty, dear," she said. "Too old to dance *all* the time, and I cannot help *thinking*, you know. And—it's no use, papa dear! I *must* do something! It *is* 'yes,' isn't it?"

"You are sure you won't mind being criticised and ridiculed?"

"Quite sure!" answered Angela.

"And sure you won't take your failures and disappointments to heart too deeply?"

"Quite sure I can bear them bravely," answered the girl. "If only one, *just one*, of those poor creatures may be helped, and lifted up, and brought out of darkness, it will be worth trying for!"

"And what does Robert Johns say about it?"

A glow kindled in Angela's face.

"Robert is in perfect sympathy with me," she said softly. Then
again, this time having risen and gone around to his side, to
speak with her face against the old banker's smoothly shaven
cheek, "It *is* 'yes,' isn't it, daddy dear?"

"Well, yes! Only you must go slow, dear. You are not over strong,
you know."

And soon it came to pass that on a vacant lot, hitherto given over
to refuse heaps, haunted by stray cats, ragpickers, and vagrant
children, in one of the vilest quarters of the metropolis, there
sprang up, with magic swiftness, a commodious frame building,
surrounded by smooth green sod, known in the lower circles as the
Locust Street Home; in upper circles, laughingly denominated
"Angela's Experiment."

Angela did not mind. It was mostly goodnatured laughter, and
many of the laughers ended by lending willing hands and hearts
to the cause. It was wonderful how the news spread through the
city's purlieus that here was a sanctuary into which cold, hunger,
and fatigue dared not intrude; a place which the lowest might
enter and be made welcome, and go unquestioned, his personal
rights as carefully respected as though he were one of the Four
Hundred.

That was Angela's theory. No man, woman, or child should
be *compelled* to anything. First make their bodies comfortable,
then surround them with ennobling influences and examples,
entertain them, arouse them, stimulate them, hold out the helping
hand, *and leave the rest to God.* "They shall not even
be *compelled* to be clean!" she said, laughing. "If the beautiful clean

bathrooms and clean clothing do not tempt them to cleanliness, then so be it! I will have no rules; only influences. You will see!"

And people did see, and wondered.

Sometimes, on warm, pleasant evenings, the spacious, cheerful hall, with its tables and chairs, would be almost empty; but on nights like that on which this story opens, a dark, cold December night, the seats were apt to be well filled, mostly with slatternly, hard-featured women, and dull-faced children, who sat staring stolidly about, while the music and speaking went on; half stupefied by the warmth and tranquillity so foreign to their lives.

Outside, a dismal sleet was falling, but from the open door of the vestibule a great sheet of light fell upon the wet pavement, and above it glowed a transparency bearing the words:

"A Merry Christmas to all! Come in!"

It was while the singing was going on, led by a high, sweet girl's voice, that a human figure came hobbling out from a side street, and stopped short at the very edge of the lighted space.

A woman by her dress, an old, old woman, with a seamed, blotched face; an ugly, human wreck, all torn and battered and discolored by the storms of life. Such was old Marg—"Luny Marg," as she was called in the haunts that knew her best. Her history? She had forgotten it herself, very likely, and there was no one to know or care—no one in the wide world to care if she should at any moment be trampled to death, or slip from the dock into the black river. The garret which lodged her would find another tenant; the children of the gutters another target for their missiles. Not that she was worse than others—only that she was old and ugly and sharp of tongue, and the world—even her world—has no use for such as she.

For some time this forlorn creature continued to hover on the edge of the lighted space. The sleet had become snow, and already a thin white film covered the pavement, promising "a white Christmas," and the cold increased from moment to moment.

The woman drew her filthy shawl closer; her jaws chattered, yet she seemed unable to tear herself from the spot. Her eyes, alert under their gray brows, as a rat's, were fixed now upon the open door, now upon the transparency, yet she made no motion toward the proffered shelter. Two men, hirsute and ragged, stopped near her and, after a moments consultation, slunk across the square of light and disappeared in the building. As the door was opened, there came a fuller burst of song, and a rush of warm air, fragrant with the aroma of coffee and oysters.

The old woman's body quivered with desire; food, warmth, rest— all that her miserable frame demanded—were there within easy reach, for the mere asking; nay for the mere taking; yet still the devils of stubbornness and spite would not let go their hold upon her. But finally, as a bitter blast swept the snow stingingly against her face, she uttered a hoarse snarl, and glancing about to see that no jeering eye was upon her, the poor creature crept across the pavement, clambered up the stone steps, and, pushing open the door, slipped into the nearest vacant seat.

The chairs and benches were unusually well filled. Numbers of women and children were in the foreground. A few men were also present, sitting with their bodies hanging forward, their hats tightly clutched between their knees, their eyes fixed on the floor. The women and children, on the contrary, followed every movement of the young women on the platform with furtive eagerness.

The simplicity of attire which Angela and her friends had assumed did not deceive even the tiniest gutter-child present—

these were "ladies," and one and all accorded them the same tribute of genuine, if reluctant, admiration.

Old Marg, after the embarrassment of the first moment, took everything in with one hawk-like glance—the Christmas greens upon the clean, white walls, the curtained space in the rear which hid some pleasant mystery, the men and women on the platform.

At the organ sat a young girl, leaning upon the now silent keys, her face toward the young man who was speaking. Old Marg could not take her eyes from this face—white, serious, sweet, set in a halo of pale golden hair. The sight of it aroused strange feelings in the bosom of the old outcast. Fascinated, tortured, bewildered, she sat and gazed. It was long since she had thought of her youth. This girl reminded her of that forgotten time. Like a violet flung upon a refuse-heap, the thought of her own innocent girlhood lay for an instant upon the foul mass of memories accumulated by sixty-miserable years. "I was light-haired, too!" ran old Marg's thoughts. "Light-haired, an' light-complected, like her!"

The perfume of that thought breathed across her soul, and was gone. Still she gazed from under her shaggy brows, and, without meaning to listen, found herself hearing what the speaker was saying. He was telling without rhetoric or cant the story of Christ, and with simplicity and tact presenting the lesson of His life.

"This joy of giving, of sacrificing for others," the young man was saying in his earnest, musical voice, "so far beyond the joy of receiving, is within the reach of every human being. Think of that! The poorest man or woman or child who breathes on earth to-night may know this joy, may give some pleasure, some help, some comfort, to some fellow-creature. Whether it be a human creature or a dumb beast, matters not. It is all one in God's sight, being an act of love and kindness and sacrifice."

Old Marg looked down upon her squalid rags; her rough features writhed with a scornful smile. "That's a lie!" she muttered. "What could the likes of *me* do for anybody, I'd like to know!"

Still she listened; but at last, as the warmth stole through her sodden garments, and into her chilled veins, and the peace of the place penetrated the turbulent recesses of her soul, the man's voice became like a voice heard in a dream, and the old outcast slept.

A confused sound greeted her awakening. Some one was playing the organ jubilantly; people were moving about—girls with trays loaded with steaming dishes; children were talking and laughing excitedly. The curtain had been drawn, and a great Christmas-tree almost blinded her with its splendor. She stared about in bewilderment. She looked at the tree, at the people, at her own foul rags. A fierce revulsion of feeling swept over her. Rage, shame, a desire to get out of sight, to be swallowed up in the darkness and misery which were her proper element, seized and mastered her. She staggered to her feet. A young girl approached her with a tray of tempting food. The sight and smell of it goaded the starved creature to madness. She could have fallen upon it like a wolf, but instead she pushed the girl roughly aside and fumbled dizzily at the door-knob.

A hand was laid upon her arm. The girl with the sweet, white face was looking at her with a friendly smile.

"Won't you stay and have something warm to eat before going into the cold?" the girl asked gently.

Old Marg shook the hand from her arm.

"No!" she snarled. "I don't want nothin'! Let me go!"

With a patient smile Angela opened the door.

"I am sorry you will not stay," she said softly. "It would give me great pleasure. There is a gift for you on the tree, too. It is Christmas Eve, you know!"

A hoarse, choking sound came from the woman's lips. She pushed by into the vestibule. Angela followed.

"If you should feel differently to-morrow," she said, in her kind, gentle voice, "come here again, about eleven o'clock. I shall be here." Without waiting for a reply, she re-entered the hall. A young man, the same who had been speaking, met her at the door.

"Angela!" he exclaimed. "You should not be out there in the cold!" She smiled absently. "Did you see her, Robert?"

"That terrible old woman? Yes, I saw her. A hopeless case, I fear."

Angela's eyes kept their absent look.

"It was awful to see her go away like that, into the cold and snow, hungry and half-clad!" she said.

The young man leaned nearer. "Angela," he whispered. "You must not let these things sink into your heart as you do, or you cannot bear the work you have undertaken. As for that old creature, it is terrible to think of her, but she seemed to me beyond our reach."

"But not beyond God's reach *through us*!" said Angela.

Meantime old Marg was facing the storm with rage and pain in her face and in her heart. The streets were deserted, and lighted only by such beams as found their way through the dirty windows of shops and saloons. From these last came sounds of revelry and contention, and at one or another the poor creature paused, listening without fear to the familiar hubbub. Should she go in? Some one might give her a drink, to ease for a time the terrible gnawing at her breast. Might? Yes; but more likely she would be thrust out with jeers and curses, and, for some reason, old Marg was in no mood to use the caustic wit and ready tongue that were her only weapons. So she staggered on until the swarming tenement was reached, stumbled up the five flights of unillumined stairs, and almost fell headlong into the dismal garret which she called her home.

Feeling about in the darkness, she found a match and lit a bit of candle which stopped the neck of an empty bottle. It burned uncertainly as if reluctant to disclose the scene upon which its light fell. A smoke-stained, sloping ceiling, a blackened floor, a shapeless mattress heaped with rags, a deal box, a rusty stove resting upon two bricks, supporting in its turn an ancient frying-pan, a chipped saucer, and a battered tin can from which, when the scavenger business was good, old Marg served afternoon tea—such were her home and all her personal belongings.

There was no fire, nor any means of producing one, but upon the box was spread a piece of paper containing a slice of bread and a soup-bone, whereto clung some fragments of meat—the gift of a neighbor hardly less wretched than herself.

The old woman's eyes glittered at the sight, and, seizing the food, she sank weakly upon the box and began gnawing at it; but her toothless jaws, stiff with cold, made no impression upon the tough meat and hard crust, and letting them drop to the floor, the poor creature fell to rocking to and fro, whimpering tearlessly, like a suffering dog. Strangely enough, within the withered bosom of this most wretched creature there had welled up, from some hidden source of womanly feeling, a passionate self-pity, a no less passionate self-loathing. This was what a moment's contact with all that she had so long abjured—purity, order, gentleness—had brought to pass.

That fair young girl-tall, pale, sweet as an Easter lily—stood before her like an incarnate memory, pointing toward the past, the far-distant past, when she, too, was young, and pretty, and innocent, and gay—too pretty and too gay for a poor working girl! That was where the trouble began.

"I was light haired, too," moaned old Marg, twisting her withered fingers restlessly. "Light-haired, and light-complected! A pretty girl, an' a good girl, too! Not like *her*. No! How could I be? Little the likes o' her knows what the likes o' me has to face! Lord!"

The bit of candle guttered and went out. The cold increased. It had ceased snowing, and a keen wind had arisen, tearing the clouds into shreds through which the stars gleamed. And presently the moon climbed up behind the belfry of the old church across the square, and sent one broad white ray through the dingy window and across the floor. All at once the great bell began to strike the midnight hour, its mingled vibrations filling the garret with tumultuous sounds. The vision of the fair girl faded, and old Marg was herself again, a hard, bitter, rebellious old woman, with a burning care where her heart had been, and only one thought, one desire, left in her desperate mind—the thought and the desire of death.

In young and passionate days she had often thought of seeking that way out of life's agonies, but at its worst there is always some sweetness left in the cup—when one is young! It was not so now. The dregs only had been hers for many a year, and she had enough. Death—yes, that was best.

~ 100 ~

Her eyes glittered as she cast a look about the silent room. Bare, even of the means to this end! Ah, the window!

With an inarticulate cry the woman arose and hobbled along the shining moon-ray to the window, and threw open the sash. Awed by the stern beauty of the heavens, the splendor of the moon tangled in the lace-like carvings of the belfry as in a net, she leaned some moments against the sill, looking out and down. Far below lay the deserted square, its white bosom traced with the sharp shadow of the tower. With a keen eye old Marg measured the distance, a sheer descent of fifty feet. Nothing to break the fall—nothing!

One movement, a swift fall, and that white surface would be broken by a black shapeless heap. A policeman would find it on his next round, or some drunken reveler would stumble over it, or the good people on their way to early mass—ah! The seamed countenance lit up suddenly with a malignant joy.

Why not wait until they began to pass—those pious, respectable people in their comfortable furs and wools—and cast herself into their midst, a ghastly Christmas offering from Poverty to Riches, from Sin to Virtue? This suggestion commended itself highly to her sense of humor. With a hoarse chuckle she was about to close the window when a portion of the shadow that lay alongside the chimney showed signs of life, and, rising on four long and skinny legs, became a cat—a lean, black cat, which crept meekly toward the window, its phosphorescent eyes gleaming, its lank jaws parted in a vain effort to mew. Startled, old Marg drew back for an instant; then, glancing from the animal to the pavement below, a brutal cunning, a malicious pleasure, lit up the witch-like features. Reaching out one skinny arm, she called coaxingly:
"Puss! Puss!"

The cat dragged herself up to the outstretched arm, rubbing her lank body caressingly against it.

The cruel, cunning old face softened suddenly. "Lord!" muttered old Marg, "if she ain't a-tryin' to purr! Wall, that beats me!"

The poor beast continued its piteous appeal for aid, arching its starved frame, waving its tail, fawning unsuspectingly against the arm that had threatened.

With an impulse new to her misery-hardened heart, old Marg drew the animal in and closed the window. Far from resisting, the cat nestled against her with every sign of pleasure.

"She's been somebody's pet," said the old woman, placing her on the floor. "She ain't always been like this."

The divine emotion of pity, so new to this forlorn creature, grew and swelled in her bosom. The man at the hall had not lied, after all. Here was another of God's creatures as miserable as herself— nay, more so, for she had a roof to shelter her! And she could share it with this homeless one.

"Poor puss!" muttered old Marg, stroking the rough fur. "You're starvin', too, ain't ye? an' I ain't got nothin' to give ye, not a bite or a sup. Ah!"

Her eyes had fallen upon the discarded food. Eagerly she seized it and placed it before the cat; the starving creature gnawed greedily at the bone an instant, then looked up with a hopeless mew.

The old woman felt a keener pang of pity.

"Poor beast!" she said, with a bitter smile. "Ye can't eat 'em, can ye? No more could I! We're in the same box, puss! Old, an' toothless, an' nobody belongin' to us. We'll have to starve together, I guess. An' it's Christmas day! Did ye know that, puss? Christmas day! Lord! Lord!"

The cat rubbed against her skirts, her eyes fixed upon her benefactor's. "Seems to understand every word I say!" old Marg muttered. "If only I had a drop o' milk for her now!"

Hobbling to the stove, she examined the battered tin can, letting the moonlight shine into its rusty depths. A little water or tea remained in it, and with this she moistened some of the bread and placed it before the cat, which devoured it now eagerly. Then she took the animal in her arms and laid herself down on the mattress, drawing the ragged covers over them. The cat nestled against her side; the warmth of the two poor bodies mingled, and both slept.

The moon-ray crept along and spread itself over the heap of rags, the knotted fingers resting on the cat's rough fur, the seamed old face; it passed away, and morning dawned, with a peal of bells and the sound of footsteps on the pavement below, and still the two slept on.

Angela stood near the door, receiving her Christmas guests. They came straggling in, in twos and threes, some boldly and impudently, some shame-faced and shy, some eager, some indifferent, but all poverty-pinched. Each one was pleasantly welcomed, and passed on to the feast. Angela watched and waited, and at last the door opened slowly to admit old Marg, who stopped short on the threshold, with a look at once stubborn, appealing, suspicious, ashamed. Like a wild animal on the alert for the faintest sign of repulsion or danger, she stood there, but Angela only smiled, proffering her white, soft hand, destitute of jewels, but the hand of a lady.

"A Merry Christmas!" she said brightly.

"I was ugly to ye last night," said old Marg huskily, ignoring the beautiful hand she dared not touch.

"Never mind!" Angela answered sweetly. "You were tired."

"I am a bad old woman!" said old Marg, mistrustfully.

"Never mind that, either!" said Angela. "Let me be your friend. If you will, you shall never be cold or hungry again."

A profound wonder came into the old face—then it began to writhe, and from each eye oozed scant tears, seeking a channel amid the seams and wrinkles of the sunken cheeks.

"You will let me be your friend," urged Angela.

Still old Marg wept silently, the scant tears of age.

"You shall have a pleasant home and——"

A swift, suspicious glance darted from the wet eyes.

"Not a 'sylum, miss, please!" said the old woman.

"No," said Angela quietly. "Not an asylum, A home—a bright, clean, comfortable home——"

"I can work, miss!" put in old Marg, doubling her knotted hands to show their strength. "I can wash, an' scrub——"

"Yes," said Angela, "you may work all you are able, helping to keep things clean and comfortable."

Still old Marg looked doubtful. Wiping her cheeks with a corner of the shawl, she half turned toward the door.

"Have you a family, or any one belonging to you?" asked Angela, thinking to have reached the root of the difficulty.

"Yes," said the old woman stoutly. "I have a cat. Where I go, she must go, too!"

Angela patted the grimy hand, with a laugh which was good to hear.

"I understand you perfectly," she said. "I have a cat of my own. You and *your* cat shall not be separated."

A half-hour later entered the young man Robert. Angela pointed silently to old Marg, sitting in a warm corner, contentedly munching her Christmas dinner. "What have you done to her?" he asked. "She looks more human already."

Angela laughed again, that same laugh which goes to one's heart so. "I have adopted her—and her cat!" she answered. "That's all!"

THE FIRST PURITAN CHRISTMAS TREE.

(ANONYMOUS.)

Mrs. Olcott called her boys, and bade them go to the pine woods and get the finest, handsomest young hemlock tree that they could find.

"Get one that is straight and tall, with well-boughed branches on it, and put it where you can draw it under the wood-shed after dark," she added.

The boys went to Pine Hill, and there they picked out the finest young tree on all the hill, and said, "We will take this one." So, with their hatchets they hewed it down and brought it safely home the next night when all was dark. And when Roger was quietly sleeping in the adjoining room, they dragged the tree into the kitchen. It was too tall, so they took it out again and cut it off two or three feet at the base. Then they propped it up, and the curtains being down over the windows, and blankets being fastened over the curtains to prevent any one looking in, and the door being doubly barred to prevent any one coming in, they all went to bed.

Very early the next morning, while the stars shone on the snow-covered hills—the same stars that shone sixteen hundred years before on the hills when Christ was born in Bethlehem—the little Puritan mother in New England arose very softly. She went out and lit the kitchen fire anew from the ash-covered embers. She fastened upon the twigs of the tree the gifts she had bought in Boston for her boys and girl. Then she took as many as twenty pieces of candle and fixed them upon the branches. After that she softly called Rupert, Robert and Lucy, and told them to get up and come into the kitchen.

Hurrying back, she began, with a bit of a burning stick, to light the candles. Just as the last one was set aflame, in trooped the three children.

Before they had time to say a word, they were silenced by their mother's warning.

"I wish to fetch Roger in and wake him up before it," she said. "Keep still until I come back!"

The little lad, fast asleep, was lifted in a blanket and gently carried by his mother into the beautiful presence.

"See! Roger, my boy, see!" she said, arousing him. "It is Christmas morning now! In England they only have Christmas-boughs, but here in New England we have a whole Christmas-tree."

"O mother!" he cried. "O Lucy! Is it really, really true, and no dream at all? Yes, I see! I see! O mother, it is so beautiful! Were all the trees on all the hills lighted up that way when Christ was born? And, mother," he added, clapping his little hands with joy at the thought, "why, yes, the stars did sing when Christ was born! They must be glad, then, and keep Christmas, too, in heaven. I know they must, and there will be good times there."

"Yes," said his mother; "there will be good times there, Roger."

"Then," said the boy, "I sha'n't mind going, now that I've seen the Christmas-bough. I—What is that, mother?"

What was it that they heard? The little Olcott home had never before seemed to tremble so. There were taps at the window, there were knocks at the door—and it was as yet scarcely the break of day! There were voices also, shouting something to somebody.

"Shall I put out the candles, mother?" whispered Robert.

"What will they do to us for having the tree? I wish we hadn't it," regretted Rupert; while Lucyclung to her mother's gown and shrieked with all her strength, "It's Indians!"

Pale and white and still, ready to meet her fate, stood Mrs. Olcott, until, out of the knocking and the tapping at her door, her heart caught a sound. It was a voice calling, "Rachel! Rachel! Rachel!"

"Unbar the door!" she cried back to her boys; "it's your father calling!" Down came the blankets; up went the curtain; open flew the door, and in walked Captain Olcott, followed by every man and woman in Plymouth who had heard at break of day the glorious news that the expected ship had arrived at Boston, and with it the long lost Captain Olcott. For an instant nothing was thought of except the joyous welcoming of the Captain in his new home.

"What's this? What is it? What does this mean?" was asked again and again, when the first excitement was passed, as the tall young pine stood aloft, its candles ablaze, its gifts still hanging.

"It's welcome home to father!" said Lucy, her only thought to screen her mother.

"No, child, no!" sternly spoke Mrs. Olcott. "Tell the truth!"

"It's—a—Christmas-tree!" faltered poor Lucy.

One and another and another, Pilgrims and Puritans all, drew near with faces stern and forbidding, and gazed and gazed, until one and another and yet another softened slowly into a smile as little Roger's piping voice sung out:

"She made it for me, mother did. But you may have it now, and all the pretty things that are on it, too, because you've brought my father back again; if mother will let you," he added.

Neither Pilgrim nor Puritan frowned at the gift. One man, the sternest there, broke off a little twig and said:

"I'll take it for the sake of the good old times at home."

THE FIRST CHRISTMAS IN NEW ENGLAND.

BY HEZEKIAH BUTTERWORTH.

They thought they had come to their port that day,

But not yet was their journey done;

And they drifted away from Provincetown Bay

In the fireless light of the sun.

With rain and sleet were the tall masts iced,

And gloomy and chill was the air,

But they looked from the crystal sails to Christ,

And they came to a harbor fair.

The white hills silent lay,—

For there were no ancient bells to ring,

No priests to chant, no choirs to sing,

No chapel of baron, or lord, or king,

That gray, cold winter day.

The snow came down on the vacant seas,

And white on the lone rocks lay,—

But rang the axe 'mong the evergreen trees

And followed the Sabbath day.

Then rose the sun in a crimson haze,

And the workmen said at dawn:

"Shall our axes swing on this day of days,

When the Lord of Life was born?"

The white hills silent lay,—

For there were no ancient bells to ring,

No priests to chant, no choirs to sing,

No chapel of baron, or lord, or king,

That gray, cold Christmas Day.

"The old town's bells we seem to hear:

They are ringing sweet on the Dee;

They are ringing sweet on the Harlem Meer,

And sweet on the Zuyder Zee.

The pines are frosted with snow and sleet.

Shall we our axes wield

When the chimes at Lincoln are ringing sweet

And the bells of Austerfield?"

The air was cold and gray,—

And there were no ancient bells to ring,

No priests to chant, no choirs to sing,

No chapel of baron, or lord, or king,

That gray, cold Christmas Day.

Then the master said, "Your axes wield,

Remember ye Malabarre Bay;

And the covenant there with the Lord ye sealed;

Let your axes ring to-day.

You may talk of the old town's bells to-night,

When your work for the Lord is done,

And your boats return, and the shallop's light

Shall follow the light of the sun.

The sky is cold and gray,—

And here are no ancient bells to ring,

No priests to chant, no choirs to sing,

No chapel of baron, or lord, or king.

This gray, cold Christmas Day.

"If Christ was born on Christmas Day,

And the day by Him is blest,

Then low at His feet the evergreens lay

And cradle His church in the West.

Immanuel waits at the temple gates

Of the nation to-day ye found,

And the Lord delights in no formal rites;

To-day let your axes sound!"

The sky was cold and gray,—

And there were no ancient bells to ring,

No priests to chant, no choirs to sing,

No chapel of baron, or lord, or king,

That gray, cold Christmas Day.

Their axes rang through the evergreen trees

Like the bells on the Thames and Tay;

And they cheerily sang by the windy seas,

And they thought of Malabarre Bay.

On the lonely heights of Burial Hill

The old Precisioners sleep;

But did ever men with a nobler will

A holier Christmas keep,

When the sky was cold and gray,—

And there were no ancient bells to ring,

No priests to chant, no choirs to sing,

No chapel of baron, or lord, or king,

That gray, cold Christmas Day?

THE CHIMES.

BY CHARLES DICKENS.

First Quarter.

There are not many people—and as it is desirable that a story-teller and a story-reader should establish a mutual understanding as soon as possible, I beg it to be noticed that I confine this observation neither to young people nor to little people, but extend it to all conditions of people: little and big, young and old: yet growing up, or already growing down again—there are not, I say, many people who would care to sleep in a church. I don't mean at sermon time in warm weather (when the thing has actually been done, once or twice), but in the night, and alone. A great multitude of persons will be violently astonished, I know, by this position, in the broad bold Day. But it applies to Night. It must be argued by night. And I will undertake to maintain it successfully on any gusty winter's night appointed for the purpose, with any one opponent chosen from the rest, who will meet me singly in an old churchyard, before an old church door; and will previously empower me to lock him in, if needful to his satisfaction, until morning.

For the night-wind has a dismal trick of wandering round and round a building of that sort, and moaning as it goes; and of trying with its unseen hand, the windows and the doors; and seeking out some crevices by which to enter. And when it has got in; as one not finding what it seeks, whatever that may be, it wails and howls to issue forth again; and not content with stalking through the aisles, and gliding round and round the pillars, and tempting the deep organ, soars up to the roof, and strives to rend the rafters; then flings itself despairingly upon the stones below, and passes, muttering, into the vaults. Ugh! Heaven preserve us, sitting snugly round the fire! It has an awful voice, that wind at midnight, singing in a church!

But, high up in the steeple! There the foul blast roars and whistles! High up in the steeple, where it is free to come and go through many an airy arch and loophole, and to twist and twine itself about the giddy stair, and twirl the groaning weathercock, and make the very tower shake and shiver!

High up in the steeple of an old church, far above the light and murmur of the town and far below the flying clouds that shadow it, is the wild and dreary place at night: and high up in the steeple of an old church, dwelt the Chimes I tell of.

They were old Chimes, trust me. Centuries ago, these Bells had been baptized by bishops: so many centuries ago, that the register of their baptism was lost long, long before the memory of man, and no one knew their names. They had had their Godfathers and Godmothers, these Bells (for my part, by the way, I would rather incur the responsibility of being Godfather to a Bell than a Boy), and had had their silver mugs, no doubt, besides. But Time had mowed down their sponsors, and Henry the Eighth had melted down their mugs; and they now hung, nameless and mugless, in the church tower.

Not speechless, though. Far from it. They had clear, loud, lusty, sounding voices, had these Bells; and far and wide they might be heard upon the wind. Much too sturdy Chimes were they, to be[Pg 108]dependent on the pleasure of the wind, moreover; for, fighting gallantly against it when it took an adverse whim, they would pour their cheerful notes into a listening ear right royally; and bent on being heard, on stormy nights, by some poor mother watching a sick child, or some lone wife whose husband was at sea, they had been sometimes known to beat a blustering

Nor'Wester; ay, "all to fits," as Toby Veck said;—for though they chose to call him Trotty Veck, his name was Toby, and nobody could make it anything else either (except Tobias); he having been as lawfully christened in his day as the bells had been in theirs, though with not quite so much of solemnity or public rejoicing.

For my part, I confess myself of Toby Veck's belief, for I am sure he had opportunities enough of forming a correct one. And whatever Toby Veck said, I say. And I take my stand by Toby Veck, although he *did* stand all day long (and weary work it was) just outside the church-door. In fact he was a ticket-porter, Toby Veck, and waited there for jobs.

And a breezy, goose-skinned, blue-nosed, red-eyed, stony-toed, tooth-chattering place it was to wait in, in the winter-time, as Toby Veck well knew. The wind came tearing round the corner—especially the east wind—as if it had sallied forth, express, from the confines of the earth, to have a blow at Toby. And oftentimes it seemed to come upon him sooner than it had expected, for bouncing round the corner, and passing Toby, it would suddenly wheel round again, as if it cried "Why, here he is!"

Toby was curious about the Bells because there were points of resemblance between them and him. They hung there in all weathers, with the wind and rain driving in upon them; facing only the outsides of all the houses; never getting anynearer to the blazing fires that gleamed and shone upon the windows or came puffing out of the chimney tops; and incapable of participating in any of the good things that were constantly being handed through the street doors and iron railings to prodigious cooks. Being but a simple man, he invested the Bells with a strange and solemn character. They were so mysterious, often heard and never seen; so high up, so far off, so full of such a deep, strong melody, that he regarded them with a species of awe; and sometimes when he looked up at the dark arched windows in the tower, he half expected to be beckoned to by something which was not a Bell, and yet was what he heard so often sounding in the Chimes. For all this Toby scouted with indignation a certain flying rumor that the Chimes were haunted, as implying the possibility of their being connected with any Evil thing. In short, they were very often in his ears, and very often in his thoughts, but always in his good opinion; and he very often got such a crick in his neck by staring with his mouth wide open, at the steeple where they hung, that he was fain to take an extra trot or two, afterward, to cure it.

The very thing he was in the act of doing one cold day, when the last drowsy sound of Twelve o'clock, just struck, was humming like a melodious monster of a Bee, and not by any means a busy Bee, all through the steeple?

"Dinner time, eh!" said Toby, trotting up and down before the church. "Ah!"

Toby's nose was very red, and his eyelids were very red, and he winked very much, and his shoulders were very near his ears, and his legs were very stiff, and altogether he was evidently a long way upon the frosty side of cool.

"Dinner time, eh!" repeated Toby, using his right hand muffler like an infantine boxing-glove, and punishing his chest for being cold. "Ah-h-h-h!"

He took a silent trot, after that, for a minute or two.

"There's nothing," said Toby, "more regular in its coming round than dinner time, and nothing less regular in its coming round than dinner. That's the great difference between 'em. It's took me a long time to find it out. I wonder whether it would be worth any gentleman's while, now, to buy that observation for the Papers; or the Parliament!"

Tony was only joking, for he gravely shook his head in self-depreciation.

"Why! Lord!" said Toby. "The Papers is full of observations as it is; and so's the Parliament. Here's last week's paper, now;" taking a very dirty one from his pocket, and holding it from him at arm's length; "full of observations! Full of observations! I like to know the news as well as any man," said Toby, slowly; folding it a little smaller, and putting it in his pocket again: "but it almost goes against the grain with me to read a paper now. It frightens me almost. I don't know what we poor people are coming to. Lord send we may be coming to something better in the New Year nigh upon us!"

"Why, father, father!" said a pleasant voice, hard by.

But Toby, not hearing it continued to trot backward and forward: musing as he went, and talking to himself.

"It seems as if we can't go right, or do right, or be righted," said Toby. "I hadn't much schooling, myself, when I was young; and I can't make out whether we have any business on the face of the earth, or not. Sometimes I think we must have—a little; and sometimes I think we must be intruding. I get so puzzled sometimes that I am not even able to make up my mind whether there is any good at all in us, or whether we are born bad. We seem to do dreadful things; we seem to give a deal of trouble; we are always being complained of and guarded against. One way or another, we fill the papers. Talk of a New Year!" said Toby, mournfully. "I can bear up as well as another man at most times; better than a good many, for I am as strong as a lion, and all men an't; but supposing it should really be that we have no right to a New Year—supposing we really *are* intruding——"

"Why, father, father!" said the pleasant voice again.

Toby heard it this time; started; stopped; and shortening his sight, which had been directed a long way off as seeking for enlightenment in the very heart of the approaching year, found himself face to face with his own child, and looking close into her eyes.

Bright eyes they were. Eyes that would bear a world of looking in, before their depth was fathomed. Dark eyes, that reflected back the eyes which searched them; not flashingly or at the owner's will, but with a clear, calm, honest, patient radiance, claiming kindred with that light which Heaven called into being. Eyes that were beautiful and true, and beaming with Hope. With Hope so young and fresh; with Hope so buoyant, vigorous and bright, despite the twenty years of work and poverty on which they had looked; that they became a voice to Trotty Veck, and said: "I think we have some business here—a little!"

Trotty kissed the lips belonging to the eyes, and squeezed the blooming face between his hands.

"Why, Pet," said Trotty. "What's to-do? I didn't expect you, to-day, Meg."

"Neither did I expect to come, father," cried the girl, nodding her head and smiling as she spoke. "But here I am! And not alone; not alone!"

"Why you don't mean to say," observed Trotty, looking curiously at a covered basket which she carried in her hand, "that you——"

"Smell it, father dear," said Meg, "Only smell it!"

Trotty was going to lift up the cover at once, in a great hurry, when she gayly interposed her hand.

"No, no, no," said Meg, with the glee of a child. "Lengthen it out a little. Let me just lift up the corner; just the lit-tle ti-ny cor-ner, you know," said Meg, suiting the action to the word with the utmost gentleness, and speaking very softly, as if she were afraid of being overheard by something inside the basket; "there. Now. What's that!"

Toby took the shortest possible sniff at the edge of the basket, and cried out in a rapture:

"Why, it's hot!"

"It is burning hot!" cried Meg. "Ha, ha, ha! It's scalding hot!"

"Ha, ha, ha!" roared Toby, with a sort of kick. "It's scalding hot!"

"But what is it father?" said Meg. "Come! you haven't guessed what it is. And you must guess what it is. I can't think of taking it out till you guess what it is. Don't be in such a hurry! Wait a minute! A little bit more of the cover. Now guess!"

Meg was in a perfect fright lest he should guess right too soon; shrinking away, as she held the basket toward him; curling up her pretty shoulders; stopping her ear with her hand, as if by so doing she could keep the right word out of Toby's lips; and laughing softly the whole time.

Meanwhile Toby, putting a hand on each knee, bent down his nose to the basket, and took a long inspiration at the lid; the grin upon his withered face expanded in the process, as if he were inhaling laughing gas.

"Ah! It's very nice," said Toby. "It ain't—I suppose it ain't Polonies?"

"No, no, no!" cried Meg, delighted. "Nothing like Polonies!"

"No," said Toby, after another sniff. "It's—it's mellower than Polonies. It's very nice. It improves every moment. It's too decided for Trotters. Ain't it?"

Meg was in ecstasy. He could not have gone wider of the mark than Trotters—except Polonies.

"Liver?" said Toby, communing with himself. "No. There's a mildness about it that don't answer to liver. Pettitoes? No. It an't faint enough for pettitoes. It wants the stringiness of Cocks' heads. And I know it an't sausages. I'll tell you what it is. It's chitterlings!"

"No, it an't!" cried Meg, in a burst of delight "No, it an't!"

"Why, what am I a thinking of!" said Toby, suddenly recovering a position as near the perpendicular as it was possible for him to assume. "I shall forget my own name next. It's tripe!"

Tripe it was; and Meg, in high joy, protested he should say, in half a minute more, it was the best tripe ever stewed.

"And so," said Meg, busying herself exultingly with her basket; "I'll lay the cloth at once, father; for I have brought the tripe in a basin, and tied the basin up in a pocket-handkerchief; and if I like to be proud for once, and spread that for a cloth, and call it a cloth, there's no law to prevent me; is there father?"

"Not that I know of, my dear," said Toby. "But they're always a bringing up some new law or other."

"And according to what I was reading you in the paper the other day, father; what the Judge said, you know; we poor people are supposed to know them all. Ha, ha! What a mistake! My goodness me, how clever they think us!"

"Yes, my dear," cried Trotty; "and they'd be very fond of any one of us that *did* know 'em all. He'd grow fat upon the work he'd get, that man, and be popular with the gentlefolks in his neighborhood. Very much so!"

"He'd eat his dinner with an appetite, whoever he was, if it smelt like this," said Meg, cheerfully. "Make haste, for there's a potato besides. Where will you dine, father? On the Post, or on the Steps? Dear, dear, how grand we are. Two places to choose from!"

"The steps to day, my Pet," said Trotty. "Steps in dry weather. Post in wet. There's a great conveniency in the steps at all times, because of the sitting down; but they're rheumatic in the damp."

"Then here," said Meg, clapping her hands, after a moment's bustle; "here it is, all ready! And beautiful it looks! Come, father. Eat it while it's hot. Come!"

Since his discovery of the contents of the basket, Trotty had been standing looking at her—and had been speaking too—in an abstracted manner, which showed that though she was the object of his thoughts and eyes, to the exclusion even of tripe, he neither saw nor thought about her as she was at that moment, but had before him some imaginary rough sketch or drama of her future life. Roused, now, by her cheerful summons, he shook off a melancholy shake of the head which was just coming upon him, and trotted to her side. As he was stooping to sit down, the Chimes rang.

"Amen!" said Trotty, pulling off his hat and looking up toward them.

"Amen to the Bells, father?" cried Meg.

"They broke in like a grace, my dear," said Trotty, taking his seat. "They'd say a good one, I am sure, if they could. Many's the kind thing they say to me."

"The Bells do, father!" laughed Meg, as she set the basin, and a knife and fork before him. "Well!"

"Seem to, my Pet," said Trotty, falling to with great vigor. "And where's the difference? If I hear 'em, what does it matter whether they speak it or not? Why bless you, my dear," said Toby, pointing at the tower with his fork, and becoming more animated under the influence of dinner, "how often have I heard them bells say, 'Toby Veck, Toby Veck, keep a good heart Toby! Toby Veck, Toby Veck, keep a good heart Toby!' A million times? More!"

"Well, I never!" cried Meg.

She had, though—over and over again. For it was Toby's constant topic.

"When things is very bad," said Trotty; "very bad indeed, I mean; almost at the worst; then it's 'Toby Veck, Toby Veck, job coming soon, Toby! Toby Veck, Toby Veck, job coming soon, Toby!' That way."

"And it comes—at last, father," said Meg, with a touch of sadness in her pleasant voice.

"Always," answered the unconscious Toby. "Never fails."

While this discourse was holding, Trotty made no pause in his attack upon the savory meat before him, but cut and ate, and cut and drank, and cut and chewed, and dodged about, from tripe to hot potato, and from hot potato back again to tripe, with an unctuous and unflagging relish. But happening now to look all round the street—in case anybody should be beckoning from any door or window, for a porter—his eyes, in coming back again, encountered Meg: sitting opposite to him, with her arms folded; and only busy in watching his progress with a smile of happiness.

"Why, Lord forgive me!" said Trotty, dropping his knife and fork. "My love! Meg! why didn't you tell me what a beast I was?"

"Father?"

"Sitting here," said Trotty, in penitent explanation, "cramming and stuffing, and gorging myself; and you before me there, never so much as breaking your precious fast, nor wanting to, when——"

"But I have broken it, father," interposed his daughter, laughing, "all to bits. I have had my dinner."

"Nonsense," said Trotty. "Two dinners in one day! It an't possible! You might as well tell me that two New Year's Days will come together, or that I have had a gold head all my life, and never changed it."

"I have had my dinner, father, for all that," said Meg, coming nearer to him. "And if you'll go on with yours, I'll tell you how and where; and how your dinner came to be brought; and—something else besides."

~ 125 ~

Toby still appeared incredulous; but she looked into his face with her clear eyes, and laying her hand upon his shoulder, motioned him to go on while the meat was hot. So Trotty took up his knife and fork again, and went to work. But much more slowly than before, and shaking his head, as if he were not at all pleased with himself.

"I had my dinner, father," said Meg, after a little hesitation, "with—with Richard. His dinner-time was early; and as he brought his dinner with him when he came to see me, we—we had it together, father."

Trotty said, "Oh!"—because she waited.

"And Richard says, father—" Meg resumed. Then stopped.

"What does Richard say, Meg?" asked Toby.

"Richard says, father—" Another stoppage.

"Richard's a long time saying it," said Toby.

"He says then, father," Meg continued, lifting up her eyes at last, and speaking in a tremble, but quite plainly; "another year is nearly gone, and where is the use of waiting on from year to year, when it is so unlikely we shall ever be better off than we are now? He says we are poor now, father, and we shall be poor then, but we are young now, and years will make us old before we know it. He says that if we wait, people in our condition, until we see our way quite clearly, the way will be a narrow one indeed—the common way—the Grave, father."

A bolder man than Trotty Veck must needs have drawn upon his boldness largely, to deny it. Trotty held his peace.

"And how hard, father, to grow old and die, and think we might have cheered and helped each other! How hard in all our lives to love each other; and to grieve, apart, to see each other working, changing, growing old and gray. Even if I got the better of it, and forgot him (which I never could), oh, father dear, how hard to have a heart so full as mine is now, and live to have it slowly drained out every drop, without the recollection of one happy moment of a woman's life, to stay behind and comfort me, and make me better!"

Trotty sat quite still, Meg dried her eyes, and said more gayly: that is to say, with here a laugh, and there a sob, and here a laugh and sob together:

"So Richard says, father; as his work was yesterday made certain for some time to come, and as I love him and have loved him fully three years—ah! longer than that, if he knew it!—will I marry him on New Year's Day; the best and happiest day, he says, in the whole year, and one that is almost sure to bring good fortune with it. It's a short notice, father—isn't it?—but I haven't my fortune to be settled, or my wedding dresses to be made, like the great ladies, father, have I? And he said so much, and said it in his way; so strong and earnest, and all the time so kind and gentle; that I said I'd come and talk to you, father. And as they paid the money for that work of mine this morning (unexpectedly, I am sure!), and as you have fared very poorly for a whole week, and as I couldn't help wishing there should be something to make this day a sort of holiday to you as well as a dear and happy day to me, father, I made a little treat and brought it to surprise you."

"And see how he leaves it cooling on the step!" said another voice.

It was the voice of the same Richard, who had come upon them unobserved, and stood before the father and daughter; looking down upon them with a face as glowing as the iron on which his stout sledge-hammer daily rung. A handsome, well-made, powerful youngster he was; with eyes that sparkled like the red-hot droppings from a furnace fire; black hair that curled about his swarthy temples rarely; and a smile—a smile that bore out Meg's eulogium on his style of conversation.

"See how he leaves it cooling on the step!" said Richard. "Meg don't know what he likes. Not she!"

Trotty, all action and enthusiasm, immediately reached up his hand to Richard, and was going to address him in a great hurry, when the house-door opened without any warning, and a footman very nearly put his foot in the tripe.

"Out of the vays here, will you! You must always go and be a-settin on our steps, must you! You can't go and give a turn to none of the neighbors never, can't you? Will you clear the road, or won't you?"

Strictly speaking, the last question was irrelevant, as they had already done it.

"What's the matter, what's the matter?" said the gentleman for whom the door was opened; coming out of the house at that kind of light, heavy pace—that peculiar compromise between a walk and jog-trot—with which a gentleman upon the smooth down-hill of life, wearing creaking boots, a watch-chain, and clean linen, may come out of his house: not only without any abatement of his dignity, but with an expression of having important and wealthy engagements elsewhere. "What's the matter? What's the matter?"

"You're always a-being begged, and prayed, upon your bended knees, you are," said the footman with great emphasis to Trotty

Veck, "to let our door-steps be. Why don't you let 'em be? Can't you let 'em be?"

"There! That'll do, that'll do!" said the gentleman, "Halloa there! Porter!" beckoning with his head to Trotty Veck, "Come here. What's that? Your dinner?"

"Yes, sir," said Trotty, leaving it behind him in a corner.

"Don't leave it there!" exclaimed the gentleman. "Bring it here, bring it here! So! this is your dinner, is it?"

"Yes, sir," repeated Trotty, looking with a fixed eye and a watery mouth at the piece of tripe he had reserved for a last delicious tit-bit, which the gentleman was now turning over and over on the end of a fork.

Two other gentlemen had come out with him. One was a low-spirited gentleman of middle age, of a meagre habit, and a disconsolate face; who kept his hands continually in the pockets of his scanty pepper-and-salt trousers, very large and dog's-eared from that custom; and was not particularly well brushed or washed. The other, a full sized, sleek, well-conditioned gentleman, in a blue coat, with bright buttons, and a white cravat. This gentleman had a very red face, as if an undue proportion of the blood in his body were squeezed up into his head, which perhaps accounted for his having also the appearance of being rather cold about the heart.

He who had Toby's meat upon the fork called to the first one by the name of Filer, and they both drew near together. Mr. Filer being exceedingly short sighted, was obliged to go so close to the remnant of Toby's dinner before he could make out what it was, that Toby's heart leaped up into his mouth. But Mr. Filer didn't eat it.

~ 129 ~

"This is a description of animal food, Alderman," said Filer, making little punches in it with a pencil-case, "commonly known to the laboring population of this country by the name of tripe."

The Alderman laughed, and winked; for he was a merry fellow. Alderman Cute. Oh, and a sly fellow too! A knowing fellow. Up to everything. Not to be imposed upon. Deep in the people's hearts! He knew them, Cute did. I believe you!

"But who eats tripe?" said Mr. Filer, looking round. "Tripe is without an exception the least economical, and the most wasteful article of consumption that the markets of this country can by possibility produce. The loss upon a pound of tripe has been found to be, in the boiling, seven-eighths of a fifth more than the loss upon a pound of any other animal substance whatever. Tripe is more expensive, properly understood, than the hot-house pine-apple. Taking into account the number of animals slaughtered yearly within the bills of mortality alone; and forming a low estimate of the quantity of tripe which the carcases of these animals, reasonably well butchered, would yield—I find that the waste on that amount of tripe, if boiled, would victual a garrison of five hundred men for five months of thirty-one days each, and a February over. The Waste, the Waste!"

Trotty stood aghast, and his legs shook under him. He seemed to have starved a garrison of five hundred men with his own hand.

"Who eats tripe?" said Mr. Filer, warmly. "Who eats tripe?"

Trotty made a miserable bow.

"You do, do you?" said Mr. Filer. "Then I'll tell you something. You snatch your tripe, my friend, out of the mouths of widows and orphans."

"I hope not, sir," said Trotty, faintly. "I'd sooner die of want!"

"Divide the amount of tripe before-mentioned, Alderman," said Mr. Filer, "by the estimated number of existing widows and orphans, and the result will be one pennyweight of tripe to each. Not a grain is left for that man. Consequently, he's a robber."

Trotty was so shocked that it gave him no concern to see the Alderman finish the tripe himself. It was a relief to get rid of it, anyhow.

"And what do you say?" asked the Alderman, jocosely, of the red-faced gentleman in the blue coat. "You have heard friend Filer. What do *you* say?"

"What's it possible to say?" returned the gentleman. "What *is* to be said? Who can take any interest in a fellow like this," meaning Trotty, "in such degenerate times as these? Look at him! What an object! The good old times, the grand old times, the great old times! *Those* were the times for a bold peasantry, and all that sort of thing. Those were the times for every sort of thing, in fact. There's nothing now-a-days. Ah!" sighed the red-faced gentleman. "The good old times, the good old times!"

It is possible that poor Trotty's faith in these very vague Old Times was not entirely destroyed, for he felt vague enough, at that moment. One thing, however, was plain to him, in the midst of his distress; to wit, that however these gentlemen might differ in details, his misgivings of that morning, and of many other mornings, were well founded. "No, no. We can't go right or do right," thought Trotty in despair. "There is no good in us. We are born bad!"

But Trotty had a father's heart within him; which had somehow got into his breast in spite of this decree; and he could not bear that

Meg, in the blush of her brief joy, should have her fortune read by these wise gentlemen. "God help her," thought poor Trotty. "She will know it soon enough."

He anxiously signed, therefore, to the young smith, to take her away. But he was so busy, talking to her softly at a little distance, that he only became conscious of this desire, simultaneously with Alderman Cute. Now, the Alderman had not yet had his say, but *he* was a philosopher, too—practical though! Oh, very practical!—and, as he had no idea of losing any portion of his audience, he cried "Stop!"

Trotty took Meg's hand and drew it through his arm. He didn't seem to know what he was doing though.

"Your daughter, eh?" said the Alderman, chucking her familiarly under the chin.

"And you're making love to her, are you?" said Cute to the young smith.

"Yes," returned Richard quickly, for he was nettled by the question. "And we are going to be married on New Year's Day."

"What do you mean?" cried Filer sharply. "Married!"

"Why, yes, we were thinking of it. Master," said Richard. "We're rather in a hurry you see, in case it should be Put Down first."

"Ah!" cried Filer, with a groan. "Put *that* down indeed. Alderman, and you'll do something. Married! Married!! The ignorance of the first principles of political economy on the part of these people; their improvidence; their wickedness is by Heavens! enough to—Now look at that couple, will you!"

Well! They were worth looking at. And marriage seemed as reasonable and fair a deed as they need have in contemplation.

"A man may live to be as old as Methuselah," said Mr. Filer, "and may labor all his life for the benefit of such people as those; and may heap up facts on figures, facts on figures, facts on figures, mountains high and dry; and he can no more hope to persuade 'em that they have no right or business to be married than he can hope to persuade 'em that they have no earthly right or business to be born. And *that* we know they haven't. We reduced that to a mathematical certainty long ago!"

"Come here, my girl!" said Alderman Cute.

The young blood of her lover had been mounting, wrathfully, within the last few minutes; and he was indisposed to let her come. But, setting a constraint upon himself, he came forward with a stride as Meg approached and stood beside her. Trotty kept her hand within his arm still, but looked from face to face as wildly as a sleeper in a dream.

"Now, I'm going to give you a word or two of good advice, my girl," said the Alderman, in his nice easy way. "It's my place to give advice, you know, because I'm a Justice. You know I'm a Justice, don't you?"

Meg timidly said, "Yes." But everybody knew Alderman Cute was a Justice! Oh dear, so active a Justice always! Who such a mote of brightness in the public eye, as Cute!

"You are going to be married, you say," pursued the Alderman. "Very unbecoming and, indelicate in one of your sex! But never mind that. After you're married, you'll quarrel with your husband, and come to be a distressed wife. You may think not; but you will, because I tell you so. Now, I give you fair warning, that I have made up my mind to Put distressed wives Down. So, don't be brought before me. You'll have children—boys. Those boys will grow up bad, of course, and run wild in the streets without shoes or stockings. Mind, my young friend! I'll convict 'em summarily every one, for I am determined to Put boys without shoes or stockings, Down. Perhaps your husband will die young (most likely) and leave you with a baby. Then you'll be turned out of doors, and wander up and down the streets. Now don't wander near me, my dear, for I am resolved to Put all wandering mothers Down. All young mothers, of all sorts and kinds, it's my determination to Put Down. Don't think to plead illness as an excuse with me; or babies as an excuse with me; for all sick persons and young children (I hope you know the church-service, but I'm afraid not) I am determined to Put Down. And if you attempt, desperately and ungratefully, and impiously, and fraudulently attempt, to drown yourself, or hang yourself, I'll have no pity on you, for I have made up my mind to Put all suicide Down! If there is one thing," said the Alderman, with his self-satisfied smile, "on which I can be said to have made up my mind more than on another, it is to Put suicide Down. So don't try it on. That's the phrase, isn't it! Ha, ha! now we understand each other."

Toby knew not whether to be agonized or glad, to see that Meg had turned deadly white, and dropped her lover's hand.

"As for you, you dull dog," said the Alderman, turning with even increased cheerfulness and urbanity to the young smith, "what are you thinking of being married for? What do you want to be married for, you silly fellow? If I was a fine, young, strapping chap like you, I should be ashamed of being milksop enough to pin myself to a woman's apron-strings! Why, she'll be an old woman before you're a middle-aged man! And a pretty figure you'll cut then, with a draggle-tailed wife and a crowd of squalling children crying after you wherever you go!"

Oh, he knew how to banter the common people, Alderman Cute!

"There! Go along with you," said the Alderman, "and repent. Don't make such a fool of yourself as to get married on New Year's Day. You'll think very differently of it, long before next New Year's Day: a trim young fellow like you, with all the girls looking after you. There! Go along with you!"

They went along. Not arm in arm, or hand in hand, or interchanging bright glances; but she in tears; he gloomy and down-looking. Were these the hearts that had so lately made old Toby's leap up from its faintness? No, no. The Alderman (a blessing on his head!) had Put *them* Down.

"As you happen to be here," said the Alderman to Toby, "you shall carry a letter for me. Can you be quick? You're an old man."

Toby, who had been looking after Meg, quite stupidly, made shift to murmur out that he was very quick, and very strong.

"How old are you?" inquired the Alderman.

"I am over sixty, sir," said Toby.

"Oh! This man's a great deal past the average age, you know," cried Mr. Filer, breaking in as if his patience would bear some trying, but this was really carrying matters a little too far.

"I feel I'm intruding, sir," said Toby. "I—I misdoubted it this morning. Oh dear me!"

The Alderman cut him short by giving him the letter from his pocket. Toby would have got a shilling too; but Mr. Filer clearly showing that in that case he would rob a certain given number of persons of ninepence-half-penny a-piece, he only got sixpence; and thought himself very well off to get that.

Then the Alderman gave an arm to each of his friends, and walked off in high feather; but, he immediately came hurrying back alone, as if he had forgotten something.

"Porter!" said the Alderman.

"Sir!" said Toby.

"Take care of that daughter of yours. She's much too handsome."

"Even her good looks are stolen from somebody or other I suppose," thought Toby, looking at the sixpence in his hand, and thinking of the tripe. "She's been and robbed five hundred ladies of a bloom a-piece, I shouldn't wonder. It's very dreadful!"

"She's much too handsome, my man," repeated the Alderman. "The chances are, that she'll come to no good, I clearly see. Observe what I say. Take care of her!" With which, he hurried off again.

"Wrong every way. Wrong every way!" said Trotty clasping his hands. "Born bad. No business here!"

The Chimes came clashing in upon him as he said the last words. Full, loud, and sounding—but with no encouragement. No, not a drop.

"The tune's changed," cried the old man, as he listened. "There's not a word of all that fancy in it. Why should there be? I have no business with the New Year nor with the old one neither. Let me die!"

Still the Bells, pealing forth their changes, made the very air spin. Put 'em down. Put 'em down! Good old Times, Good old Times! Facts and Figures, Facts and Figures! Put 'em down, Put 'em down! If they said anything they said this, until the brain of Toby reeled.

He pressed his bewildered head between his hands as if to keep it from splitting asunder. A well-timed action, as it happened; for finding the letter in one of them, and being by that means reminded of his charge, he fell, mechanically, into his usual trot, and trotted off.

Second Quarter.

The letter Toby had received from Alderman Cute, was addressed to a great man in the great district of the town. The greatest district of the town. It must have been the greatest district of the town, because it was commonly called "the world" by its inhabitants.

The Year was Old, that day. The patient Year had lived through the reproaches and misuses of its slanderers, and faithfully performed its work. Spring, summer, autumn, winter. It had labored through the destined round, and now laid down its weary head to die.

Trotty had no portion, to his thinking, in the New Year or the Old.

"Put 'em down. Put 'em down! Facts and Figures, Facts and Figures! Good old Times, Good old Times! Put 'em down, Put 'em down!"—his trot went to that measure, and would fit itself to nothing else.

But, even that one, melancholy as it was, brought him, in due time, to the end of his journey. To the mansion of Sir Joseph Bowley, Member of Parliament.

The door was opened by a Porter. Such a Porter! Not of Toby's order. Quite another thing. His place was the ticket, though; not Toby's.

This Porter underwent some hard panting before he could speak; having breathed himself by coming incautiously out of his chair, without first taking time to think about it and compose his mind. When he had found his voice—which it took him some time to do, for it was a long way off and hidden under a load of meat—he said in a fat whisper:

"Who's it from?"

Toby told him.

"You're to take it in yourself," said the Porter, pointing to a room at the end of a long passage, opening from the hall. "Everything goes straight in, on this day of the year. You're not a bit too soon; for the carriage is at the door now, and they have only come to town for a couple of hours, a'purpose."

Toby wiped his feet (which were quite dry already) with great care, and took the way pointed out to him, observing as he went that it was an awfully grand house, but hushed and covered up, as if the family were in the country. Knocking at the room door, he was told to enter from within; and doing so found himself in a spacious library, where, at a table strewn with files and papers, were a stately lady in a bonnet, and a not very stately gentleman in black, who wrote from her dictation; while another, and an older, and a much statelier gentleman, whose hat and cane were on the table, walked up and down, with one hand in his breast, and looked complacently from time to time at his own picture—a full length; a very full length—hanging over the fire-place.

"What is this?" said the last-named gentleman. "Mr. Fish, will you have the goodness to attend?"

Mr. Fish begged pardon, and taking the letter from Toby, handed it, with great respect.

"From Alderman Cute, Sir Joseph."

"Is this all? Have you nothing else, Porter?" inquired Sir Joseph.

Toby replied in the negative.

"You have no bill or demand upon me—my name is Bowley, Sir Joseph Bowley—of any kind from anybody, have you?" said Sir Joseph. "If you have, present it. There is a cheque-book by the side of Mr. Fish. I allow nothing to be carried into the New Year. Every description of account is settled in this house at the close of the old one. So that if death was to—to—"

"To cut," suggested Mr. Fish.

"To sever, sir," returned Sir Joseph, with great asperity, "the cord of existence—my affairs would be found, I hope, in a state of preparation."

"My dear Sir Joseph!" said the lady, who was greatly younger than the gentleman. "How shocking!"

"My Lady Bowley," returned Sir Joseph, floundering now and then, as in the great depth of his observations, "at this season of the year we should think of—of—ourselves. We should look into our—our accounts. We should feel that every return of so eventful a period in human transactions involves matter of deep moment between a man and his—and his banker."

Sir Joseph delivered these words as if he felt the full morality of what he was saying, and desired that even Trotty should have an opportunity of being improved by such discourse. Possibly he had this end before him in still forbearing to break the seal of the letter, and in telling Trotty to wait where he was a minute.

"I am the Poor Man's Friend," observed Sir Joseph, glancing at the poor man present. "As such I may be taunted. As such I have been taunted. But I ask no other title."

"Bless him for a noble gentleman!" thought Trotty.

"I don't agree with Cute here, for instance," said Sir Joseph, holding out the letter. "I don't agree with the Filer party. I don't agree with any party. My friend, the Poor Man, has no business with any thing of that sort, and nothing of that sort has any business with him. My friend, the Poor Man, in my district, is my business. No man or body of men has any right to interfere between my friend and me. That is the ground I take. I assume a—a paternal character toward my friend. I say, 'My good fellow, I will treat you paternally.'"

With that great sentiment, he opened the Alderman's letter, and read it.

"Very polite and attentive, I am sure!" exclaimed Sir Joseph. "My lady, the Alderman is so obliging as to remind me that he has had 'the distinguished honor'—he is very good—of meeting me at the house of our mutual friend Deedles, the banker, and he does me the favor to inquire whether it will be agreeable to me to have Will Fern put down. He came up to London, it seems, to look for employment (trying to better himself—that's his story), and being found at night asleep in a shed, was taken into custody, and carried next morning before the Alderman. The Alderman observes (very properly) that he is determined to put this sort of thing down, and that if it will be agreeable to me to have Will Fern put down, he will be happy to begin with him."

"Let him be made an example of, by all means," returned the lady. "Last winter, when I introduced pinking and eyelet-holing among the men and boys in the village as a nice evening employment, and had the lines,

Oh let us love our occupations,

Bless the squire and his relations,

~ 141 ~

Live upon our daily rations,

And always know our proper stations,

set to music on the new system, for them to sing the while; this
very Fern—I see him now—touched that hat of his, and said, 'I
humbly ask your pardon, my lady, but an't I something
different from a great girl?' I expected it, of course; who can expect
anything but insolence and ingratitude from that class of people?
That is not to the purpose, however. Sir Joseph! Make an example of
him!"

Trotty, who had long ago relapsed, and was very low-spirited,
stepped forward with a rueful face to take the letter Sir Joseph held
out to him.

"You have heard, perhaps," said Sir Joseph, oracularly, "certain
remarks into which I have been led respecting the solemn period of
time at which we have arrived, and the duty imposed upon us of
settling our affairs, and being prepared. Now, my friend, can you
lay your hand upon your heart, and say that you also have made
preparation for a New Year?"

"I am afraid, sir," stammered Trotty, looking meekly at him, "that
I am a—a—little behind-hand with the world."

"Behind-hand with the world!" repeated Sir Joseph Bowley, in a
tone of terrible distinctness.

"I am afraid, sir," faltered Trotty, "that there's a matter of ten or
twelve shillings owing to Mrs. Chickenstalker."

"To Mrs. Chickenstalker!" repeated Sir Joseph, in the same tone as
before.

"A shop, sir," exclaimed Toby, "in the general line. Also a—a little money on account of rent. A very little, sir. It oughtn't to be owing, I know, but we have been hard put to it, indeed!"

Sir Joseph looked at his lady, and at Mr. Fish, and at Trotty, one after another, twice all round. He then made a despondent gesture with both hands at once, as if he gave the thing up altogether.

"How a man, even among this improvident and impracticable race; an old man; a man grown grey; can look a New Year in the face with his affairs in this condition; how he can lie down on his bed at night, and get up again in the morning, and—There!" he said, turning his back on Trotty.

"Take the letter! Take the letter!"

"I heartily wish it was otherwise, sir," said Trotty, anxious to excuse himself. "We have been tried very hard."

Sir Joseph still repeating "Take the letter, take the letter!" and Mr. Fish not only saying the same thing, but giving additional force to the request by motioning the bearer to the door, he had nothing for it but to make his bow and leave the house. And in the street, poor Trotty pulled his worn old hat down on his head to hide the grief he felt at getting no hold on the New Year, anywhere.

He didn't even lift his hat to look up at the Bell tower when he came to the old church on his return. He halted there a moment, from habit; and knew that it was growing dark and that the steeple rose above him indistinct and faint in the murky air. He knew, too, that the Chimes would ring immediately, and that they sounded to his fancy, at such a time, like voices in the clouds. But he only made the more haste to deliver the Alderman's letter and get out of the way before they began; for he dreaded to hear them tagging

"Friends and Fathers, Friends and Fathers," to the burden they had rung out last.

Toby discharged himself of his commission, therefore, with all possible speed and set off trotting homeward. But what with his pace, which was at best an awkward one in the street; and what with his hat, which didn't improve it; he trotted against somebody in less than no time and was sent staggering out into the road.

"I beg your pardon, I'm sure!" said Trotty, pulling up his hat in great confusion, and between[Pg 133] the hat and the torn lining, fixing his head into a kind of bee-hive. "I hope I haven't hurt you."

As to hurting anybody, Toby was not such an absolute Samson, but that he was much more likely to be hurt himself; and indeed he had flown out into the road like a shuttle-cock. He had such an opinion of his own strength, however, that he was in real concern for the other party, and said again,

"I hope I haven't hurt you?"

The man against whom he had run, a sun-browned, sinewy, country-looking man, with grizzled hair and a rough chin, stared at him for a moment, as if he suspected him to be in jest. But, satisfied of his good faith, he answered:

"No, friend. You have not hurt me."

"Nor the child, I hope?" said Trotty.

"Nor the child," returned the man. "I thank you kindly."

As he said so, he glanced at a little girl he carried in his arms, asleep, and shading her face with the long end of the poor handkerchief he wore about his throat, went slowly on.

The tone in which he said "I thank you kindly," penetrated Trotty's heart. He was so jaded and foot sore, and so soiled with travel, and looked about him so forlorn and strange, that it was a comfort to him to be able to thank anyone, no matter for how little. Toby stood gazing after him as he plodded wearily away, with the child's arm clinging round his neck.

At the figure in the worn shoes—now the very shade and ghost of shoes—rough leather leggings, common frock and broad slouched hat, Trotty stood gazing, blind to the whole street. And at the child's arm, clinging round its neck.

Before he merged into the darkness the traveler stopped, and looking round and seeing Trotty standing there yet, seemed undecided whether to[Pg 134] return or go on. After doing first the one and then the other, he came back, and Trotty went half way to meet him.

"You can tell me, perhaps," said the man with a faint smile, "and if you can I am sure will, and I'd rather ask you than another— where Alderman Cute lives."

"Close at hand," replied Toby, "I'll show you his house with pleasure."

"I was to have gone to him elsewhere to-morrow," said the man, accompanying Toby, "but I am uneasy under suspicion, and want to clear myself and to be free to go and seek my bread—I don't know where. So, maybe he'll forgive my going to his house to-night."

"It's impossible," cried Toby with a start, "that your name's Fern!"

"Eh!" cried the other, turning on him in astonishment.

"Fern! Will Fern!" said Trotty.

"That's my name," replied the other.

"Why, then," cried Trotty, seizing him by the arm and looking cautiously round, "for Heaven's sake don't go to him! Don't go to him! He'll put you down as sure as ever you were born. Here, come up this alley, and I'll tell you what I mean. Don't go to *him.*"

His new acquaintance looked as if he thought him mad, but he bore him company, nevertheless. When they were shrouded from observation, Trotty told him what he knew, and what character he had received, and all about it.

The subject of his history listened to it with a calmness that surprised him. He did not contradict or interrupt it once. He nodded his head now and then—more in corroboration of an old and worn-out story, it appeared, than in refutation of it; and once or twice threw back his hat, and passed his freckled hand over a brow, where every furrow he had ploughed seemed to have set its image in little. But he did no more.

"It's true enough in the main," he said, "master, I could sift grain from the husk here and there, but let it be as 'tis. What odds? I have gone against his plans; to my misfortun'. I can't help it; I should do the like to-morrow. As to character, them gentlefolks will search and search, and pry and pry, and have it as free from spot or speck in us, afore they'll help us to a dry good word!—Well! I hope they don't lose good opinion as easy as we do, or their lives is strict indeed, and hardly worth the keeping. For myself, master, I never took with that hand"—holding it before him—"what wasn't my own; and never held it back from work, however hard, or poorly paid. Whoever can deny it, let him chop it off! But when work won't maintain me like a human creetur; when my living is so bad, that I am Hungry, out of doors and in; when I see a whole working life begin that way, go on that way, and end that way, without a chance or change; then I say to the gentlefolks 'Keep away from me! Let my cottage be. My doors is dark enough without your darkening of 'em more. Don't look for me to come up into the Park to help the show when there's a Birthday, or a fine Speechmaking, or what not. Act your Plays and Games without me, and be welcome to 'em and enjoy 'em. We've now to do with one another. I'm best let alone!'"

Seeing that the child in his arms had opened her eyes, and was looking about in wonder, he checked himself to say a word or two of foolish prattle in her ear, and stand her on the ground beside him. Then slowly winding one of her long tresses round and round his rough forefinger like a ring, while she hung about his dusty leg, he said to Trotty,

"I'm not a cross-grained man by natur', I believe; and easy satisfied, I'm sure. I bear no ill will against none of 'em. I only want to live like one of the Almighty's creeturs. I can't—I don't— and so there's a pit dug between me, and them that can and do. There's others like me. You might tell 'em off by hundreds and by thousands, sooner than by ones."

Trotty knew that he spoke the truth in this, and shook his head to signify as much.

"I've got a bad name this way," said Fern; "and I'm not likely, I'm afeared, to get a better. 'Tan't lawful to be out of sorts, and I AM out of sorts, though God knows, I'd sooner bear a cheerful spirit if I could. Well! I don't know as this Alderman could hurt me much by sending me to gaol; but without a friend to

~ 147 ~

speak a word for me, he might do it; and you see—!" pointing downward with his finger, at the child.

He sunk his voice so low, and gazed upon her with an air so stern and strange, that Toby, to divert the current of his thoughts, inquired if his wife were living.

"I never had one," he returned, shaking his head. "She's my brother's child: a orphan. Nine year old, though you'd hardly think it; but she's tired and worn out now. They'd have taken care on her in the Union—eight and twenty mile away from where we live—between four walls (as they took care of my old father when he couldn't work no more, though he didn't trouble 'em long); but I took her instead, and she's lived with me ever since. Her mother had a friend once, in London here. We are trying to find her, and to find work too; but it's a large place. Never mind. More room for us to walk about in, Lilly!"

Meeting the child's eyes with a smile which melted Toby more than tears, he shook him by the hand.

"I don't so much as know your name," he said, "but I've opened my heart free to you, for I'm thankful to you; with good reason. I'll take your advice and keep clear of this—"

"Justice," suggested Toby.

"Ah!" he said. "If that's the name they give him. This Justice. And to-morrow will try whether there's better fortun' to be met with somewheres near London. Goodnight. A Happy New Year!"

"Stay!" cried Trotty, catching at his hand, as he relaxed his grip. "Stay! The New Year never can be happy to me, if we part like this. The New Year can never be happy to me, if I see the child and you go wandering away, you don't know where, without a shelter for your heads. Come home with me! I'm a poor man, living in a poor place; but I can give you lodging for one night and never miss it. Come home with me! Here! I'll take her!" cried Trotty, lifting up the child. "A pretty one! I'd carry twenty times her weight, and never know I'd got it. Tell me if I go too quick for you. I'm very fast. I always was!" Trotty said this, taking about six of his trotting paces to one stride of his fatigued companion; and with his thin legs quivering again, beneath the load he bore.

"Down the Mews here, Uncle Will, and step at the black door, with 'T. Veck, Ticket Porter,' wrote upon a board; and here we are, and here we go, and here we are indeed, my precious Meg, surprising you!"

With which words Trotty, in a breathless state, set the child down before his daughter in the middle of the floor. The little visitor looked once at Meg; and doubting nothing in that face, but trusting everything she saw there; ran into her arms.

"Here we are, and here we go!" cried Trotty, running round the room and choking audibly. "Here, Uncle Will, here's a fire you know! Why don't you come to the fire? Oh here we are and here we go! Meg, my precious darling, where's the kettle? Here it is and here it goes, and it'll bile in no time!"

Trotty really had picked up the kettle somewhere or other in the course of his wild career, and now put it on the fire; while Meg, seating the child in a warm corner, knelt down on the ground before her, and pulled off her shoes, and dried her wet feet on a cloth. Ay, and she laughed at Trotty too—so pleasantly, so cheerfully, that Trotty could have blessed her where she kneeled; for he had seen that, when they entered, she was sitting by the fire in tears.

"Why, father!" said Meg. "You're crazy to-night, I think. I don't know what the Bells would say to that."

Meg looked toward him and saw that he had elaborately stationed himself behind the chair of their male visitor, where with many mysterious gestures he was holding up the six-pence he had earned.

"I see, my dear," said Trotty, "as I was coming in, half an ounce of tea lying somewhere on the stairs; and I'm pretty sure there was a bit of bacon too. As I don't remember where it was exactly, I'll go myself and try to find 'em."

With this inscrutable artifice, Toby withdrew to purchase the viands he had spoken of, for ready money, at Mrs. Chickenstalker's; and presently came back, pretending that he had not been able to find them, at first in the dark.

"But here they are at last," said Trotty, setting out the tea things, "all correct! I was pretty sure it was tea and a rasher. So it is. Meg my pet, if you'll just make the tea, while your unworthy father toasts the bacon, we shall be ready immediate. It's a curious circumstance," said Trotty, proceeding in his cookery, with the assistance of the toasting-fork, "curious, but well known to my friends, that I never care, myself, for rashers, nor for tea. I like to see other people enjoy 'em," said Trotty, speaking very loud to impress the fact upon his guest, "but to me, as food, they are disagreeable."

Yet Trotty sniffed the savor of the hissing bacon—ah!—as if he liked it; and when he poured the boiling water in the tea-pot, looked lovingly down into the depths of that snug caldron, and suffering the fragrant steam to curl about his nose, and wreathe his head and face in a thick cloud. However, for all this, he neither ate nor drank, except at the very beginning, a mere morsel for

~ 150 ~

form's sake, which he appeared to eat with infinite relish, but declared was perfectly uninteresting to him.

"Now, I'll tell you what," said Trotty after tea. "The little one, she sleeps with Meg, I know."

"With good Meg!" cried the child, caressing her. "With Meg."

"That's right," said Trotty. "And I shouldn't wonder if she'll kiss Meg's father, won't she? I'm Meg's father."

Mightily delighted Trotty was, when the child went timidly toward him, and having kissed him, fell back upon Meg again.

Meg looked toward their guest, who leaned upon her chair, and with his face turned from her, fondled the child's head, half hidden in her lap.

"To be sure," said Toby. "To be sure! I don't know what I am rambling on about, to-night. My wits are wool-gathering, I think. Will Fern, you come along with me. You're tired to death, and broken down for want of rest. You come along with me."

The hand released from the child's hair, had fallen, trembling, into Trotty's hand. So Trotty, talking without intermission, led him out as tenderly and easily as if he had been a child himself.

Returning before Meg, he listened for an instant at the door of her little chamber; an adjoining room. The child was murmuring a simple Prayer before lying down to sleep; and when she had remembered Meg's name, "Dearly, Dearly"—so her words ran— Trotty heard her stop and ask for his.

It was some short time before the foolish little old fellow could compose himself to mend the fire, and draw his chair to the warm hearth. But when he had done so, and had trimmed the light, he took his newspaper from his pocket and began to read. Carelessly at first, and skimming up and down the columns; but with an earnest and a sad attention, very soon.

For this same dreaded paper re-directed Trotty's thoughts into the channel they had taken all that day, and which the day's events had so marked out and shaped. His interest in the two wanderers had set him on another course of thinking, and a happier one, for the time; but being alone again, and reading of the crimes and violences of the people, he relapsed into his former train.

"It's too true, all I've heard to-day," Toby muttered; "too just, too full of proof. We're Bad!"

The Chimes took up the words so suddenly—burst out so loud, and clear, and sonorous—that the Bells seemed to strike him in his chair.

And what was that, they said?

"Toby Veck, Toby Veck, waiting for you Toby! Toby Veck, Toby Veck, waiting for you Toby! Come and see us, come and see us, Drag him to us, drag him to us, Haunt and hunt him, haunt and hunt him, Break his slumbers, break his slumbers! Toby Veck, Toby Veck, door open wide Toby, Toby Veck, Toby Veck, door open wide Toby—" then fiercely back to their impetuous strain again, and ringing in the very bricks and plaster on the walls.

Toby listened. Fancy, fancy! His remorse for having run away from them that afternoon! No, no. Nothing of the kind. Again, again, and yet a dozen times again. "Haunt and hunt him, haunt and hunt him, Drag him to us, drag him to us!" Deafening the whole town!

"Meg," said Trotty, softly; tapping at her door. "Do you hear anything?"

"I hear the Bells, father. Surely they're very loud to-night."

"Is she asleep?" said Toby, making an excuse for peeping in.

"So peacefully and happily! I can't leave her yet though, father. Look how she holds my hand!"

"Meg!" whispered Trotty. "Listen to the Bells!"

She listened, with her face toward him all the time. But it underwent no change. She didn't understand them.

Trotty withdrew, resumed his seat by the fire, and once more listened by himself. He remained here a little time.

It was impossible to bear it; their energy was dreadful.

"If the tower-door is really open," said Toby, hastily laying aside his apron, but never thinking of his hat, "what's to hinder me from going up in the steeple and satisfying myself? If it's shut, I don't want any other satisfaction. That's enough."

He was pretty certain as he slipped out quietly into the street that he should find it shut and locked, for he knew the door well, and had so rarely seen it open, that he couldn't reckon above three times in all. It was a low-arched portal outside the church, in a dark nook behind a column; and had such great iron hinges, and such a monstrous lock, that there was more hinge and lock than door.

But what was his astonishment when, coming bare-headed to the church, and putting his hand into this dark nook, with a certain misgiving that it might be unexpectedly seized, and a shivering propensity to draw it back again, he found that the door, which opened outward, actually stood ajar!

He thought, on the first surprise, of going back; or of getting a light, or a companion; but his courage aided him immediately, and he determined to ascend alone.

"What have I to fear?" said Trotty. "It's a church! Besides the ringers may be there, and have forgotten to shut the door."

So he went in, feeling his way as he went, like a blind man; for it was very dark. And very quiet, for the Chimes were silent.

The dust from the street had blown into the recess; and lying there, heaped up, made it so soft and velvet-like to the foot, that there was something startling even in that. The narrow stair was so close to the door, too, that he stumbled at the very first; and shutting the door upon himself by striking it with his foot, and causing it to rebound back heavily, he couldn't open it again.

This was another reason, however, for going on. Trotty groped his way, and went on. Up, up, up, and round and round; and up, up, up, higher, higher, higher up!

Until, ascending through the floor, and pausing with his head just raised above its beams, he came among the Bells. It was barely possible to make out their great shapes in the gloom; but there they were. Shadowy, and dark, and dumb.

A heavy sense of dread and loneliness fell instantly upon him, as he climbed into this airy nest of stone and metal. His head went round and [Pg 143] round. He listened and then raised a wild "Halloa!"

Halloa! was mournfully protracted by the echoes.

~ 154 ~

Giddy, confused, and out of breath, and frightened, Toby looked about him vacantly, and sunk down in a swoon.

Third Quarter.

When and how the darkness of the night-black steeple changed to shining light; and how the solitary tower was peopled with a myriad figures; when and how the whispered "Haunt and hunt him," breathing monotonously through his sleep or swoon, became a voice exclaiming in the waking ears of Trotty, "Break his slumbers;" when and how he ceased to have a sluggish and confused idea that such things were, companioning a host of others that were not; there are no dates or means to tell. But, awake, and standing on his feet upon the boards where he had lately lain, he saw this Goblin Sight.

Then and not before, did Trotty see in every Bell a bearded figure of the bulk and stature of the Bell—incomprehensibly, a figure and the Bell itself. Gigantic, grave, and darkly watchful of him, as he stood rooted to the ground.

Mysterious and awful figures! Resting on nothing; poised in the night air of the tower, with their draped and hooded heads merged in the dim roof; motionless and shadowy. Shadowy and dark, although he saw them by some light belonging to themselves— none else was there—each with its muffled hand upon its goblin mouth.

He could not plunge down wildly through the opening in the floor; for, all power of motion had deserted him. Otherwise he would have done so—ay, would have thrown himself, head-foremost, from the steeple-top, rather than have seen them watching him with eyes that would have waked and watched, although the pupils had been taken out.

A blast of air—how cold and shrill!—came moaning through the tower. As it died away, the Great Bell, or the Goblin of the Great Bell, spoke.

~ 156 ~

"What visitor is this?" it said. The voice was low and deep, and Trotty fancied that it sounded in the other figures as well.

"I thought my name was called by the Chimes!" said Trotty, raising his hands in an attitude of supplication. "I hardly know why I am here, or how I came. I have listened to the Chimes these many years. They have cheered me often."

"And you have thanked them?" said the bell.

"A thousand times!" cried Trotty.

"How?"

"I am a poor man," faltered Trotty, "and could only thank them in words."

"And always so?" inquired the Goblin of the Bell. "Have you never done us wrong in words?"

"No!" cried Trotty, eagerly.

"Never done us foul, and false, and wicked wrong, in words?" pursued the Goblin of the Bell.

Trotty was about to answer "Never!" But he stopped and was confused.

"The voice of Time," said the Phantom, "cries to man, Advance! Time is for his advancement and improvement; for his greater worth, his greater happiness, his better life; his progress onward to that goal within its knowledge and its view, and set there, in the period when Time and he began. Ages of darkness, wickedness, and violence, have come and gone—millions uncountable, have suffered, lived, and died—to point the way before him. Who seeks to turn him back, or stay him on his course, arrests a mighty engine which will strike the meddler dead; and be the fiercer and the wilder, ever, for its momentary check!"

"I never did so to my knowledge, sir," said Trotty. "It was quite by accident if I did. I wouldn't go to do it, I'm sure."

"Who puts into the mouth of Time, or of its servants," said the Goblin of the Bell, "a cry of lamentation for days which have had their trial and their failure, and have left deep traces of it which the blind may see—a cry that only serves the present time, by showing men how much it needs their help when any ears can listen to regrets for such a past—who does this, does a wrong. And you have done that wrong to us, the Chimes."

Trotty's first excess of fear was gone. But he had felt tenderly and gratefully toward the Bells, as you have seen; and when he heard himself arraigned as one who had offended them so weightily, his heart was touched with penitence and grief.

"If you knew," said Trotty, clasping his hands earnestly—"or perhaps you do know—if you know how often you have kept me company; how often you have cheered me up when I've been low; how you were quite the plaything of my little daughter Meg (almost the only one she ever had) when first her mother died, and she and me were left alone; you won't bear malice for a hasty word!"

"Who hears in us, the Chimes, one note bespeaking disregard, or stern regard, of any hope, or joy, or pain, or sorrow, of the many-sorrowed throng; who hears us make response to any creed that gauges human passions and affections, as it gauges the amount of miserable food on which humanity may pine and wither; does us wrong. That wrong you have done us!" said the Bell.

"I have!" said Trotty. "Oh, forgive me!"

"Spare me," cried Trotty, falling on his knees; "for Mercy's sake!"

"Listen!" said the Shadow.

"Listen!" cried the other Shadows.

"Listen!" said a clear and child-like voice, which Trotty thought he recognized as having heard before.

The organ sounded faintly in the church below. Swelling by degrees, the melody ascended to the roof, and filled the choir and nave. Expanding more and more, it rose up, up, up, up; higher, higher, higher up; awakening agitated hearts within the burly piles of oak, the hollow bells, the iron-bound doors, the stairs of solid stone; until the tower walls were insufficient to contain it, and it soared into the sky.

No wonder that an old man's breast could not contain a sound so vast and mighty. It broke from that weak prison in a rush of tears; and Trotty put his hands before his face.

"Listen!" said the Shadow.

"Listen!" said the other Shadows.

"Listen!" said the child's voice.

A solemn strain of blended voices rose into the tower.

It was a very low and mournful strain—a Dirge—and as he listened, Trotty heard his child among the singers.

"She is dead!" exclaimed the old man. "Meg is dead. Her spirit calls to me. I hear it!"

"The Spirit of your child bewails the dead, and mingles with the dead—dead hopes, dead fancies, dead imaginings of youth," returned the Bell, "but she is living. Learn from her life, a living truth. Learn from the creature dearest to your heart, how bad the bad are born. See every bud and leaf plucked one by one from off the fairest stem, and know how bare and wretched it may be. Follow her! To desperation!"

Each of the shadowy figures stretched its right arm forth, and pointed downward.

"The Spirit of the Chimes is your companion," said the figure. "Go! It stands behind you!"

Trotty turned, and saw—the child! The child Will Fern had carried in the street; the child whom Meg had watched, but now, asleep!

"I carried her myself, to-night," said Trotty. "In these arms!"

"Show him what he calls himself," said the dark figures, one and all.

The tower opened at his feet. He looked down, and beheld his own form, lying at the bottom, on the outside: crushed and motionless.

"No more a living man!" cried Trotty. "Dead!"

"Dead!" said the figures altogether.

"Gracious Heaven! And the New Year—'

"Past," said the figures.

"What!" he cried, shuddering, "I missed my way, and coming on the outside of this tower in the dark, fell down—a year ago?"

"Nine years ago!" replied the figures.

As they gave the answer, they recalled their outstretched hands; and where their figures had been, there the Bells were.

"What are these?" he asked his guide. "If I am not mad, what are these?"

"Spirits of the Bells. Their sound upon the air," returned the child. "They take such shapes and occupations as the hopes and thoughts of mortals, and the recollections they have stored up, give them."

"And you," said Trotty, wildly. "What are you?"

"Hush, hush!" returned the child. "Look here!"

In a poor, mean room; working at the same kind of embroidery, which he had often, often, seen before her; Meg, his own dear daughter, was presented to his view. He made no effort to imprint his kisses on her face; he did not strive to clasp her to his loving heart; he knew that such endearments were, for him, no more. But he held his trembling breath, and brushed away the blinding tears, that he might look upon her; that he might only see her.

Ah! Changed. Changed. The light of the clear eye, how dimmed. The bloom, how faded from the cheek. Beautiful she was, as she had ever been, but Hope, Hope, Hope, oh, where was the fresh Hope that had spoken to him like a voice!

She looked up from her work, at a companion. Following her eyes, the old man started back.

In the woman grown, he recognized her at a glance. In the long silken hair, he saw the self-same curls; around the lips, the child's expression lingering still. See! In the eyes, now turned inquiringly on Meg, there shone the very look that scanned those features when he brought her home!

Then what was this, beside him?

Looking with awe into its face, he saw a something reigning there: a lofty something, undefined and indistinct, which made it hardly more than a remembrance of that child—as yonder figure might be—yet it was the same: the same: and wore the dress.

Hark! They were speaking!

"Meg," said Lilian, hesitating. "How often you raise your head from your work to look at me!"

"Are my looks so altered, that they frighten you?" asked Meg.

"Nay, dear! But you smile at that yourself! Why not smile when you look at me, Meg?"

"I do so. Do I not?" she answered: smiling on her.

"Now you do," said Lilian, "but not usually. When you think I'm busy, and don't see you, you look so anxious and so doubtful, that I hardly like to raise my eyes. There is little cause for smiling in this hard and toilsome life, but you were once so cheerful."

"Am I not now?" cried Meg, speaking in a tone of strange alarm, and rising to embrace her. "Do *I* make our weary life more weary to you, Lilian?"

"You have been the only thing that made it life," said Lilian, fervently kissing her; "sometimes the only thing that made me care to live so, Meg. Such work, such work! So many hours, so many days, so many long, long nights of hopeless, cheerless, never-ending work—not to heap up riches, not to live grandly or gayly, not to live upon enough, however coarse; but to earn bare bread; to scrape together just enough to toil upon, and want upon, and keep alive in us the consciousness of our hard fate! Oh, Meg, Meg!" she raised her voice and twined her arms about her as she spoke, like one in pain. "How can the cruel world go round, and bear to look upon such lives!"

"Lilly!" said Meg, soothing her, and putting back her hair from her wet face. "Why, Lilly! You! So pretty and so young!"

"Oh, Meg!" she interrupted, holding her at arm's-length, and looking in her face imploringly. "The worst of all! The worst of all! Strike me old, Meg! Wither me and shrivel me, and free me from the dreadful thoughts that tempt me in my youth!"

Trotty turned to look upon his guide. But, the Spirit of the child had taken flight. Was gone.

*   *   *   *   *

~ 163 ~

Fourth Quarter.

Some new remembrance of the ghostly figures in the Bells; some faint impression of the ringing of the Chimes; some giddy consciousness of having seen the swarm of phantoms reproduced and [Pg 150] reproduced until the recollection of them lost itself in the confusion of their numbers; some hurried knowledge, how conveyed to him he knew not, that more years had passed; and Trotty, with the Spirit of the child attending him, stood looking on at mortal company.

Fat company, rosy-cheeked company, comfortable company. They were but two, but they were red enough for ten. They sat before a bright fire, with a small low table between them; and unless the fragrance of hot tea and muffins lingered longer in that room than in most others, the table had seen service very lately. But all the cups and saucers being clean, and in their proper places in the corner cupboard; and the brass toasting fork hanging in its usual nook, and spreading its four idle fingers out, as if it wanted to be measured for a glove; there remained no other visible tokens of the meal just finished, than such as purred and washed their whiskers in the person of the basking cat, and glistened in the gracious, not to say the greasy, faces of her patrons.

This cosy couple (married, evidently) had made a fair division of the fire between them, and sat looking at the glowing sparks that dropped into the grate; now nodding off into a doze; now waking up again when some hot fragment, larger than the rest, came rattling down, as if the fire were coming with it.

It was in no danger of sudden extinction, however; for it gleamed not only in the little room, and on the panes of window-glass in the door, and on the curtain half drawn across them, but in the little shop beyond. A little shop, quite crammed and choked with the abundance of its stock; a perfectly voracious little shop, with a maw as accommodating and full as any shark's. Cheese, butter, firewood, soap, pickles, matches, bacon, table-beer, peg-tops, sweetmeats, boys' kites, bird-seed, cold ham, birch brooms, hearth-stones, salt, vinegar, blacking, red herrings, stationery, lard, mushroom ketchup, stay-laces, loaves of bread, shuttlecocks, eggs, and slate-pencils; everything was fish that came to the net of this greedy little shop, and all articles were in its net.

Glancing at such of these items as were visible in the shining of the blaze, and the less cheerful radiance of two smoky lamps which burnt but dimly in the shop itself, as though its plethora sat heavy on their lungs; and glancing, then, at one of the two faces by the parlor-fire, Trotty had small difficulty in recognizing in the stout old lady, Mrs. Chickenstalker: always inclined to corpulency, even in the days when he had known her as established in the general line, and having a small balance against him in her books.

The features of her companion were less easy to him. The great broad chin, with creases in it large enough to hide a finger in; the astonished eyes, that seemed to expostulate with themselves for sinking deeper and deeper into the yielding fat of the soft face; the nose afflicted with that disordered action of its functions which is generally termed The Snuffles; the short thick throat and laboring chest, with other beauties of the like description, though calculated to impress the memory, Trotty could at first allot to nobody he had ever known: and yet he had some recollection of them too. At length, in Mrs. Chickenstalker's partner in the general line, and in the crooked and eccentric line of life, he recognized the former porter of Sir Joseph Bowley; an apoplectic innocent, who had connected himself in Trotty's mind with Mrs. Chickenstalker years ago, by giving him admission to the mansion where he had confessed his obligations to that lady, and drawn on his unlucky head such grave reproach.

~ 165 ~

Trotty had little interest in a change like this, after the changes he had seen; but association is very strong sometimes; and he looked involuntarily behind the parlor-door, where the accounts of credit customers were usually kept in chalk. There was no record of his name. Some names were there, but they were strange to him, and infinitely fewer than of old; from which he argued that the porter was an advocate of ready money transactions, and on coming into the business had looked pretty sharp after the Chickenstalker defaulters.

So desolate was Trotty, and so mournful for the youth and promise of his blighted child, that it was a sorrow to him, even to have no place in Mrs. Chickenstalker's ledger.

"What sort of a night is it, Anne?" inquired the former porter of Sir Joseph Bowley, stretching out his legs before the fire, and rubbing as much of them as his short arms could reach; with an air that added, "Here I am if it's bad, and I don't want to go out if it's good."

"Hard weather indeed," returned his wife, shaking her head.

"Ay, ay! Years," said Mr. Tugby, "are like Christians in that respect. Some of 'em die hard; some of 'em die easy. This one hasn't many days to run, and is making a fight for it. I like him all the better. There's a customer, my love!"

Attentive to the rattling door, Mrs. Tugby had already risen.

"Now, then!" said that lady, passing out into the little shop. "What's wanted? Oh! I beg your pardon, sir, I'm sure. I didn't think it was you."

She made this apology to a gentleman in black, who, with his wristbands tucked up, and his hat cocked loungingly on one side, and his hand in his pocket, sat down astride on the table-beer barrel, and nodded in return.

"This is a bad business up-stairs, Mrs. Tugby," said the gentleman. "The man can't live."

"Not the back-attic can't!" cried Tugby, coming out into the shop to join the conference.

"The back-attic, Mr. Tugby," said the gentleman, "is coming down-stairs fast, and will be below the basement very soon."

Looking by turns at Tugby and his wife, he sounded the barrel with his knuckles for the depth of beer, and having found it, played a tune upon the empty part.

"The back-attic, Mr. Tugby," said the gentleman: Tugby having stood in silent consternation for some time; "is Going."

"Then," said Tugby, turning to his wife, "he must Go, you know, before he's Gone."

"I don't think you can move him," said the gentleman, shaking his head. "I wouldn't take the responsibility of saying it could be done, myself. You had better leave him where he is. He can't live long."

"It's the only subject," said Tugby, bringing the butter-scale down upon the counter with a crash, by weighing his fist on it, "that we've ever had a word upon; she and me; and look what it comes to! He's going to die here, after all. Going to die upon the premises. Going to die in our house!"

"And where should he have died, Tugby?" cried his wife.

"In the workhouse," he returned. "What are workhouses made for?"

"Not for that!" said Mrs. Tugby, with great energy. "Not for that! Neither did I marry you for that. Don't think it, Tugby. I won't have it. I won't allow it. I'd be separated first, and never see your face again. When my widow's name stood over that door, as it did for many, many years: the house being known as Mrs. Chickenstalker's far and wide, and never known but to its honest credit and its good report: when my widow's name stood over that door, Tugby, I knew him as a handsome, steady, manly, independent youth; I knew her as the sweetest looking, sweetest tempered girl, eyes ever saw; I knew her father (poor old creetur, he fell down from the steeple walking in his sleep, and killed himself), for the simplest, hardest working, childest-hearted man, that ever drew the breath of life; and when I turn them out of house and home, may angels turn me out of heaven. As they would! And serve me right!"

Her old face, which had been a plump and dimpled one before the changes which had come to pass, seemed to shine out of her as she said these words; and when she dried her eyes, and shook her head and her handkerchief at Tugby, with an expression of firmness which it was quite clear was not to be easily resisted, Trotty said, "Bless her! Bless her!"

Then he listened, with a panting heart, for what should follow. Knowing nothing yet, but that they spoke of Meg.

The gentleman upon the table-beer cask, who appeared to be some authorized medical attendant upon the poor, was far too well accustomed, evidently, to little differences of opinion between man and wife, to interpose any remark in this instance. He sat softly whistling, and turning little drops of beer out of the tap upon the ground, until there was a perfect calm: when he raised his head and said to Mrs. Tugby, late Chickenstalker:

"There's something interesting about the woman, even now. How did she come to marry him?"

"Why, that," said Mrs. Tugby, taking a seat near him, "is not the least cruel part of her story, sir. You see they kept company, she and Richard, many years ago. When they were a young and beautiful couple, everything was settled, and they were to have been married on a New Year's Day. But, somehow, Richard got it into his head, through what the gentleman told him, that he might do better, and that he'd soon repent it, and that she wasn't good enough for him, and that a young man of spirit had no business to be married. And the gentleman frightened her, and made her melancholy, and timid of his deserting her, and of her children coming to the gallows, and of its being wicked to be man and wife, and a good deal more of it. And in short, they lingered and lingered, and their trust in one another was broken, and so at last was the match. But the fault was his. She would have married him, sir, joyfully. I've seen her heart swell, many times afterwards, when he passed her in a proud and careless way; and never did a woman grieve more truly for a man, than she for Richard when he first went wrong."

"Oh! he went wrong, did he?" said the gentleman, pulling out the vent-peg of the table-beer, and trying to peep down into the barrel through the hole.

"Well, sir, I don't know that he rightly understood himself, you see. I think his mind was troubled by their having broke with one another; and that but for being ashamed before the gentlemen, and perhaps for being uncertain too, how she might take it, he'd have gone through any suffering or trial to have had Meg's promise, and Meg's hand again. That's my belief. He never said so; more's the pity! He took to drinking, idling, bad companions: all the fine resources that were to be so much better for him than the Home he might have had. He lost his looks, his character, his health, his strength, his friends, his work: everything!"

"He didn't lose everything, Mrs. Tugby," returned the gentleman, "because he gained a wife; and I want to know how he gained her."

"I'm coming to it, sir, in a moment. This went on for years and years; he sinking lower and lower; she enduring, poor thing, miseries enough to wear her life away. At last he was so cast down, and cast out, that no one would employ or notice him; and doors were shut upon him, go where he would. Applying from place to place, and door to door; and coming for the hundredth time to one gentleman, who had often and often tried him (he was a good workman to the very end); that gentleman, who knew his history, said, 'I believe you are incorrigible; there's only one person in the world who has a chance of reclaiming you; ask me to trust you no more, until she tries to do it.' Something like that, in his anger and vexation."

"Ah!" said the gentleman. "Well?"

"Well, sir, he went to her, and kneeled to her; said it was so; said it ever had been so; and made a prayer to her to save him."

"And she?—Don't distress yourself, Mrs. Tugby."

"She came to me that night to ask me about living here. 'What he was once to me,' she said, 'is buried in a grave, side by side with what I was to him. But I have thought of this; and I will make the trial. In the hope of saving him; for the love of the light-hearted girl (you remember her) who was to have been married on a New Year's Day; and for the love of her Richard.' And he said he had come to her from Lilian, and Lilian had trusted to him, and she never could forget that. So they were married; and when they came home here, and I saw them, I hoped that such prophecies as parted

~ 170 ~

them when they were young, may not often fulfill themselves as[Pg 157] they did in this case, or I wouldn't be the makers of them for a Mine of Gold."

The gentleman got off the cask, and stretched himself, observing:

"I suppose he used her ill, as soon as they were married?"

"I don't think he ever did that," said Mrs. Tugby, shaking her head and wiping her eyes. "He went on better for a short time; but, his habits were too old and strong to be got rid of; he soon fell back a little; and was falling fast back, when his illness came so strong upon him. I think he has always felt for her. I am sure he has. I've seen him in his crying fits and tremblings, try to kiss her hand; and I have heard him call her 'Meg,' and say it was her nineteenth birthday. There he has been lying, now, these weeks and months. Between him and her baby, she has not been able to do her old work; and by not being able to be regular, she has lost it, even if she could have done it. How they have lived, I hardly know!"

"/ know," muttered Mr. Tugby, looking at the till, and round the shop, and at his wife; and rolling his head with immense intelligence.

He was interrupted by a cry—a sound of lamentation—from the upper story of the house. The gentleman moved hurriedly to the door.

"My friend," he said, looking back, "you needn't discuss whether he shall be removed or not. He has spared you that trouble, I believe."

Saying so, he ran up-stairs, followed by Mrs. Tugby; while Mr. Tugby panted and grumbled after them at leisure: being rendered more than commonly short-winded by the weight of the till, in

~ 171 ~

which there had been an inconvenient quantity of copper. Trotty, with the child beside him, floated up the staircase like mere air.

"Follow her! Follow her! Follow her!" He heard the ghostly voices in the Bells repeat their words as he ascended. "Learn it, from the creature dearest to your heart!"

It was over. It was over. And this was she, her father's pride and joy! This haggard, wretched woman, weeping by the bed, if it deserved that name, and pressing to her breast, and hanging down her head upon, an infant? Who can tell how spare, how sickly, and how poor an infant? Who can tell how dear?

"Thank God!" cried Trotty, holding up his folded hands. "O, God be thanked! She loves her child!"

Again Trotty heard the voices, saying, "Follow her!" He turned toward his guide, and saw it rising from him, passing through the air. "Follow her!" it said. And vanished.

He hovered round her; sat down at her feet; looked up into her face for one trace of her old self; listened for one note of her old pleasant voice. He flitted round the child: so wan, so prematurely old, so dreadful in its gravity, so plaintive in its feeble, mournful, miserable wail. He almost worshiped it. He clung to it as her only safeguard; as the last unbroken link that bound her to endurance. He set his father's hope and trust on the frail baby; watched her every look upon it as she held it in her arms; and cried a thousand times, "She loves it! God be thanked, she loves it!"

He saw the woman tend her in the night; return to her when her grudging husband was asleep, and all was still; encourage her, shed tears with her, set nourishment before her. He saw the day come, and the night again; the day, the night; the time go by; the house of death relieved of death; the room left to herself and to the child; he heard it moan and cry; he saw it harass her, and tire her out, and when she slumbered in exhaustion, drag her back to consciousness, and hold her with its little hands upon the rack; but she was constant to it, gentle with it, patient with it. Patient! Was its loving mother in her inmost heart and soul, and had its Being knitted up with hers as when she carried it unborn.

All this time, she was in want: languishing away, in dire and pining want. With the baby in her arms, she wandered here and there in quest of occupation; and with its thin face lying in her lap, and looking up in hers, did any work for any wretched sum: a day and night of labor for as many farthings as there were figures on the dial. If she had quarreled with it; if she had neglected it; if she had looked upon it with a moment's hate! if, in the frenzy of an instant, she had struck it! No! His comfort was, She loved it always.

She told no one of her extremity, and wandered abroad in the day lest she should be questioned by her only friend: for any help she received from her hands, occasioned fresh disputes between the good woman and her husband; and it was new bitterness to be the daily cause of strife and discord, where she owed so much.

She loved it still. She loved it more and more. But a change fell on the aspect of her love.

One night she was singing faintly to it in its sleep and walking to and fro to hush it, when her door was softly opened, and a man looked in.

"For the last time," he said.

"William Fern!"

"For the last time."

~ 173 ~

He listened like a man pursued: and spoke in whispers.

"Margaret, my race is nearly run, I couldn't finish it, without a parting word with you. Without one grateful word."

"What have you done?" she asked: regarding him with terror.

He looked at her but gave no answer.

After a short silence, he made a gesture with his hand, as if he set her question by; as if he brushed it aside; and said:

"It's long ago, Margaret, now; but that night is as fresh in my memory as ever 'twas. We little thought then," he added, looking round, "that we should ever meet like this. Your child, Margaret? Let me have it in my arms. Let me hold your child."

He put his hat upon the floor, and took it. And he trembled as he took it, from head to foot.

"Is it a girl?"

"Yes."

He put his hand before its little face.

"See how weak I'm grown, Margaret, when I want the courage to look at it! Let her be, a moment. I won't hurt her. It's long ago, but—What's her name?"

"Margaret," she answered quickly.

"I'm glad of that," he said. "I'm glad of that!"

He seemed to breathe more freely; and after pausing for an instant, took away his hand, and looked upon the infant's face. But covered it again, immediately.

"Margaret!" he said; and gave her back the child. "It's Lilian's."

"Lilian's!"

"I held the same face in my arms when Lilian's mother died and left her."

"When Lilian's mother died and left her!" she repeated, wildly.

"How shrill you speak! Why do you fix your eyes upon me so? Margaret!"

She sunk down in a chair, and pressed the infant to her breast, and wept over it. Sometimes, she released it from her embrace, to look anxiously in[Pg 161] its face: then strained it to her bosom again. At those times, when she gazed upon it, then it was that something fierce and terrible began to mingle with her love. Then it was that her old father quailed.

"Follow her!" was sounded through the house. "Learn it, from the creature dearest to your heart!"

"Margaret," said Fern, bending over her, and kissing her upon the brow: "I thank you for the last time. Good night. Good bye! Put your hand in mine, and tell me you'll forget me from this hour, and try to think the end of me was here."

She called to him; but he was gone. She sat down stupefied, until her infant roused her to a sense of hunger, cold, and darkness. She paced the room with it the livelong night, hushing it and soothing it. She said at intervals, "Like Lilian when her mother

~ 175 ~

died and left her!" Why was her step so quick, her eyes so wild, her love so fierce and terrible, whenever she repeated those words?

"But, it is Love," said Trotty. "It is Love. She'll never cease to love it. My poor Meg!"

She dressed the child next morning with unusual care—ah, vain expenditure of care upon such squalid robes!—and once more tried to find some means of life. It was the last day of the Old Year. She tried till night, and never broke her fast. She tried in vain.

She mingled with an abject crowd, who tarried in the snow, until it pleased some officer appointed to dispense the public charity (the lawful charity; not that once preached upon a Mount), to call them in, and question them, and say to this one, "Go to such a place," to that one, "Come next week;" to make a foot-ball of another wretch, and pass him here and there, from hand to hand, from house[Pg 162] to house, until he wearied and lay down to die; or started up and robbed, and so became a higher sort of criminal, whose claims allowed of no delay. Here, too, she failed.

She loved her child, and wished to have it lying on her breast. And that was quite enough.

It was night: a bleak, dark, cutting night: when pressing the child close to her for warmth, she arrived outside the house she called her home. She was so faint and giddy, that she saw no one standing in the doorway until she was close upon it, and about to enter. Then, she recognized the master of the house, who had so disposed himself—with his person it was not difficult—as to fill up the whole entry.

"Oh!" he said softly. "You have come back?"

She looked at the child and shook her head.

"Don't you think you have lived here long enough without paying any rent? Don't you think that, without any money, you've been a pretty constant customer at this shop, now?" said Mr. Tugby.

She repeated the same mute appeal.

"Suppose you try and deal somewhere else," he said. "And suppose you provide yourself with another lodging. Come! Don't you think you could manage it?"

She said, in a low voice, that it was very late. To-morrow.

"Now I see what you want," said Tugby; "and what you mean. You know there are two parties in this house about you, and you delight in setting them by the ears. I don't want any quarrels; I'm speaking softly to avoid a quarrel; but if you don't go away, I'll speak out loud, and you shall cause words loud enough to please you. But you shan't come in, that I am determined."

She put her hair back with her hand, and looked in a sudden manner at the sky, and the dark lowering distance.

"This is the last night of an Old Year, and I won't carry ill-blood and quarrelings and disturbances into a New One, to please you nor anybody else," said Tugby, who was quite a retail Friend and Father. "I wonder you an't ashamed of yourself, to carry such practices into a New Year. If you haven't any business in the world, but to be always giving way, and always making disturbances between man and wife, you'd be better out of it. Go along with you!"

"Follow her! To desperation!"

~ 177 ~

Again the old man heard the voices. Looking up, he saw the figures hovering in the air, and pointing where she went, down the dark street.

"She loves it!" he exclaimed in agonized entreaty for her. "Chimes! she loves it still!"

"Follow her!" The shadows swept upon the track she had taken like a cloud.

Oh, for something to awaken her! For any sight or sound, or scent, to call up tender recollections in a brain on fire! For any gentle image of the Past, to rise up before her!

"I was her father! I was her father!" cried the old man, stretching out his hands to the dark shadows flying on above. "Have mercy on her, and on me! Where does she go? Turn her back! I was her father!"

But, they only pointed to her, as she hurried on; "To desperation! Learn it from the creature dearest to your heart!"

A hundred voices echoed it. The air was made of breath expended in those words. He seemed to take them in, at every gasp he drew. They were everywhere, and not to be escaped. And still she hurried on; the same light in her eyes.

All at once she stopped.

"Now, turn her back!" exclaimed the old man, tearing his white hair. "My child! Meg! Turn her back! Great Father, turn her back!"

In her own scanty shawl, she wrapped the baby warm. With her fevered hands, she smoothed its limbs, composed its face, arranged its mean attire. In her wasted arms she folded it, as though she never would resign it more. And with her dry lips, kissed it in a final pang, and last long agony of Love.

Putting its tiny hand up to her neck, and holding it there, within her dress, next to her distracted heart, she set its sleeping face against her: closely, steadily against her: and sped onward to the river.

To the rolling River, swift and dim, where Winter Night sat brooding like the last dark thoughts of many who had sought a refuge there before her. Where scattered lights upon the banks gleamed sullen, red and dull, as torches that were burning there to show the way to Death. Where no abode of living people cast its shadow, on the deep, impenetrable, melancholy shade.

To the River! To that portal of Eternity, her desperate footsteps tended with the swiftness of its rapid waters running to the sea. He tried to touch her as she passed him, going down to its dark level; but, the wild distempered form, the fierce and terrible love, the desperation that had left all human check or hold behind, swept by him like the wind.

He followed her. She paused a moment on the brink, before the dreadful plunge. He fell down on his knees, and in a shriek addressed the figures in the Bells now hovering above them.

"Have mercy on her!" he exclaimed, "as one in whom this dreadful crime has sprung from Love perverted; from the strongest, deepest Love we fallen creatures know! Think what her misery must have been, when such seed bears such fruit. Heaven meant her to be good. There is no loving mother on the earth who might not come to this, if such a life had gone before. Oh, have mercy on my child, who, even at this pass, means mercy to her own, and dies herself, and perils her immortal soul, to save it!"

~ 179 ~

She was in his arms. He held her now. His strength was like a giant's.

He might have said more; but the Bells, the old familiar Bells, his own dear, constant, steady friends, the Chimes, began to ring the joy-peals for a New Year; so lustily, so merrily, so happily, so gayly, that he leapt upon his feet, and broke the spell that bound him.

"And whatever you do, father," said Meg, "don't eat tripe again without asking some doctor whether it's likely to agree with you; for how you *have* been going on, Good gracious!"

She was working with her needle at the little table by the fire, dressing her simple gown with ribbons for her wedding. So quietly happy, so blooming and youthful, so full of beautiful promise, that he uttered a great cry as if it were an Angel in his house; then flew to clasp her in his arms.

But he caught his feet in the newspaper, which had fallen on the hearth, and somebody came rushing in between them.

"No!" cried the voice of this same somebody; a generous and jolly voice it was. "Not even you. Not even you. The first kiss of Meg in the New Year is mine. Mine! I have been waiting outside the house this hour to hear the Bells and claim it. Meg, my precious prize, a happy year! A life of happy years, my darling wife!"

And Richard smothered her with kisses.

You never in all your life saw anything like Trotty after this. I don't care where you have lived or what you have seen, you never in all your life saw anything at all approaching him! He sat

~ 180 ~

down in his chair and beat his knees and cried; he sat[Pg 166] down in his chair and beat his knees and laughed; he sat down in his chair and beat his knees and laughed and cried together; he got out of his chair and hugged Meg; he got out of his chair and hugged Richard; he got out of his chair and hugged them both at once; he kept running up to Meg and squeezing her fresh face between his hands and kissing it, going from her backward not to lose sight of it, and running up again like a figure in a magic lantern; and whatever he did, he was constantly sitting himself down in this chair, and never stopping in it for one single moment, being—that's the truth—beside himself with joy.

"And to-morrow's your wedding-day, my pet!" cried Trotty. "Your real, happy wedding-day!"

"To-day!" cried Richard, shaking hands with him. "To-day. The Chimes are ringing in the New Year. Hear them!"

They WERE ringing! Bless their sturdy hearts, they WERE ringing! Great Bells as they were; melodious, deep-mouthed, noble Bells; cast in no common metal; made by no common founder; when had they ever chimed like that before?

"But to-day, my pet," said Trotty. "You and Richard had some words to-day."

"Because he's such a bad fellow, father," said Meg. "An't you, Richard? Such a headstrong, violent man! He'd have made no more of speaking his mind to that great Alderman, and putting *him*down I don't know where, than he would of—"

"—Kissing Meg," suggested Richard. Doing it, too.

"No. Not a bit more," said Meg. "But I wouldn't let him, father. Where would have been the use?"

"Richard, my boy!" cried Trotty. "You was turned up Trumps originally, and Trumps you must be until you die! But you were crying by the fire to-night, my pet, when I came home. Why did you cry by the fire?"

"I was thinking of the years we've passed together, father. Only that. And thinking you might miss me, and be lonely."

Trotty was backing off to that extraordinary chair again, when the child, who had been awakened by the noise, came running in, half dressed.

"Why, here she is!" cried Trotty catching her up. "Here's little Lilian! Ha, ha, ha! Here we are and here we go! O, here we are and here we go again! And here we are and here we go! And Uncle Will, too!" Stopping in his trot to greet him heartily. "O, Uncle Will, the vision that I've had to-night, through lodging you! O, Uncle Will, the obligations that you've laid me under by your coming, my good friend!"

Before Will Fern could make the least reply, a band of music burst into the room, attended by a flock of neighbors, screaming: "A Happy New Year, Meg!" "A Happy Wedding!" "Many of 'em!" and other fragmentary good wishes of that sort. The Drum (who was a private friend of Trotty's) then stepped forward and said:

"Trotty Veck, my boy! It's got about that your daughter is going to be married to-morrow. There an't a soul that knows you that don't wish you well, or that knows her and don't wish her well. Or that knows you both and don't wish you both all the happiness the New Year can bring. And here we are, to play it in accordingly."

"What a happiness it is, I'm sure," said Trotty, "to be so esteemed. How kind and neighborly you are! It's all along of my dear daughter. She deserves it."

At this moment a combination of prodigious sounds was heard outside, and a good-humored, comely woman of some fifty years of age, or thereabouts, came running in, closely followed by the[Pg 168]marrow-bones and cleavers and the bells— not *the* Bells, but a portable collection on a frame.

Trotty said: "It's Mrs. Chickenstalker!" And sat down and beat his knees again.

"Married, and not tell me, Meg!" cried the good woman. "Never! I couldn't rest on the last night of the Old Year without coming to wish you joy. I couldn't have done it, Meg. Not if I had been bed-ridden. So here I am."

"Mrs. Tugby," said Trotty, who had been going round and round her in an ecstasy—"I *should* say Chickenstalker—bless your heart and soul! A happy New Year, and many of 'em! Mrs. Tugby," said Trotty, when he had saluted her—"I *should* say Chickenstalker—this is William Fern and Lilian."

The worthy dame, to his surprise, turned very pale and very red.

"Not Lilian Fern, whose mother died in Dorsetshire?" said she.

Her uncle answered "Yes," and meeting hastily they exchanged some hurried words together, of which the upshot was that Mrs. Chickenstalker shook him by both hands, saluted Trotty on his cheek again of her own free will, and took the child to her capacious breast.

~ 183 ~

"Will Fern," said Trotty, pulling on his right-hand muffler. "Not the friend that you was hoping to find?"

"Ay," returned Will, putting a hand on each of Trotty's shoulders. "And like to prove a'most as good a friend, if that can be, as one I found."

"O!" said Trotty. "Please to play up there. Will you have the goodness?"

Had Trotty dreamed? Or are his joys and sorrows, and the actors in them, but a dream; himself a dream; the teller of this tale a dreamer, waking but now? If it be so, O listener, dear to him in all his visions, try to bear in mind the stern realities [Pg 169] from which these shadows come; and in your sphere—none is too wide and none too limited for such an end—endeavor to correct, improve and soften them. So may the New Year be a happy one to you, happy to many more whose happiness depends on you! So may each year be happier than the last, and not the meanest of our brethren or sisterhood debarred their rightful share in what our great Creator formed them to enjoy.

BILLY'S SANTA CLAUS EXPERIENCE.

BY CORNELIA REDMOND.

Of course I don't believe in any such person as Santa Claus, but
Tommy does. Tommy is my little brother, aged six. Last
Christmas I thought I'd make some fun for the young one by
playing Santa Claus, but as always happens when I try to amuse
anybody I jes' got myself into trouble.

I went to bed pretty early on Christmas Eve so as to give my
parents a chance to get the presents out of the closet in mamma's
room, where they had been locked up since they were bought. I kep'
my clo'es on except my shoes, and put my nightgown over them
so as I'd look white if any of them came near me. Then I waited,
pinchin' myself to keep awake. After a while papa came into the
room with a lot of things that he dumped on Tommy's bed. Then
mamma came in and put some things on mine and in our two
stockings that were hung up by the chimney. Then they both
went out very quiet, and soon all the lights went out too.

I kep' on pinchin' myself and waitin' for a time, and then when I
was sure that everybody was asleep I got up. The first thing I went
into was my sister's room and got her white fur rug that mamma
gave her on her birthday, and her sealskin cape that was hanging
on the closet door. I tied the cape on my head with shoestrings and
it made a good big cap. Then I put the fur rug around me and
pinned it with big safety pins what I found on Tommy's garters.
Then I got mamma's new scrap-basket, trimmed with roses, what
Mrs. Simmons 'broidered for the church fair and piled all of the
kid's toys into it. I fastened it to my back with papa's suspenders,
and then I started for the roof.

I hurt my fingers some opening the scuttle, but kept right on. It
was snowing hard and I stood and let myself get pretty well

covered with flakes. Then I crawled over to the chimney that went down into our room and climbed up on top of it. I had brought my bicycle lantern with me and I lighted it so as Tommy could see me when I came down the chimney into the room.

There did not seem to be any places inside the chimney where I could hold on by my feet, but the ceiling in our room was not very high and I had often jumped most as far, so I jes' let her go, and I suppose I went down. Anyway, I did not know about anything for a long time. Then I woke up all in the dark with my head feeling queer, and when I tried to turn over in bed I found I wasn't in bed at all, and then my arms and legs began to hurt terrible, mostly one arm that was doubled up. I tried to get up but I couldn't because my bones hurt so and I was terrible cold and there was nothing to stand on. I was jes' stuck. Then I began to cry, and pretty soon I heard mamma's voice saying to papa:

"Those must be sparrers that are making that noise in the chimney. Jes' touch a match to the wood in the boys' fireplace."

I heard papa strike a light and then the wood began to crackle. Then, by jinks! it began to get hot and smoky and I screamed:

"Help! Murder! Put out that fire lest you want to burn me up!"

Then I heard papa stamping on the wood and mamma calling out:

"Where's Billy? Where is my chile?"

Next Tommy woke up and began to cry and everything was terrible, specially the pains all over me. Then papa called out very stern:

"William, if you are in that chimney come down at once!" and I answered, cryin', that I would if I could, but I was stuck and couldn't.

Then I heard papa gettin' dressed, and pretty soon he and John from the stable went up on the roof and let down ropes what I put around me and they hauled me up.

It was jes' daylight and I was all black and sooty and scratched and my arm was broken.

Everybody scolded me excep' mamma. I had spoiled my sister's white rug and broken all of Tommy's toys, and the snow what went in through the scuttle melted and marked the parlor ceiling, besides I guess it cost papa a good deal to get my arm mended. Nobody would believe that I had jes' meant to make some fun for Tommy, and my arm and all my bruised places hurt me awful for a long time. If I live to be a million I am never goin' to play Santa Claus ag'in.

CHRISTMAS IN POGANUC.

BY HARRIET BEECHER STOWE.

The First Christmas.

Can any of us look back to the earlier days of our mortal pilgrimage and remember the helpless sense of desolation and loneliness caused by being forced to go off to the stillness and darkness of a solitary bed far from all the beloved voices and employments and sights of life? Can we remember lying, hearing distant voices, and laughs of more fortunate, older people and the opening and shutting of distant doors, that told of scenes of animation and interest from which we were excluded? How doleful sounded the tick of the clock, and how dismal was the darkness as sunshine faded from the window, leaving only a square of dusky dimness in place of daylight!

All who remember these will sympathize with Dolly, who was hustled off to bed by Nabby the minute supper was over, that she might have the decks clear for action.

"Now be a good girl; shut your eyes, and say your prayers, and go right to sleep," had been Nabby's parting injunction as she went out, closing the door after her.

The little head sunk into the pillow, and Dolly recited her usual liturgy of "Our Father who art in heaven," and "I pray God to bless my dear father and mother and all my dear friends and relations, and make me a good girl," and ending with

"'Now I lay me down to sleep.'"

But sleep she could not. The wide, bright, wistful blue eyes lay shining like two stars toward the fading light in the window, and the little ears were strained to catch every sound. She heard the shouts of Tom and Bill and the loud barking of Spring as they swept out of the door; and the sound went to her heart. Spring—her faithful attendant, the most loving and sympathetic of dogs, her friend and confidential counselor in many a solitary ramble—Spring had gone with the boys to see the sight, and left her alone. She began to pity herself and cry softly on her pillow. For a while she could hear Nabby's energetic movements below, washing up dishes, putting back chairs, and giving energetic thumps and bangs here and there, as her way was of producing order. But by and by that was all over, and she heard the loud shutting of the kitchen door and Nabby's voice chatting with her attendant as she went off to the scene of gaiety.

In those simple, innocent days in New England villages nobody thought of locking house doors at night. There was in those times no idea either of tramps or burglars, and many a night in summer had Dolly lain awake and heard the voices of tree-toads and whip-poor-wills mingling with the whisper of leaves and the swaying of elm boughs, while the great outside door of the house lay broad open in the moonlight. But then this was when everybody was in the house and asleep, when the door of her parents' room stood open on the front hall, and she knew she could run to the paternal bed in a minute for protection. Now, however, she knew the house was empty. Everybody had gone out of it; and there is something fearful to a little lonely body in the possibilities of a great, empty house. She got up and opened her door, and the "tick-tock" of the old kitchen clock for a moment seemed like company; but pretty soon its ticking began to strike louder and louder with a nervous insistency on her ear, till the nerves quivered and vibrated, and she couldn't go to sleep. She lay and listened to all the noises outside. It was a still, clear, freezing night, when the least sound clinked with a metallic resonance.

~ 189 ~

She heard the runners of sleighs squeaking and crunching over the frozen road, and the lively jingle of bells. They would come nearer, nearer, pass by the house, and go off in the distance. Those were the happy folks going to see the gold star and the Christmas greens in the church. The gold star, the Christmas greens, had all the more attraction from their vagueness. Dolly was a fanciful little creature, and the clear air and romantic scenery of a mountain town had fed her imagination. Stories she had never read, except in the Bible and the Pilgrim's Progress, but her very soul had vibrated with the descriptions of the celestial city—something vague, bright, glorious, lying beyond some dark river; and Nabby's rude account of what was going on in the church suggested those images.

Finally a bright thought popped into her little head. She could see the church from the front windows of the house; she would go there and look. In haste she sprang out of bed and dressed herself. It was sharp and freezing in the fireless chamber, but Dolly's blood had a racing, healthy tingle to it; she didn't mind cold. She wrapped her cloak around her and tied on her hood and ran to the front windows. There it was, to be sure—the little church with its sharp-pointed windows, every pane of which was sending streams of light across the glittering snow. There was a crowd around the door, and men and boys looking in at the windows. Dolly's soul was fired. But the elm boughs a little obstructed her vision; she thought she would go down and look at it from the yard. So down-stairs she ran, but as she opened the door the sound of the chant rolled out into the darkness with sweet and solemn cadence:

"Glory be to God on high; and on earth peace, good will toward men."

Dolly's soul was all aglow—her nerves tingled and vibrated; she thought of the bells ringing in the celestial city; she could no longer contain herself, but faster and faster the little hooded form

~ 190 ~

scudded across the snowy plain and pushed in among the dark cluster of spectators at the door. All made way for the child, and in a moment, whether in the body or out she could not tell, Dolly was sitting in a little nook under a bower of spruce, gazing at the star and listening to the voices:

"We praise Thee, we bless Thee, we worship Thee, we glorify Thee, we give thanks to Thee for Thy great glory, O Lord God, Heavenly King, God, the Father Almighty."

Her heart throbbed and beat; she trembled with a strange happiness and sat as one entranced till the music was over. Then came reading, the rustle and murmur of people kneeling, and then they all rose and there was the solemn buzz of voices repeating the Creed with a curious lulling sound to her ear. There was old Mr. Danforth with his spectacles on, reading with a pompous tone, as if to witness a good confession for the church; and there were Squire Lewis and old Ma'am Lewis; and there was one place where they all bowed their heads and all the ladies made courtesies—all of which entertained her mightily.

When the sermon began Dolly got fast asleep, and slept as quietly as a pet lamb in a meadow, lying in a little warm roll back under the shadows of the spruces. She was so tired and so sound asleep that she did not wake when the service ended, lying serenely curled up, and having perhaps pleasant dreams. She might have had the fortunes of little Goody Two-Shoes, whose history was detailed in one of the few children's books then printed, had not two friends united to find her out.

Spring, who had got into the slip with the boys, and been an equally attentive and edified listener, after service began a tour of investigation, dog-fashion, with his nose; for how could a minister's dog form a suitable judgment of any new procedure if he was repressed from the use of his own leading faculty? So,

Spring went round the church conscientiously, smelling at pew doors, smelling of the greens, smelling at the heels of gentlemen and ladies, till he came near the door of the church, when he suddenly smelt something which called for immediate attention, and he made a side dart into the thicket where Dolly was sleeping, and began licking her face and hands and pulling her dress, giving short barks occasionally, as if to say, "Come, Dolly, wake up!" At the same instant Hiel, who had seen her from the gallery, came down just as the little one was sitting up with a dazed, bewildered air.

"Why, Dolly, how came you out o' bed this time o' night? Don't ye know the nine o'clock bell's jest rung?"

Dolly knew Hiel well enough—what child in the village did not? She reached up her little hands, saying in an apologetic fashion:

"They were all gone away, and I was so lonesome!"

Hiel took her up in his long arms and carried her home, and was just entering the house door with her as the sleigh drove up with Parson Cushing and his wife.

"Wal, Parson, your folks has all ben to the 'lumination—Nabby and Bill and Tom and Dolly here; found her all rolled up in a heap like a rabbit under the cedars."

"Why, Dolly Cushing!" exclaimed her mother. "What upon earth got you out of bed this time of night? You'll catch your death o' cold."

"I was all alone," said Dolly, with a piteous bleat.

"Oh, there, there, wife; don't say a word," put in the parson. "Get her off to bed. Never mind, Dolly, don't you cry;" for Parson Cushing was a soft-hearted gentleman and couldn't bear the sight of Dolly's quivering under lip. So Dolly told her little story, how she had been promised a sugar dog by Nabby if she'd be a good girl and go to sleep, and how she couldn't go to sleep, and how she just went down to look from the yard, and how the music drew her right over.

"There, there," said Parson Cushing, "go to bed, Dolly; and if Nabby don't give you a sugar dog, I will. This Christmas dressing is all nonsense," he added, "but the child's not to blame—it was natural."

"After all," he said to his wife the last thing after they were settled for the night, "our little Dolly is an unusual child. There were not many little girls that would have dared to do that. I shall preach a sermon right away that will set all this Christmas matter straight," said the Doctor. "There is not a shadow of evidence that the first Christians kept Christmas. It wasn't kept for the first three centuries, nor was Christ born anywhere near the 25th of December."

*   *   *   *   *

The next morning found little Dolly's blue eyes wide open with all the wondering eagerness of a new idea.

Dolly had her wise thoughts about Christmas. She had been terribly frightened at first, when she was brought home from the church; but when her papa kissed her and promised her a sugar dog she was quite sure that, whatever the unexplained mystery might be, he did not think the lovely scene of the night before a wicked one. And when Mrs. Cushing came and covered the little girl up warmly in bed, she only said to her, "Dolly, you must never get out of bed again at night after you are put there; you might have caught a dreadful cold and been sick and died, and then we should have lost our little Dolly." So Dolly promised quite readily to be good and lie still ever after, no matter what attractions might be on foot in the community.

Much was gained, however, and it was all clear gain; and forthwith the little fanciful head proceeded to make the most of it, thinking over every feature of the wonder. The child had a vibrating, musical organization, and the sway and rush of the chanting still sounded in her ears and reminded her of that wonderful story in the "Pilgrim's Progress", where the gate of the celestial city swung open, and there were voices that sung, "Blessing and honor and glory and power be unto Him who sitteth on the throne." And then that wonderful star, that shone just as if it were a real star—how could it be! For Miss Ida Lewis, being a young lady of native artistic genius, had cut a little hole in the centre of her gilt paper star, behind which was placed a candle, so that it gave real light, in a way most astonishing to untaught eyes. In Dolly's simple view it verged on the supernatural—perhaps it was *the* very real star read about in the Gospel story. Why not? Dolly was at the happy age when anything bright and heavenly seemed credible, and had the child-faith to which all things were possible.

"I wish, my dear," said Mrs. Cushing, after they were retired to their room for the night, "that to-morrow morning you would read the account of the birth of Christ in St. Matthew, and give the children some advice upon the proper way of keeping Christmas."

"Well, but you know we don't *keep* Christmas; nobody knows anything about Christmas," said the Doctor.

"You know what I mean, my dear," replied his wife. "You know that my mother and her family *do* keep Christmas. I always heard of it when I was a child; and even now, though I have been out of the way of it so long, I cannot help a sort of kindly feeling toward these ways. I am not surprised at all that the children got drawn over last night to the service. I think it's the most natural thing in the world, and I know by experience just how attractive such things are. I shouldn't wonder if this other church should draw very seriously on your congregation; but I don't want it to begin by taking away our own children. Dolly is an inquisitive child; a child that thinks a good deal, and she'll be asking all sorts of questions about the why and wherefore of what she saw last night."

"Oh, yes, Dolly is a bright one. Dolly's an uncommon child," said the Doctor, who had a pardonable pride in his children—they being, in fact, the only worldly treasure that he was at all rich in.

He rose up early on the following Sabbath and proceeded to buy a sugar dog at the store of Lucius Jenks, and when Dolly came down to breakfast he called her to him and presented it, saying as he kissed her:

"Papa gives you this, not because it is Christmas, but because he loves his little Dolly."

"But *isn't it* Christmas?" asked Dolly with a puzzled air.

"No, child; nobody knows when Christ was born, and there is nothing in the Bible to tell us *when* to keep Christmas."

And then in family worship the Doctor read the account of the birth of Christ and of the shepherds abiding in the fields who came at the call of the angels, and they sung the old hymn:

"While shepherds watched their flocks by night."

"Now, children," he said when all was over, "you must be good children and go to school. If we are going to keep any day on

~ 195 ~

account of the birth of Christ, the best way to keep it is by doing all our duties on that day better than any other. Your duty is to be good children, go to school and mind your lessons."

Tom and Bill were quite ready to fall in with their father's view of the matter. As for Dolly, she put her little tongue advisedly to the back of her sugar dog and found that he was very sweet indeed—a most tempting little animal. She even went so far as to nibble off a bit of the green ground he stood on—yet resolved heroically not to eat him at once, but to make him last as long as possible. She wrapped him tenderly in cotton and took him to the school with her, and when her confidential friend, Bessie Lewis, displayed her Christmas gifts, Dolly had something on her side to show, though she shook her curly head and informed Bessie in strict confidence that there wasn't any such thing as Christmas, her papa had told her so—a heresy which Bessie forthwith reported when she went home at noon.

"Poor little child—and did she say so?" asked gentle old Grandmamma Lewis. "Well, dear, you mustn't blame her—she don't know any better. You bring the little one in here to-night and I'll give her a Christmas cooky. I'm sorry for such children."

And so, after school, Dolly went in to see dear old Madam Lewis, who sat in her rocking-chair in the front parlor, where the fire was snapping behind great tall brass andirons and all the pictures were overshadowed with boughs of spruce and pine. Dolly gazed about her with awe and wonder. Over one of the pictures was suspended a cross of green with flowers of white everlasting.

"What is *that* for?" asked Dolly, pointing solemnly with her little forefinger, and speaking under her breath.

"Dear child, that is the picture of my poor boy who died—ever so many years ago. That is my cross—we have all one—to carry."

Dolly did not half understand these words, but she saw tears in the gentle old lady's eyes and was afraid to ask more.

She accepted thankfully and with her nicest and best executed courtesy a Christmas cooky representing a good-sized fish, with fins all spread and pink sugar-plums for eyes, and went home marveling yet more about this mystery of Christmas.

As she was crossing the green to go home the Poganuc stage drove in, with Hiel seated on high, whipping up his horses to make them execute that grand *entrée* which was the glory of his daily existence.

Now that the stage was on runners, and slipped noiselessly over the smooth frozen plain, Hiel cracked his whip more energetically and shouted louder, first to one horse then to another, to make up for the loss of the rattling wheels; and he generally had the satisfaction of seeing all the women rushing distractedly to doors and windows, and imagined them saying, "There's Hiel; the stage is in!"

"Hulloa, Dolly!" he called out, drawing up with a suddenness which threw the fore-horses back upon their haunches. "I've got a bundle for your folks. Want to ride? You may jest jump up here by me and I'll take you 'round to your father's door;" and so Dolly reached up her little red-mittened hand, and Hiel drew her up beside him.

"'Xpect ye want a bit of a ride, and I've got a bundle for Widder Badger, down on South Street, so I guess I'll go 'round that way to make it longer. I 'xpect this 'ere bundle is from some of your ma's folks in Boston—'Piscopals they be and keeps Christmas. Good-sized bundle 'tis; reckon it'll come handy in a good many ways."

So, after finishing his detour, Hiel landed his little charge at the parsonage door.

"Reckon I'll be over when I've put up my hosses," he said to Nabby when he handed down the bundle to her. "I hain't been to see you much lately, Nabby, and I know you've been a-pinin' after me, but fact is—"

"Well, now, Hiel Jones, you jest shet up with your imperence," said Nabby, with flashing eyes; "you jest look out or you'll get suthin."

"I 'xpect to get a kiss when I come 'round to-night," said Hiel, composedly. "Take care o' that air bundle, now; mebbe there's glass or crockery in't."

"Hiel Jones," said Nabby, "don't give me none o' your saace, for I won't take it. Jim Sawin said last night you was the brassiest man he ever see. He said there was brass enough in your face to make a kettle of."

"You tell him there's sap enough in his head to fill it, anyway," said Hiel. "Good bye, Nabby, I'll come 'round this evenin'," and he drove away at a rattling pace, while Nabby, with flushed cheeks and snapping eyes, soliloquized:

"Well, I hope he will come! I'd jest like a chance to show him how little I care for him."

Meanwhile the bundle was soon opened, and contained a store of treasures: a smart little red dress and a pair of red shoes for Dolly, a half dozen pocket-handkerchiefs for Dr. Cushing, and "Robinson Crusoe" and "Sanford and Merton," handsomely bound, for the boys, and a bonnet trimming for Mrs. Cushing. These were accompanied by a characteristic letter from Aunt Debby Kittery, opening as follows:

"Dear Sister:

"Mother worries because she thinks you won't get any Christmas presents. However, this comes to give every one of you some of the crumbs which fall from the church's table, and Mother says she wishes you all a pious Christmas, which she thinks is better than a merry one. If I didn't lay violent hands on her she would use all our substance in riotous giving of Christmas presents to all the beggars and chimney sweeps in Boston. She is in good health and talks daily of wanting to see you and the children; and I hope before long you will bring some of them, and come and make us a visit.

"Your affectionate sister,

"Debby Kittery."

There was a scene of exultation and clamor in the parsonage as these presents were pulled out and discussed; and when all possible joy was procured from them in the sitting-room, the children rushed in a body into the kitchen and showed them to Nabby, calling on her to join their acclamations.

On the whole, when Dolly had said her prayers that night and thought the matter over, she concluded that her Christmas Day had been quite a success.

The Second Christmas.

Once more had Christmas come round in Poganuc; once more the Episcopal church was being dressed with ground-pine and spruce; but this year economy had begun to make its claims felt. An illumination might do very well to open a church, but there were many who said "to what purpose is this waste?" when the proposition was made to renew it yearly. Consequently it was resolved to hold the Christmas Eve service with only that necessary amount of light which would enable the worshipers to read the prayers.

On this Christmas Eve Dolly went to bed at her usual hour with a resigned and quiet spirit. She felt herself a year older, and more than a year wiser, than when Christmas had first dawned upon her consciousness.

Mis' Persis appeared on the ground by day-dawn. A great kettle was slung over the kitchen fire, in which cakes of tallow were speedily liquefying; a frame was placed quite across the kitchen to sustain candle-rods, with a train of boards underneath to catch the drippings, and Mis' Persis, with a brow like one of the Fates, announced: "Now we can't hev any young 'uns in this kitchen to-day;" and Dolly saw that there was no getting any attention in that quarter.

Mis' Persis, in a gracious Saturday afternoon mood, sitting in her own tent-door dispensing hospitalities and cookies, was one thing; but Mis' Persis in her armor, with her loins girded and a hard day's work to be conquered, was quite another: she was terrible as Minerva with her helmet on.

Dinner-baskets for all the children were hastily packed, and they were sent off to school with the injunction on no account to show their faces about the premises till night. The Doctor, warned of what was going on, retreated to his study at the top of the house, where, serenely above the lower cares of earth, he sailed off into President Edwards' treatise on the nature of true virtue, concerning which he was preparing a paper to read at the next association meeting.

That candles were a necessity of life he was well convinced, and by faith he dimly accepted the fact that one day in the year the whole house was to be devoted and given up to this manufacture; and his part of the business, as he understood it, was, clearly, to keep himself out of the way till it was over.

"There won't be much of a dinner at home, anyway," said Nabby to Dolly, as she packed her basket with an extra doughnut or two. "I've got to go to church to-day, 'cause I'm one of the singers, and your ma'll be busy waitin' on her; so we shall just have a pick-up dinner, and you be sure not to come home till night; by that time it'll be all over."

Dolly trotted off to school well content with the prospect before her: a nooning, with leave to play with the girls at school, was not an unpleasant idea.

But the first thing that saluted her on her arrival was that Bessie Lewis—her own dear, particular Bessie—was going to have a Christmas party at her house that afternoon, and was around distributing invitations right and left among the scholars with a generous freedom.

"We are going to have nuts, and raisins, and cakes, and mottoes," said Bessie, with artless triumph. The news of this bill of fare spread like wildfire through the school.

Never had a party been heard of which contemplated such a liberal entertainment, for the rising generation of Poganuc were by no means wearied with indulgence, and raisins and almonds stood for grandeur with them. But these *mottoes*, which consisted of bits of confectionery wrapped up in printed couplets of sentimental poetry, were an unheard-of refinement. Bessie assured them that her papa had sent clear to Boston for them, and whoever got one would have his or her fortune told by it.

The school was a small, select one, comprising the children of all ages from the best families of Poganuc. Both boys and girls, and all with great impartiality, had been invited. Miss Titcome, the teacher, quite readily promised to dismiss at three o'clock that afternoon any scholar who should bring a permission from parents, and the children nothing doubted that such a permission was obtainable.

Dolly alone saw a cloud in the horizon. She had been sent away with strict injunctions not to return till evening, and children in those days never presumed to make any exceptions in obeying an absolute command of their parents.

"But, of course, you will go home at noon and ask your mother, and of course she'll let you; won't she, girls?" said Bessie.

"Oh, certainly; of course she will," said all the older girls, "because you know a party is a thing that don't happen every day, and your mother would think it strange if you *didn't* come and ask her." So, too, thought Miss Titcome, a most exemplary, precise and proper young lady, who always moved and spoke and thought as became a schoolmistress, so that, although she was in reality only twenty years old, Dolly considered her as a very advanced and ancient person—if anything, a little older than her father and mother.

Even she was of opinion that Dolly might properly go home to lay a case of such importance before her mother; and so Dolly rushed home after the morning school was over, running with all her might, and increasing in mental excitement as she ran. Her bonnet blew off upon her shoulders, her curls flew behind her in the wind, and she most inconsiderately used up the little stock of breath that she would want to set her cause in order before her mother.

Just here we must beg any mother and housekeeper to imagine herself in the very midst of the most delicate, perplexing and laborious of household tasks, when interruption is most irksome and perilous, suddenly called to discuss with a child some new and startling proposition to which at the moment she cannot even give a thought.

Mrs. Cushing was sitting in the kitchen with Mis' Persis, by the side of a caldron of melted tallow, kept in a fluid state by the heat of a portable furnace on which it stood. A long train of half-dipped candles hung like so many stalactites from the frames on which the rods rested, and the two were patiently dipping set after set and replacing them again on the frame.

"As sure as I'm alive! if there isn't Dolly Cushing comin' back—runnin' and tearin' like a wild cretur'," said Mis' Persis. "She'll be in here in a minute and knock everything down!"

Mrs. Cushing looked, and with a quick movement stepped to the door.

"Dolly! what are you here for? Didn't I tell you not to come home this noon?"

"Oh, mamma, there's going to be a party at General Lewis'—Bessie's party—and the girls are all going; mayn't I go?"

"No, you can't; it's impossible," said her mother. "Your best dress isn't ready to wear, and there's nobody can spend time to get you ready. Go right back to school."

"But, mamma—"

"Go!" said her mother, in the decisive tone that mothers used in the old days, when arguing with children was not a possibility.

"What's all this about?" asked the Doctor, looking out of the door.

"Why," said Mrs. Cushing, "there's going to be a party at General Lewis', and Dolly is wild to go. It's just impossible for me to attend to her now."

"Oh, I don't want her intimate at Lewis's," said the Doctor, and immediately he came out behind his wife.

"There; run away to school, Dolly," he said. "Don't trouble your mother; you don't want to go to parties; why, it's foolish to think of it. Run away now, and don't think any more about it—there's a good girl!"

Dolly turned and went back to school, the tears freezing on her cheek as she went. As for not thinking any more about it—that was impossible.

When three o'clock came, scholar after scholar rose and departed, until at last Dolly was the only one remaining in the school-room.

When Dolly came home that night the coast was clear, and the candles were finished and put away to harden in a freezing cold room; the kitchen was once more restored, and Nabby bustled about getting supper as if nothing had happened.

"I really feel sorry about poor little Dolly," said Mrs. Cushing to her husband.

"Do you think she cared much?" asked the Doctor, looking as if a new possibility had struck his mind.

"Yes, indeed, poor child, she went away crying; but what could I do about it? I couldn't stop to dress her."

"Wife, we must take her somewhere to make up for it," said the Doctor.

Just then the stage stopped at the door and a bundle from Boston was handed in. Dolly's tears were soon wiped and dried, and her mourning was turned into joy when a large jointed London doll emerged from the bundle, the Christmas gift of her grandmother in Boston.

Dolly's former darling was old and shabby, but this was of twice the size, and with cheeks exhibiting a state of the most florid health.

Besides this there was, as usual in grandmamma's Christmas bundle, something for every member of the family; and so the evening went on festive wings.

Poor little Dolly! only that afternoon she had watered with her tears, at school, the dismal long straight seam, which stretched on before her as life sometimes does to us, bare, disagreeable and cheerless. She had come home crying, little dreaming of the joy just approaching; but before bed-time no cricket in the hearth was cheerier or more noisy. She took the new dolly to bed with her, and could hardly sleep, for the excitement of her company.

Meanwhile, Hiel had brought the Doctor a message to the following effect:

"I was drivin' by Tim Hawkins', and Mis' Hawkins she comes out and says they're goin' to hev an apple-cuttin' there to-morrow night, and she would like to hev you and Mis' Cushin' and all your folks come—Nabby and all."

The Doctor and his lady of course assented.

"Wal, then, Doctor—ef it's all one to you," continued Hiel, "I'd like to take ye over in my new double sleigh. I've jest got two new strings o' bells up from Boston, and I think we'll sort o' make the snow fly. S'pose there'd be no objections to takin' my mother 'long with ye?"

"Oh, Hiel, we shall be delighted to go in company with your mother, and we're ever so much obliged to you," said Mrs. Cushing.

"Wal, I'll be round by six o'clock," said Hiel.

"Then, wife," said the Doctor, "we'll take Dolly, and make up for the loss of her party."

Punctually at six, Hiel's two horses, with all their bells jingling, stood at the door of the parsonage, whence Tom and Bill, who had been waiting with caps and mittens on for the last half hour, burst forth with irrepressible shouts of welcome.

"Take care now, boys; don't haul them buffalo skins out on t' the snow," said Hiel. "Don't get things in a muss gen'ally; wait for your ma and the[Pg 191] Doctor. Got to stow the grown folks in fust; boys kin hang on anywhere."

And so first came Mrs. Cushing and the Doctor, and were installed on the back seat, with Dolly in between. Then hot bricks were handed in to keep feet warm, and the buffalo robe was tucked down securely. Then Nabby took her seat by Hiel in front, and the sleigh drove round for old Mrs. Jones. The Doctor insisted on giving up his place to her and tucking her warmly under the buffalo robe, while he took the middle seat and acted as moderator between the boys, who were in a wild state of hilarity. Spring, with explosive barks, raced first on this and then on that side of the sleigh as it flew swiftly over the smooth frozen road.

The stars blinked white and clear out of a deep blue sky, and the path wound up-hill among cedars and junipers and clumps of mountain laurel, on whose broad green leaves the tufts of snow lay like clusters of white roses. The keen clear air was full of stimulus and vigor; and so Hiel's proposition to take the longest way met with enthusiastic welcome from all the party. Next to being a bird, and having wings, is the sensation of being borne over the snow by a pair of spirited horses who enjoy the race, apparently, as much as those they draw. Though Hiel contrived to make the ride about eight miles, it yet seemed but a short time before the party drove up to the great red farmhouse, whose lighted windows sent streams of radiant welcome far out into the night.

Our little Dolly had had an evening of unmixed bliss. Everybody had petted her, and talked to her, and been delighted with her sayings and doings, and she was carrying home a paper parcel of sweet things which good Mrs. Hawkins had forced into her hand at parting. She had spent a really happy Christmas!

THE CHRISTMAS PRINCESS.

BY MRS. MOLESWORTH.

In the olden times there lived a king who was worthy of the name. He loved his people, and his people loved him in return. His kingdom must have been large; at least it appears to be beyond doubt that it extended a good way in different directions, for it was called the Kingdom of the Four Orts, which, of course, as everybody knows, means that he had possessions north, south, east, and west.

It was not so large, however, but that he was able to manage it well for himself—that is to say, with certain help which I will tell you of. A year never passed without his visiting every part of his dominions and inquiring for himself into the affairs of his subjects. Perhaps—who can say?—the world was not so big in those days; doubtless, however that may have been, there were not so many folk living on it.

Many things were different in those times: many things existed which nowadays would be thought strange and incredible. Human beings knew much more than they do now about the other dwellers on the earth. For instance, it was no uncommon case to find learned men who were able to converse with animals quite as well as with each other. Fairies, of course, were often visible to mortal eyes, and it was considered quite natural that they should interfere for good—sometimes, perhaps, for evil; as to that I cannot say—in human affairs. And good King Brave-Heart was especially favored in this way. For the help which, as I said, was his in governing his people was that of four very wise counselors indeed—the four fairies of the North and the South, the East and the West.

These sisters were very beautiful as well as very wise. Though older than the world itself, they always looked young. They were very much attached to each other, though they seldom met, and it must be confessed that sometimes on such occasions there were stormy scenes, though they made it up afterward. And the advice they gave was always to be relied upon.

Now, King Brave-Heart was married. His wife was young and charming, and devotedly fond of him. But she was of a rather jealous and exacting disposition, and she had been much spoilt in her youth at her own home. She was sweet and loving, however, which makes up for a good deal, and always ready to take part in any scheme for the good of their people, provided it did not separate her from her husband.

They had no children, though they had been married for some years; but at last there came the hope of an heir, and the Queen's delight was unbounded—nor was the King's joy less than hers.

It was late autumn, or almost winter, when a great trouble befell the pretty Queen. The weather had grown suddenly cold, and a few snowflakes even had fallen before their time. But Queen Claribel only clapped her hands at the sight, for with the winter she hoped the baby would come, and she welcomed the signs of its approach on this account. The King, however, looked grave, and when the next morning the ground was all white, the trees and the bushes covered with silvery foliage, he looked graver still.

"Something is amiss," he said. "The Fairy of the North must be on her way, and it is not yet time for her visit."

And that very afternoon the snow fell again, more heavily than before, and the frost-wind whistled down the chimneys and burst open the doors and windows, and all the palace servants went hurrying and scurrying about to make great fires and hang up thick curtains and get everything in order for the cold season, which they had not expected so soon.

"It will not last," said the King, quietly. "In a few days there will be milder weather again." But, nevertheless, he still looked grave.

And early the next morning, as he was sitting with the Queen, who was beginning to feel a little frightened at the continuance of the storm, the double doors of her boudoir suddenly flew open, an icy blast filled the room, and a tall, white-shrouded figure stood before them.

"I have come to fetch you, Brave-Heart," she said abruptly. "You are wanted, sorely wanted, in my part of the world. The people are starving: the season has been a poor one, and there has been bad faith. Some few powerful men have bought up the grain, which was already scarce, and refuse to let the poor folk have it. Nothing will save their lives or prevent sad suffering but your own immediate presence. Are you ready? You must have seen I was coming."

She threw off her mantle as she spoke and sank on to a couch. Strong as she was, she seemed tired with the rate at which she had traveled, and the warm air of the room was oppressive to her. Her clear, beautiful features looked harassed; her gray eyes full of anxiety. For the moment she took no notice of the Queen.

"Are you ready?" she repeated.

"Yes, I am ready!" said Brave-Heart, as he rose to his feet.

But the Queen threw herself upon him, with bitter crying and reproaches. Would he leave *her*, and at such a time, a prey to all kinds of terrible anxiety? Then she turned to the fairy and upbraided her in unmeasured language. But the spirit of the North glanced at her with calm pity.

"Poor child!" she said, "I had almost forgotten you. The sights I have seen of late have been so terrible that they absorb me. Take courage, Claribel! Show yourself a queen. Think of the suffering mothers and their little ones whom your husband hastens to aid. All will be well with you, believe me. But you, too, must be brave and unselfish."

It was no use. All she said but made the Queen more indignant. She would scarcely bid her husband farewell: she turned her back to the fairy with undignified petulance.

"Foolish child," said the Northern spirit. "She will learn better some day."

Then she gave all her attention to the matter she had come about, explaining to the King as they journeyed exactly the measures he must take and the difficulties to be overcome. But though the King had the greatest faith in her advice, and never doubted that it was his duty to obey, his heart was sore, as you can understand.

Things turned out as he had said. The severe weather disappeared again as if by magic, and some weeks of unusually mild days followed. And when the winter did set in for good at last, it was with no great rigor. From time to time news reached the palace of the King's welfare. The tidings were cheering. His presence was effecting all that the fairy had hoped.

So Queen Claribel ought to have been happy. But she was determined not to be. She did nothing but cry and abuse the fairy, declaring that she would never see her dear Brave-Heart again, and that if ever her baby came she was sure it would not live, or that there would be something dreadful the matter with it.

"It is not fair," she kept saying, "it is a shame that I should suffer so."

And even when on Christmas Eve a beautiful little girl was born, as pretty and lively and healthy as could be wished, and even though the next day brought the announcement of the King's immediate return, Claribel still nursed her resentment, though in the end it came to be directed entirely against the fairy. For when she saw Brave-Heart again, his tender affection and his delight in his little daughter made it impossible for her not to "forgive him," as she expressed it, though she could not take any interest in his accounts of his visit to the north and all he had been able to do there.

A great feast was arranged in honor of the christening of the little Princess. All the grand people of the neighborhood were bidden to it, nor, you may be sure, did the good King forget the poorer folk. The four fairies were invited, for it was a matter of course that they should be the baby's godmothers. And though the Queen would gladly have excluded the Northern fairy, she dared not even hint at such a thing.

But she resolved in her own mind to do all in her power to show that she was not the welcome fairy.

On such occasions, when human beings were honored by the presence of fairy visitors, these distinguished guests were naturally given precedence of all others, otherwise very certainly they would never have come again. Even among fairies themselves there are ranks and formalities, and the Queen well knew that the first place was due to the Northern spirit. But she gave instructions that this rule should be departed from, and the Snow fairy, as she was sometimes called, found herself placed at the King's left hand, separated from him by her sister of the West, instead of next to him on the right, which seat, on the contrary, was occupied by the fairy of the South. She glanced round her calmly, but took no notice; and the King, imagining that by her own choice perhaps, she had chosen the unusual position, made no remark. And the feast progressed with the accustomed splendor and rejoicing.

But at the end, when the moment arrived at which the four godmothers were expected to state their gifts to the baby, the Queen's spite could be no longer concealed.

"I request," she exclaimed, "that for reasons well known to herself, to the King, and to myself, the Northern fairy's gift may be the last in order instead of the first."

The King started and grew pale. The beautiful, soft-voiced fairy of the South, in her glowing golden draperies, would fain have held back, for her affection for her sterner sister was largely mingled with awe. But the Snow fairy signed to her imperiously to speak.

"I bestow upon the Princess Sweet-Heart," she said, half tremblingly, "the gift of great beauty."

"And I," said the spirit of the East, who came next, her red robes falling majestically around her, her dark hair lying smoothly in its thick masses on her broad, low forehead, "I give her great powers of intellect and intelligence."

"And I," said the Western fairy, with a bright, breezy flutter of her sea-green garments, "health—perfect health and strength of body, as my gift to the pretty child."

"And you," said the Queen bitterly, "you, cold-hearted fairy, who have done your best to kill me with misery, who came between my husband and me, making him neglect me as he never would have done but for your influence—what will *you* give my child? Will you do something to make amends for the suffering you caused? I would rather my pretty baby were dead than that she lived to endure what I have of late endured."

"Life and death are not mine to bestow or to withhold," said the Northern spirit calmly, as she drew her white garments more closely round her with a majestic air. "So your rash words, foolish woman, fortunately for you all, cannot touch the child. But something—much—I can do, and I will. She shall not know the suffering you dread for her with so cowardly a fear. She shall be what you choose to fancy *I* am. And instead of the name you have given her, she shall be known for what she is—Princess Ice-Heart."

She turned to go, but the King on one hand, her three sisters on the other, started forward to detain her.

"Have pity!" exclaimed the former.

"Sister, bethink you," said the latter; the Western fairy adding beseechingly, the tears springing in her blue eyes, which so quickly changed from bright to sad, "Say something to soften this hard fate. Undo it you cannot, I know. Or, at least, allow me to mitigate it if I can."

The Snow fairy stopped; in truth, she was far from hard-hearted or remorseless, and already she was beginning to feel half sorry for what she had done.

"What would you propose?" she said coldly.

The fairy of the West threw back her auburn hair with a gesture of impatience.

"I would I knew!" she said. "'Tis a hard knot you have tied, my sister. For that which would mend the evil wrought seems to me impossible while the evil exists—the cure and the cessation of the disease are one. How could the heart of ice be melted till tender feelings warm it, and how can tender feelings find entrance into a feelingless heart? Alas! alas! I can but predict what sounds like a mockery of your trouble," she went on, turning to the King, though indeed by this time she might have included the Queen in her sympathy, for Claribel stood, horrified at the result of her mad resentment, as pale as Brave-Heart himself. "Hearken!" and her expressive face, over which sunshine and showers were wont to chase each other as on an April day—for such, as all know, is the nature of the changeful, lovable spirit of the West—for once grew still and statue-like, while her blue eyes pierced far into the distance. "The day on which the Princess of the Icy Heart shall shed a tear, that heart shall melt—but then only."

The Northern fairy murmured something under her breath, but what the words were no one heard, for it was not many that dared stand near to her, so terribly cold was her presence. The graceful spirit of the South fluttered her golden locks, and with a little sigh drew her radiant mantle round her, and kissed her hand in farewell, while the thoughtful-eyed, mysterious Eastern fairy linked her arm in that of her Western sister, and whispered that the solution of the problem should have her most earnest study. And the green-robed spirit tried to smile through her tears in farewell as she suffered herself to be led away.

So the four strange guests departed; but their absence was not followed by the usual outburst of unconstrained festivity. On the contrary, a sense of sorrow and dread hung over all who remained, and before long everyone not immediately connected with the palace respectfully but silently withdrew, leaving the King and Queen to their mysterious sorrow.

Claribel flew to the baby's cradle. The little Princess was sleeping soundly; she looked rosy and content—a picture of health. Her mother called eagerly to the King.

"She seems just as usual," she exclaimed. "Perhaps—oh! perhaps after all I have done no harm."

For, strange to say, her resentment against the Northern fairy had died away. She now felt nothing but shame and regret for her own wild temper. "Perhaps," she went on, "it was but to try me, to teach me a lesson, that the Snow fairy uttered those terrible words."

Brave-Heart pitied his wife deeply, but he shook his head.

"I dare not comfort you with any such hopes," he said, "my poor Claribel. The fairy is true—true as steel—if you could but have trusted her! Had you seen her, as I have done—full of tenderest pity for suffering—you could never have so maligned her."

Claribel did not answer, but her tears dropped on the baby's face. The little Princess seemed annoyed by them. She put up her tiny hand and, with a fretful expression, brushed them off.

And that very evening the certainty came.

The head nurse sent for the Queen while she was undressing the child, and the mother hastened to the nursery. The attendants were standing round in the greatest anxiety, for, though the baby looked quite well otherwise, there was the strangest coldness over her left side, in the region of the heart. The skin looked perfectly colorless, and the soft cambric and still softer flannel of the finest which had covered the spot were stiff, as if they had been exposed to a winter night's frost.

"Alas!" exclaimed Claribel, but that was all. It was no use sending for doctors—no use doing anything. Her own delicate hand when she laid it on the baby's heart was, as it were, blistered with cold. The next morning she found it covered with chilblains.

But the baby did not mind. She flourished amazingly, heart or no heart. She was perfectly healthy, ate well, slept well, and soon gave signs of unusual intelligence. She was seldom put out, but when angry she expressed her feelings by loud roars and screams, though with never a tear! At first this did not seem strange, as no infant sheds tears during the earliest weeks of its life. But when she grew to six months old, then to a year, then to two and three, and was near her fourth birthday without ever crying, it became plain that the prediction was indeed to be fulfilled.

And the name "Ice-Heart" clung to her. In spite of all her royal parents' commands to the contrary, "Princess Ice-Heart" she was called far and near. It seemed as if people could not help it. "Sweet-Heart we cannot name her, for sweet she is not," was murmured by all who came in contact with her.

And it was true. Sweet she certainly was not. She was beautiful and healthy and intelligent, but she had no feeling. In some ways she gave little trouble. Her temper, though occasionally violent, was, as a rule, placid; she seemed contented in almost all circumstances. When her good old nurse died, she remarked coolly that she hoped her new attendant would dress her hair more becomingly; when King Brave-Heart started on some of his distant journeys she bade him good-bye with a smile, observing that if he never came home again it would be rather amusing, as she would then reign instead of him, and when she saw her mother break into sobs at her unnatural speech she stared at her in blank astonishment.

And so things went on until Ice-Heart reached her seventeenth year. By this time she was, as regarded her outward appearance, as beautiful as the fondest of parents could desire; she was also exceedingly strong and healthy, and the powers of her mind were unusual. Her education had been carefully directed, and she had learnt with ease and interest. She could speak in several languages, her paintings were worthy of admiration, as they were skillful and well executed; she could play with brilliancy on various instruments. She had also been taught to sing, but her voice was metallic and unpleasing. But she could discuss scientific and philosophical subjects with the sages of her father's kingdom like one of themselves.

And besides all this care bestowed upon her training, no stone had been left unturned in hopes of awakening in the unfortunate girl some affection or emotion. Every day the most soul-stirring poetry was read aloud to her by the greatest elocutionists, the most exciting and moving dramas were enacted before her; she was taken to visit the poor of the city in their pitiable homes; she was encouraged to see sad sights from which most soft-hearted maidens would instinctively flee. But all was in vain. She would express interest and ask intelligent questions with calm, unmoved features and dry eyes. Even music, from which much had been hoped, was powerless to move her to aught but admiration of the performers' skill or curiosity as to the construction of their instruments. There was but one peculiarity about her, which sometimes, though they could not have explained why, seemed to Ice-Heart's unhappy parents to hint at some shadowy hope. The sight of tears was evidently disagreeable to her. More certainly than anything else did the signs of weeping arouse one of her rare fits of anger—so much so that now and then, for days together, the poor Queen dared not come near her child, and tears were to her a frequent relief from her lifelong regrets.

So beautiful and wealthy and accomplished a maiden was naturally not without suitors; and from this direction, too, at first, Queen Claribel trusted fondly that cure might come.

"If she could but fall in love," she said, the first time the idea struck her.

"My poor dear!" replied the King, "to see, you must have eyes; to love, you must have a heart."

"But a heart she has," persisted the mother. "It is only, as it were, asleep—frozen, like the winter stream which bursts forth again into ever fresh life and movement with the awaking spring."

So lovers were invited, and lovers came and were made welcome by the dozen. Lovers of every description—rich and poor, old and young, handsome and ugly—so long as they were of passable birth and fair character, King Brave-Heart was not too particular—in the forlorn hope that among them one fortunate wight might rouse some sentiment in the lovely statue he desired to win. But all in vain. Each prince, or duke, or simple knight, duly instructed in the sad case, did his best: one would try poetry, another his lute, a third sighs and appeals, a fourth, imagining he had made some way, would attempt the bold stroke of telling Ice-Heart that unless she could respond to his adoration he would drown himself. She only smiled, and begged him to allow her to witness the performance—she had never seen anyone drown. So, one by one, the troupe of aspirants—some in disgust, some in strange fear, some in annoyance—took their departure, preferring a more ordinary spouse than the bewitched though beautiful Princess.

And she saw them go with calmness, though, in one or two cases she had replied to her parents that she had no objection to marry Prince So-and-so, or Count Such-another, if they desired it—it would be rather agreeable to have a husband if he gave her plenty of presents and did all she asked. "Though a sighing and moaning lover, or a man who is always twiddling a fiddle or making verses I could not stand," she would add contemptuously.

So King Brave-Heart thought it best to try no such experiment. And in future no gentleman was allowed to present himself except with the understanding that he alone who should succeed in making Princess Ice-Heart shed a tear would be accepted as her betrothed.

This proclamation diminished at once the number of suitors. Indeed, after one or two candidates had failed, no more appeared— so well did it come to be known that the attempt was hopeless.

And for more than a year Princess Ice-Heart was left to herself— very much, apparently, to her satisfaction.

But all this time the mystic sisters were not idle or forgetful. Several of the aspirants to Ice-Heart's hand had been chosen by them and conveyed to the neighborhood of the palace by their intermediacy from remote lands. And among these, one of the few who had found some slight favor in the maiden's eyes was a special protégé of the Western fairy—the young and spirited Prince Francolin.

He was not one of the sighing or sentimental order of swains; he was full of life and adventure and brightness, and his heart was warm and generous. He admired the beautiful girl, but he pitied her still more, and this pity was the real motive which made him yield to the fairy's proposal that he should try again.

"You pleased the poor child," she said, when she arrived one day at the Prince's home to talk over her new idea. "You made her smile by your liveliness and fun. For I was there when you little knew it. The girl has been overdosed with sentimentality and doleful strains. I believe we have been on a wrong track all this time."

"What do you propose?" said Francolin, gravely, for he could be serious enough when seriousness was called for. "She did not actually dislike me, but that is the most that can be said; and however I may feel for her, however I may admire her beauty and intelligence, nothing would induce me to wed a bride who could not return my affection. Indeed, I could scarcely feel any for such a one."

"Ah no! I agree with you entirely," said the fairy. "But listen—my power is great in some ways. I am well versed in ordinary enchantment, and am most willing to employ my utmost skill for my unfortunate god-daughter."

She then unfolded to him her scheme, and obtained his consent to it.

"Now is your time," she said, in conclusion. "I hear on the best authority that Ice-Heart is feeling rather dull and bored at present. It is some time since she has had the variety of a new suitor, and she will welcome any distraction."

And she proceeded to arrange all the details of her plan.

So it came to pass that very shortly after the conversation I have related there was great excitement in the capital city of the Kingdom of the Four Orts. After an interval of more than a year a new suitor had at length presented himself for the hand of the Princess Ice-Heart. Only the King and Queen received the news with melancholy indifference.

"He may try as the others have done," said Brave-Heart to the messenger announcing the arrival of the stranger at the gates, accompanied by a magnificent retinue; "but it is useless." For the poor King was fast losing all hope of his daughter's case; he was growing aged and care-worn before his time.

"Does he know the terms attached to his acceptance?" inquired the Queen.

Yes, the messenger from the unknown candidate for the hand of the beautiful Ice-Heart had been expressly charged to say that the Prince Jocko such was the new-comer's name—was fully informed as to all particulars, and prepared to comply with the conditions.

The Princess' parents smiled somewhat bitterly. They had no hope, but still they could not forbid the attempt.

"Prince Jocko?" said the King, "not a very prince-like name. However, it matters little."

A few hours later the royal pair and their daughter, with all their attendants, in great state and ceremony, were awaiting their guest. And soon a blast of trumpets announced his approach. His retinue was indeed magnificent; horsemen in splendid uniforms, followed by a troop of white mules with negro riders in gorgeous attire, then musicians, succeeded by the Prince's immediate attendants, defiled before the great marble steps in front of the palace, at the summit of which the King, with the Queen and Princess, was seated in state.

Ice-Heart clapped her hands.

"'Tis as good as a show," she said, "but where is the Prince?"

~ 222 ~

As she said the word the cortége halted. A litter, with closely drawn curtains, drew up at the foot of the steps.

"Gracious!" exclaimed the Princess, "I hope he is not a molly-coddle;" but before there was time to say more the curtains of the litter were drawn aside, and in another moment an attendant had lifted out its occupant, who forthwith proceeded to ascend the steps.

The parents and their daughter stared at each other and gasped.

Prince Jocko was neither more nor less than a monkey!

But such a monkey as never before had been seen. He was more comical than words can express, and when at last he stood before them, and bowed to the ground, a three-cornered hat in his hand, his sword sticking straight out behind, his tail sweeping the ground, the effect was irresistible. King Brave-Heart turned his head aside. Queen Claribel smothered her face in her handkerchief. Princess Ice-Heart opened her pretty mouth wide and forgot to close it again, while a curious expression stole into her beautiful eyes.

Was it a trick?

No; Prince Jocko proceeded to speak.

He laid his little brown paw on his heart, bowed again, coughed, sneezed, and finally began an oration. If his appearance was too funny, his words and gestures were a hundred times more so. He rolled his eyes, he declaimed, he posed and pirouetted like a miniature dancing-master, and his little cracked voice rose higher and higher as his own fine words and expressions increased in eloquence.

And at last a sound—which never before had been heard, save faintly—made everyone start. The Princess was laughing as if

~ 223 ~

she could no longer contain herself. Clear, ringing, merry laughter, which it did one's heart good to hear. And on she went, laughing ever, till—she flung herself at her mother's feet, the tears rolling down her cheeks.

"Oh, mamma!" she exclaimed, "I never—" and then she went off again.

But Prince Jocko suddenly grew silent. He stepped up to Ice-Heart and, respectfully raising her hand to his lips, gazed earnestly, beseechingly into her face, his own keen sharp eyes gradually growing larger and deeper in expression, till they assumed the pathetic, wistful look of appeal one often sees in those of a noble dog.

"Ah, Princess!" he murmured.

And Ice-Heart stopped laughing. She pressed her hand to her side.

"Father! mother!" she cried, "help me! help me! Am I dying? What has happened to me?" And, with a strange, long drawn sigh she sank fainting to the ground.

There was great excitement in the palace, hurrying to and fro, fetching of doctors, and much alarm. But when the Princess had been carried indoors and laid on a couch, she soon revived. And who can describe the feelings of the King and Queen when she turned to them with a smile such as they had never seen on her face before.

"Dearest father, dearest mother," she said, "how I love you! Those strange warm drops that filled my eyes seem to have brought new life to me," and as the Queen passed her arm round the maiden she felt no chill of cold such as used to thrill her with misery every time she embraced her child.

"Sweet-Heart! my own Sweet-Heart!" she whispered.

And the Princess whispered back, "Yes, call me by that name always."

All was rejoicing when the wonderful news of the miraculous cure spread through the palace and the city. But still the parents' hearts were sore, for was not the King's word pledged that his daughter should marry him who had effected this happy change? And this was no other than Jocko, the monkey!

The Prince had disappeared at the moment that Ice-Heart fainted, and now with his retinue he was encamped outside the walls. All sorts of ideas occurred to the King.

"I cannot break my word," he said, "but we might try to persuade the little monster to release me from it."

But the Princess would not hear of this.

"No," she said. "I owe him too deep a debt of gratitude to think of such a thing. And in his eyes I read more than I can put in words. No, dear father! you must summon him at once to be presented to our people as my affianced husband."

So again the cortége of Prince Jocko made its way to the palace, and again the litter, with its closely drawn curtains, drew up at the marble steps. And Sweet-Heart stood, pale, but calm and smiling, to welcome her ridiculous betrothed.

But who is this that quickly mounts the stairs with firm and manly tread? Sweet-Heart nearly swooned again.

"Jocko?" she murmured. "Where is Jocko? Why, this is Prince Francolin!"

~ 225 ~

"Yes, dear child," said a bright voice beside her; and, turning round, Sweet-Heart beheld the Western fairy, who, with her sisters, had suddenly arrived. "Yes, indeed! Francolin, and no other!"

The universal joy may be imagined. Even the grave fairy of the North smiled with pleasure and delight, and, as she kissed her pretty god-daughter, she took the girl's hand and pressed it against her own heart.

"Never misjudge me, Sweet-Heart," she whispered. "Cold as I seem to those who have not courage to approach me closely, my heart, under my icy mantle, is as warm as is now your own."

And so it was.

Where can we get a better ending than the time-honored one? Francolin and Sweet-Heart were married, and lived happy ever after, and who knows but what, in the Kingdom of the Four Orts, they are living happily still?

If only we knew the way thither, we might see for ourselves if it is so.

WIDOW TOWNSEND'S VISITOR.

The fire crackled cheerfully on the broad hearth of an old-fashioned fireplace in an old-fashioned public house in an old fashioned village, down in that part of the Old Dominion called the "Eastern Shore." A cat and three kittens basked in the warmth, and a decrepit yellow dog, lying full in the reflection of the blaze, wrinkled his black nose approvingly, as he turned his hind feet where his fore feet had been. Over the chimney hung several fine hams and pieces of dried beef. Apples were festooned along the ceiling, and other signs of plenty and good cheer were scattered profusely about. There were plants, too, on the window ledges, horse-shoe geraniums, and dew-plants, and a monthly rose, just budding, to say nothing of pots of violets that perfumed the whole place whenever they took it into their purple heads to bloom. The floor was carefully swept, the chairs had not a speck of dust upon leg or round, the long settle near the fireplace shone as if it had been just varnished, and the eight-day clock in the corner had had its white face newly washed, and seemed determined to tick the louder for it.

Two arm-chairs were drawn up at cozy distance from the hearth and each other; a candle, a newspaper, a pair of spectacles, a dish of red cheeked apples, and a pitcher of cider, filled a little table between them. In one of these chairs sat a comfortable-looking woman about forty-five, with cheeks as red as the apples, and eyes as dark and bright as they had ever been, resting her elbow on the table and her head upon her hand, and looking thoughtfully into the fire.

This was Widow Townsend, "relict" of Mr. Levi Townsend, who had been mouldering into dust in the neighboring churchyard for seven years and more. She was thinking of her dead husband, possibly because all her work being done, and the servant gone to bed, the sight of his empty chair at the other side of the table, and the silence of the room, made her a little lonely.

"Seven years," so the widow's reverie ran; "it seems as if it were more than fifty, and Christmas nigh here again, and yet I don't look so very old neither. Perhaps it's not having any children to bother my life out, as other people have. They may say what they like—children are more plague than profit, that's my opinion. Look at my sister Jerusha, with her six boys. She's worn to a shadow, and I am sure they have done it, though she never will own it."

The widow took an apple from the dish and began to peel it.

"How fond Mr. Townsend used to be of these apples! He'll never eat any more of them, poor fellow, for I don't suppose they have apples where he has gone to. Heigho! I remember very well how I used to throw apple-peel over my head when I was a girl to see who I was going to marry."

Mrs. Townsend stopped short and blushed, for in those days she did not know Mr. T., and was always looking eagerly to see if the peel had formed a capital S. Her meditations took a new turn.

"How handsome Sam Payson was, and how much I use to care about him! I wonder what has become of him! Jerusha says he went away from our village just after I did, and no one has ever heard of him since. What a silly thing that quarrel was! If it had not been for that—"

Here came a long pause, during which the widow looked very steadfastly at the empty arm-chair of Levi Townsend, deceased. Her fingers played carelessly with the apple-peel: she drew it safely towards her, and looked around the room.

~ 228 ~

"Upon my word, it is very ridiculous, and I don't know what the neighbors would say if they saw me."

Still the plump fingers drew the red peel nearer.

"But then they can't see me, that's a comfort; and the cat and old Bose never will know what it means. Of course I don't *believe* anything about it."

The peel hung gracefully from her hand.

"But still, I should like to try; it would seem like old times, and—"

Over her head it went, and curled up quietly on the floor at a little distance. Old Bose, who always slept with one eye open, saw it fall, and marched deliberately up to smell it.

"Bose—Bose—don't touch!" cried his mistress, and bending over it with beating heart, she turned as red as fire. There was as handsome a capital S as any one could wish to see.

A great knock came suddenly at the door. Bose growled, and the widow screamed and snatched up the apple-peel.

"It's Mr. T.—it's his spirit come back again, because I tried that silly trick," she thought fearfully to herself.

Another knock—louder than the first, and a man's voice exclaimed:

"Hello—the house!"

"Who is it?" asked the widow, somewhat relieved to find that the departed Levi was still safe in his grave on the hillside.

"A stranger," said the voice.

"What do you want?"

"To get a lodging here for the night."

The widow deliberated.

"Can't you go on? There's a house half a mile farther, if you keep to the right-hand side of the road, and turn to the left after you get by—"

"It's raining cats and dogs, and I'm very delicate," said the stranger, coughing. "I'm wet to the skin: don't you think you can accommodate me?—I don't mind sleeping on the floor."

"Raining, is it? I didn't know that," and the kind-hearted little woman unbarred the door very quickly. "Come in, whoever you may be; I only asked you to go on because I am a lone woman, with only one servant in the house."

The stranger entered, shaking himself like a Newfoundland dog upon the step, and scattering a little shower of drops over his hostess and her nicely swept floor.

"Ah, that looks comfortable after a man has been out for hours in a storm," he said, as he caught sight of the fire; and striding along toward the hearth, followed by Bose, who sniffed suspiciously at his heels, he stationed himself in the arm-chair—Mr. Townsend's arm-chair! which had been kept "sacred to his memory" for seven years. The widow was horrified, but her guest looked so weary and worn-out that she could not ask him to move, but busied herself in stirring up the blaze that he might the sooner dry his dripping clothes.

A new thought struck her: Mr. T. had worn a comfortable dressing-gown during his illness, which still hung in the closet at her right. She could not let this poor man catch his death, by sitting in that wet coat. If he was in Mr. Townsend's chair, why should he not be in Mr. Townsend's wrapper? She went nimbly to the closet, took it down, fished out a pair of slippers from a boot-rack below, and brought them to him.

"I think you had better take off your coat and boots—you will have the rheumatic fever, or something like it, if you don't. Here are some things for you to wear while they are drying. And you must be hungry, too; I will go into the pantry and get you something to eat."

She bustled away, "on hospitable thoughts intent," and the stranger made the exchange with a quizzical smile playing around his lips. He was a tall, well-formed man, with a bold but handsome face, sun-burned and heavily bearded, and looking anything but "delicate," though his blue eyes glanced out from under a forehead as white as snow. He looked around the kitchen with a mischievous air, and stretched out his feet decorated with the defunct Boniface's slippers.

"Upon my word, this is stepping into the old man's shoes with a vengeance! And what a hearty, good-humored looking woman she is! Kind as a kitten," and he leaned forward and stroked the cat and her brood, and then patted old Bose upon the head. The widow, bringing in sundry good things, looked pleased at his attention to her dumb friends.

"It's a wonder Bose does not growl; he generally does if strangers touch him. Dear me, how stupid!"

The last remark was neither addressed to the stranger nor to the dog but to herself She had forgotten that the little stand was not empty, and there was no room on it for the things she held.

"Oh, I'll manage it," said her guest, gathering up paper, candle, apples, and spectacles (it was not without a little pang that she saw them in his hand, for they had been her husband's, and were placed each night, like the arm-chair, beside her) and depositing them on the settle.

"Give me the table-cloth, ma'am, I can spread it as well as any woman; I've learned that along with scores of other things, in my wanderings. Now let me relieve you of those dishes; they are far too heavy for those hands"—the widow blushed; "and now please, sit down with me, or I cannot eat a morsel."

"I had supper long ago, but really I think I can take something more," said Mrs. Townsend, drawing her chair nearer to the table.

"Of course you can, my dear lady; in this cold fall weather people ought to eat twice as much as they do in warm. Let me give you a piece of this ham, your own curing, I dare say."

"Yes: my poor husband was very fond of it. He used to say that no one understood curing ham and drying beef better than I."

"He was a most sensible man, I am sure. I drink your health, ma'am, in this cider."

He took a long draught, and set down his glass.

"It is like nectar."

The widow was feeding Bose and the cat (who thought they were entitled to a share of every meal eaten in the house), and did not quite hear what he said.

"Fine dog, ma'am, and a very pretty cat."

"They were my husband's favorites," and a sigh followed the answer.

"Ah, your husband must have been a very happy man."

The blue eyes looked at her so long, that she grew flurried.

"Is there anything more I can get for you, sir?" she asked, at last.

"Nothing, thank you; I have finished."

She rose to clear the things away. He assisted her, and somehow their hands had a queer knack of touching as they carried the dishes to the pantry shelves. Coming back to the kitchen, she put the apples and cider in their old places, and brought out a clean pipe and a box of tobacco from an arched recess near the chimney.

"My husband always said he could not sleep after eating supper late unless he smoked," she said. "Perhaps you would like to try it."

"Not if it is to drive you away," he answered, for she had her candle in her hand.

"Oh, no; I do not object to smoke at all." She put the candle down; some faint suggestion about "propriety" troubled her, but she glanced at the old clock, and felt reassured. It was only half-past nine.

~ 233 ~

The stranger pushed the stand back after the pipe was lit, and drew her easy-chair a little nearer the fire, and his own.

"Come, sit down," he said, pleadingly; "it's not late, and when a man has been knocking about in California and all sorts of places, for a score of years, he is glad enough to get into a berth like this, and to have a pretty woman to speak to once again."

"California! Have you been in California?" she exclaimed, dropping into the chair at once. Unconsciously, she had long cherished the idea that Sam Payson, the lover of her youth, with whom she had so foolishly quarreled, had pitched his tent, after many wanderings, in that far-off land. Her heart warmed to one who, with something of Sam's looks and ways about him, had also been sojourning in that country, and who very possibly had met him—perhaps had known him intimately! At that thought her heart beat quick, and she looked very graciously at the bearded stranger, who, wrapped in Mr. Townsend's dressing-gown, wearing Mr. Townsend's slippers, and sitting in Mr. Townsend's chair, beside Mr. Townsend's wife, smoked Mr. Townsend's pipe with such an air of feeling most thoroughly and comfortably at home!

"Yes, ma'am. I've been in California for the last six years. And before that I went quite round the world in a whaling ship!"

"Good gracious!"

The stranger sent a puff of smoke curling gracefully over his head.

"It's very strange, my dear lady, how often you see one thing as you go wandering about the world after that fashion."

"And what is that?"

"Men, without house or home above their heads, roving here and there, and turning up in all sorts of odd places; caring very little for life as a general thing, and making fortunes just to fling them away again, and all for one reason. You don't ask me what *that* is? No doubt you know already very well."

"I think not, sir."

"Because a woman has jilted them!"

Here was a long pause, and Mr. Townsend's pipe emitted short puffs with surprising rapidity. A guilty conscience needs no accuser, and the widow's cheek was dyed with blushes as she thought of the absent Sam.

"I wonder how women manage when *they* get served in the same way," said the stranger musingly; "you never meet *them* roaming up and down in that style."

"No," said Mrs. Townsend, with some spirit, "if a woman is in trouble she must stay at home and bear it, the best way she can. And there's more women bearing such things than we know of, I dare say."

"Like enough. We never know whose hand gets pinched in a trap unless they scream. And women are too shy or too sensible—which you choose—for that."

"Did you ever, in all your wanderings, meet any one by the name of Samuel Payson?" asked the widow, unconcernedly.

The stranger looked toward her; she was rummaging the table-drawer for her knitting work, and did not notice him. When it was found, and the needles in motion, he answered her.

~ 235 ~

"Payson—Sam Payson? Why, he was my most intimate friend! Do you know him?"

"A little—that is, I used to, when I was a girl. Where did you meet him?"

"He went with me on the whaling voyage I told you of, and afterward to California. We had a tent together, and some other fellows with us, and we worked the same claim for more than six months."

"I suppose he was quite well?"

"Strong as an ox."

"And—and happy?" pursued the widow, bending closer over her knitting.

"Hum—the less said about that the better, perhaps. But he seemed to enjoy life after a fashion of his own. And he got rich out there, or rather, I will say, well off."

Mrs. Townsend did not pay much attention to that part of the story. Evidently she had not finished asking questions, but she was puzzled about her next one. At last she brought it out beautifully:

"Was his wife with him in California?"

The stranger looked at her with twinkling eyes.

"His wife, ma'am! Why, bless you, he has not got any wife."

"Oh, I thought—I mean I heard"—here the little widow remembered the fate of Ananias and Sapphira, and stopped short before she told such a tremendous fib.

"Whatever you heard of his marrying was all nonsense, I can assure you. I knew him well, and he had no thoughts of the kind about him. Some of the boys used to tease him about it, but he soon made them stop."

"How?"

"He just told them frankly that the only woman he ever loved had jilted him years before, and married another man. After that no one ever mentioned the subject to him, except me."

Mrs. Townsend laid her knitting aside, and looked thoughtfully into the fire.

"He was another specimen of the class of men I was speaking of. I have seen him face death a score of times as quietly as I face the fire. 'It matters very little what takes me off,' he used to say; 'I've nothing to live for, and there's no one that will shed a tear for me when I am gone.' It's a sad thought for a man to have, isn't it?"

Mrs. Townsend sighed as she said she thought it was.

"But did he ever tell you the name of the woman who jilted him?"

"I know her *first* name."

"What was it?"

"Maria."

The plump little widow almost started out of her chair, the name was spoken so exactly as Sam would have said it.

"Did you know her, too?" he asked, looking keenly at her.

"Yes."

"Intimately?"

"Yes."

"Where is she now? Still happy with her husband, I suppose, and never giving a thought to the poor fellow she drove out into the world?"

"No," said Mrs. Townsend, shading her face with her hand, and speaking unsteadily; "no, her husband is dead."

"Ah! but still she never thinks of Sam."

There was a dead silence.

"Does she?"

"How can I tell?"

"Are you still friends?"

"Yes."

"Then you ought to know, and you do. Tell me."

"I'm sure I don't know why I should. But if I do, you must promise me, on your honor, never to tell him, if you ever meet him again."

"Madam, what you say to me never shall be repeated to any mortal man, upon my honor."

"Well, then, she does remember him."

"But how?"

"As kindly, I think, as he could wish."

"I am glad to hear it, for his sake. You and I are the friends of both parties: we can rejoice with each other."

He drew his chair much nearer hers, and took her hand. One moment the widow resisted, but it was a magnetic touch, the rosy palm lay quietly in his, and the dark beard bent so low that it nearly touched her shoulder. It did not matter much. Was he not Samuel's dear friend? If he was not the rose, had he not dwelt very near it, for a long, long time?

"It was a foolish quarrel that parted them," said the stranger, softly.

"Did he tell you about it?"

"Yes, on board the whaler."

"Did he blame her much?"

"Not so much as himself. He said that his jealousy and ill-temper drove her to break off the match; but he thought sometimes if he had only gone back and spoken kindly to her, she would have married him after all."

"I am sure she would," said the widow piteously. "She has owned it to me more than a thousand times."

"She was not happy, then, with another."

"Mr.—that is to say, her husband—was very good and kind," said the little woman, thinking of the lonely grave out on the hillside rather penitently, "and they lived very pleasantly together. There never was a harsh word between them."

"Still—might she not have been happier with Sam? Be honest, now, and say just what you think."

"Yes."

"Bravo! that is what I wanted to come at. And now I have a secret to tell you, and you must break it to her."

Mrs. Townsend looked rather scared.

"What is it?"

"I want you to go and see her, wherever she may be, and say to her, 'Maria,'—what makes you start so?"

"Nothing; only you speak so like some one I used to know, once in a while."

"Do I? Well, take the rest of the message. Tell her that Sam loved her through the whole; that, when he heard she was free, he began to work hard at making a fortune. He has got it; and he is coming to share it with her, if she will let him. Will you tell her this?"

The widow did not answer. She had freed her hand from his, and covered her face with it. By and by she looked up again—he was waiting patiently.

"Well?"

"I will tell her."

He rose from his seat, and walked up and down the room. Then he came back, and leaning on the mantel-piece, stroked the yellow hide of Bose with his slipper.

"Make her quite understand that he wants her for his wife. She may live where she likes and how she likes, only it must be with him."

"I will tell her."

"Say he has grown old, but not cold; that he loves her now perhaps better than he did twenty years ago; that he has been faithful to her all through his life, and that he will be faithful till he dies."

The Californian broke off suddenly. The widow answered still, "I will tell her."

"And what do you think she will say?" he asked, in an altered tone.

"What *can* she say but *Come!*"

"Hurrah!"

The stranger caught her out of her chair as if she had been a child, and kissed her.

"Don't—oh, don't!" she cried out. "I am Sam's Maria!"

"Well—I am Maria's Sam!"

Off went the dark wig and the black whiskers—there smiled the dear face she had not forgotten! I leave you to imagine the tableau;

~ 241 ~

even the cat got up to look, and Bose sat on his stump of a tail, and wondered if he was on his heels or his head.

The widow gave one little scream, and then she—

But, stop! Quiet people like you and me, dear reader, who have got over all these follies, and can do nothing but turn up our noses at them, have no business here. I will only add that two hearts were very happy, that Bose concluded after a while that all was right, and so lay down to sleep again, and that one week afterward, on Christmas Eve, there was a wedding at the house that made the neighbors stare. The widow had married her First Love!

THE OLD MAN'S CHRISTMAS.

BY ELLA WHEELER WILCOX.

I.

Though there was wrong on both sides, they never would have separated had it not been for the old man.

He was Ben's father, and Ben was an only child—a spoiled, selfish, high-tempered lad, who had grown up with the idea that his father, Anson English, or the "old man," as his dutiful son called him, was much richer than he really was, and that he had no need of any personal effort—any object in life, aside from the pursuit of pleasure.

Ben's mother had died when he was fifteen years old and his father had never married again. Yet it was not any allegiance to her memory which had kept Anson English from a second marriage. He remembered her, to be sure, and scarcely a day passed without his mentioning her. But after her death, as during her weary life, he used her name as a synonym for all that was undesirable. He compared everybody to "'Liz'beth," and always to her disadvantage. He had a word of praise and encouragement and approval for every housewife in the neighborhood except—his own. Whatever went wrong, in doors or out, "'Liz'beth" was the direct or indirect cause.

During the first five years of her married life, Elizabeth made strenuous exertions to please her husband. She wept her sweet eyes dim over her repeated failures. Then she found that she had been attempting an impossible labor, and grew passively indifferent—an indifference which lasted until death kindly released her.

Elizabeth had been a tidy housekeeper during these first years.

~ 243 ~

"You'd scrub and scour a man out 'er house an' home!" was all the praise her husband gave her for her order and cleanliness; and to his neighbors, to whom he was fond of paying informal visits, he would often say—"'Liz'beth's at it again—sweepin' and cleanin', so I cleared out. Never see *her* without out a broom in her hand. I'd a good deal rather have a little more dirt, than so much tearin' 'round. 'Liz'beth tires me, with her ways."

Yet, when in the indifference of despair which seized upon Elizabeth before her death, she allowed her house to look after itself, Anson was no better satisfied.

"I've come over to find a place to set down," he would tell his neighbors. "'Liz'beth's let things 'cumulate, till the house is a sight to see—she's gettin' dreadful slack, somehow. A man likes order when he goes home to rest from all his cares."

Even when she died she displeased him by choosing a busy season for the occasion.

"Just like 'Liz'beth, to die in hayin' time," he said. "Everything got to stop—hay spoilin'—men idle. Women never seem to have no system about work matters—no power of plannin' things, to make it convenient like for men folks."

Yet after she was gone, Anson found how much help she had been to him, how wonderful her economy had been, how light her expenditures. He knew he could never find any one to replace her, in these respects, and as money considerations were the main ones in his mind he believed it would be the better economy to remain a widower, and hire his work done.

So during those most critical years of Ben's life, he had been without a woman's guidance or care.

~ 244 ~

At eighteen he was all that arrogance, conceit, selfishness, and high temper could render him. Yet he was a favorite with the fair sex for all that, as he had a manly figure, and a warm, caressing way when he chose, that won their admiration and pleased their vanity.

Anson English favored early marriages, and began to think it would be better all around if Ben should bring a wife home.

She could do the work better than hired help, and keep the money all in the family. And Ben would not waste his time and means on half a dozen, as he was now doing, but would stay at home, no doubt, and settle down into a sensible, practical business man. Yes, Ben ought to marry, and his father told him so.

Ben smiled.

"I'm already thinking of it," he said. He had expected opposition from his father, and was surprised at his suggestion.

"Yes," continued the "old man," as Ben already designated him, "I'd like to see you settle down before you're twenty-one. But you want to make a good choice. There's Abby Wilson, now. She's got the muscle of a man, and ain't afraid of anything. And her father has a fine property—a growin' property. Abby'll make a man a good, vigorous helpmate, and she'll bring him money in time. You'd better shine up to Abby, Ben."

Ben gave a contemptuous laugh. "I'd as soon marry a dressed-up boy," he said. "She's more like a boy than a girl in her looks and in her ways. I have other plans in my mind, father, more to my taste. I mean to marry Edith Gilman, if she'll take me, and I think she will."

A dark frown contracted Anson English's brow.

"Edith Gilman?" he repeated; "why, that puny schoolma'm, with her baby face and weak voice, 'll never help *you* to get a livin', Ben. What are you thinkin' of?"

"Of love, father, I guess. I love her, and that's all there is of it. And I shall marry her, if she'll take me, and you can like it or lump it, as you please. She's a good girl, and if she's treated well all round, she'll make a good wife, and she's the only woman that can put the check rein on me, when I get in my tempers. She'll make a man of me yet."

"But she can't work," insisted the father. "She looks as white and puny as 'Liz'beth did the year she died."

"She's overworked in the school-room. I mean to take her home, and give her a rest. I don't ask any woman to marry me and be my drudge. I expect my wife will keep help."

The old man groaned aloud. Ben's ideas were positively ruinous. If he married this girl, it would add to, not decrease, the family expenses. But it was useless to oppose. Ben would do as he pleased, the old man saw that plainly, and he might as well submit.

He did submit, and Ben married Edith on his twenty-first birthday, and brought her home.

Edith was a quiet little creature, with a soft voice, and a pale, sweet face, and frail figure. She came up to Anson English when she entered the house, and put her hands timidly upon his arms.

"I want you to love me," she said; "I have had no father or mother since I can remember. I want to call you father, and I want to make you happy if I can."

"Well, I'll tell you how," the old man retorted. "Discharge the hired girl, and make good bread. That'll make me happy,"—and he laughed harshly.

Edith shrank from his rough words, so void of the sympathy and love she longed for. But she discharged the girl within a week, and tried to make good bread. It was not a success, however, and the old man was not slow to express his dissatisfaction. Edith left the table in tears.

"Another dribbler—'Liz'beth was always cryin' just that way over every little thing," sighed the old man.

Edith eventually conquered the difficulties of bread making, and became a famous cook. But she did not please her husband's father any the better by this achievement.

"You're always a-fixin' up some new sort of trash for the table," he said to her one day. "Dessert is it, you call it? 'Nuff to make a man's patience desert him to see sugar and flour wasted so. 'Liz'beth liked your fancy cooking, but I cured her of it."

"Yes, and you killed her too," cried Edith, for the first time since her marriage losing control of her temper and answering back. "Everybody says you worried her into the grave. But you won't succeed so well with me. I will live just to defy you, if no more. And I'll show you that I'll not bear everything, too."

It was all over in a moment, and it was not repeated. Indeed, Edith was kinder and gentler and more submissive in her manner after that for days, as sweet natures always are when they have once broken over the rules which govern their lives.

Yet the old man always spoke of Edith as a virago after that.

"She's worse'n 'Liz'beth," he said, "and she had a temper of her own at times that would just *singe* things."

Ben passed most of his evenings and a good part of his days at the village "store." He came home the worse for drink occasionally, and he was absolutely indifferent to all the work and care of the farm and family.

"She's just like 'Liz'beth," the old man said to his neighbors; "she don't make home entertainin' for her husband. But Ben isn't balanced like me, and he goes wrong. He's excitable. I never was. The right kind of a woman could keep him at home."

After a child came to them matters seemed to mend for a time. So long as the infant lay pink and helpless in its mother's arms or in its crib, it was a bond to unite them all.

So soon as it began to be an active child, with naughty ways which needed correction, it was another element of discord.

The old man did not think Edith capable of controlling the child, and Ben was hasty and harsh, and he did not like to hear the baby cry. So he stayed more and more at the store, and was an object of fear to the child and of reproach to the mother when he did return.

They drifted farther apart, and the old man constantly widened the breach between them. They had been married six years, and the baby girl was four years old, when Ben struck Edith a blow, one day, and told her to take her child and leave the house.

In less than an hour she had gone, no one knew whither.

"She'll come back, more's the pity," the old man said. "'Liz'beth, she started off to leave me once, but she concluded to come back and try it over again."

But Edith did not come back. Months afterward they heard of her in a distant part of the State teaching school and supporting her child.

Ben applied for a divorce on the plea of desertion. Edith never appeared against him, and he obtained it.

III.

One year from the time Edith left him, he married Abby Wilson. She had grown into a voluptuous though coarse maturity, and was dashing in dress and manner. Her father had recently died, leaving her a fine property. She had always coveted Ben, and did not delay the nuptials from any sense of delicacy, but rather hastened the hour which should make him legally her own.

The old man was highly pleased at the turn affairs had taken. After all these years Ben was united to the woman he had chosen for him so long ago, and now surely Ben would settle down, and take the care off his shoulders—shoulders which were beginning to feel the weight of years of labor. In truth, the old man was breaking down.

He fell ill of a low fever soon after Ben's second marriage, and when he rose from his bed he seemed to have grown ten years older. He was more childish in his fault-finding, and more irritable than ever before, and this new wife of Ben's had little patience with him. She was not at all like Edith. She bullied him, and frightened him into silence when he began to find fault with her extravagances. For she was extravagant—there was no denying that. She cared only for show and outward appearance. She neglected her home duties, and often left the old man to prepare his own food, while she and Ben dashed over the country, or through the neighboring villages, behind the blooded span she had insisted upon his purchasing soon after their marriage.

Poor old Anson English! He was nearing his sixtieth year now, and he looked and seemed much older. Ben was his only earthly tie, and the hope and stay of his old age. And he was but a reed—a reed. His father saw that at last. Ben would never develop into a practical business man. He was unstable, lazy, and selfish. And this new wife seemed to encourage him in every extravagant folly, instead of restraining him as the old man had hoped. And someway Ben had never been the same since Edith went away. He had been none too good or kind to his father before that; but since then—well, when she went, it seemed to Anson that she took with her whatever of gentleness or kindness lurked in Ben's nature, and left only its brutality and selfishness.

And strive as he would to banish the feeling, the old man missed the child.

Ah, no! he was not happy in this new state of affairs, which he had so rejoiced over at the first. He grew very old during the next two years. Like all men who worry the lives of women in the domestic circle, he was cowardly at heart. And Ben's new wife frightened him into silent submission by her masculine assumption of authority and her loud voice and well-defined muscle.

He spoke little at home now, but he still paid frequent visits to his neighbors, and he remained firm in the Adam-like idea that Elizabeth had been the root of all evil in his life.

"Yes, Ben's letting the place run down pretty bad," he confessed to a neighbor who had broached the subject. "Ben's early trainin' wasn't right. 'Liz'beth, she let him do 'bout as he pleased. Liz'beth never had no notions of how a boy should be trained. He'd a' come out all right if I'd a' managed him from the start."

Strange to say, he never was known to speak one disparaging word of Abby, Ben's second wife. Her harshness and neglect were matters of common discussion in the neighborhood, but the old man, who had been so bitter and unjust toward his own wife and Edith, seemed to feel a curious respect for this Amazon who had subjugated him. Or, perhaps, he remembered how eager he had been for the marriage, and his pride kept him silent. Certain it is that he bore her neglect, and later her abuse, with no word of complaint, and even spoke of her sometimes with praise.

"She's a brave one, Abby is," he would say. "She ain't afraid of nothin' or nobody. Ef she'd a' been a man, she'd a' made a noise in the world."

Ben drank more and more, and Abby dressed and drove in like ratio. The farm ran down, and debts accumulated—debts which Abby refused to pay with her money, and the old man saw the savings of a long life of labor squandered in folly and vice.

People said it was turning his brain, for he talked constantly of his poverty, often walking the streets in animated converse with himself. And at length he fell ill again, and was wildly delirious for weeks. It was a high fever; and when it left him, he was totally blind, and quite helpless.

He needed constant care and attention. He could not be left alone even for an hour; Ben was seldom at home, and Abby rebelled at the confinement and restraint it imposed upon her. Hired help refused to take the burden of the care of the troublesome old man without increased wages, and Ben could not and Abby would not incur this added expense. Servants gave warning; Ben drank more deeply and prolonged his absences from home, and Abby finally carried out a resolve which had at first caused even her hard heart some twinges.

She made an application to the keeper of the County Poor to admit her husband's father to the department of the incurably insane, which was adjacent to the Poor House.

"He's crazy," she said, "just as crazy as can be. We can't do anything with him. He needs a strong man to look after him. Ben's never at home, and he has everything to look after any way, and can't be broken of his rest, and the old man talks and cries half the night. I'm not able to take care of him—I seem to be breaking down myself, with all I have to endure, and besides it isn't safe to have him in the house. I think he's getting worse all the time. He'd be better off, and we all would, if he was in the care of the county."

The authorities looked into the matter, and found that at least a portion of the lady's statements were true. It was quite evident that the old man would be better off in the County House than he was in the home of his only son. So he was taken away, and Abby had her freedom at last.

"We are going to take you where you will have medical treatment and care; it is your daughter's request," they told him in answer to his trembling queries.

"Oh! yes, yes—Abby thinks I'll get my sight back, I suppose, if I'm doctored up. Well, maybe so, but I'm pooty old—pooty old for the doctors to patch up. But Abby has a powerful mind to plan things—a powerful mind. 'Liz'beth never would a' thought of sending me away—'Liz'beth was so easy like. Abby ought to a' been a man, she had. She'd a' flung things."

So he babbled on as they carried him to the Poor House.

It was November, and the holidays were close at hand. Thanksgiving, Christmas, New Year. Abby meant to enjoy them, and invited all her relatives to a time of general feasting and merrymaking.

"I feel as if a great nightmare were lifted off my heart and brain, now the old man has gone," she said. "He will be so much better off, and get so much more skillful treatment, you know, in a place like that. They are very kind in that institution, and so clean and

~ 253 ~

nice, and he will have plenty of company to keep him from being lonesome. We have been all through it, during the last year, or else we never should have sent him there. It is really an excellent home for him."

IV.

It was just a year later when a delicate, sweet-faced woman was shown through the wards of that "excellent home" for the poor and unfortunate. She walked with nervous haste, and her eyes glanced from room to room, and from face to face, as if seeking, yet dreading, some object.

Presently the attendant pushed open a partly closed door, which led into a small, close room, ventilated only by one high, narrow window.

"This is the room, I believe," he said, and the lady stepped in—and paused. The air was close and impure, and almost stifled her.

On the opposite side of the room she saw a large crib with a cover or lid which could be closed and locked when necessary, but which was raised now. In this crib, upon a hard mattress and soiled pillow, lay the emaciated form of an old man. He turned his sightless eyes toward the door as he heard the sound of footsteps.

"What is wanted?" he asked, feebly; "does anybody want me? Has anybody come for me?"

"O father, father!" cried the woman in a voice choked with sobs. "Don't you know me? It is I—and I have come to take you away— to take you away home with me. Will you go?"

A glow of delight shone over the old man's wasted face, like the last rays of the sunlight over a winter landscape. He half arose upon his elbow, and leaned forward as if trying to see the speaker.

"Why, it's Abby, it's Abby, come at last!" he said. "You called me father, didn't you—and you was crying, and it made your voice sound kind[Pg 234] o' strange and broken like. But you must be

~ 255 ~

Abby come to take me home. Oh, I thought you'd come at last, Abby. It seems a long, long time since I came away. And you've never been to see me; no, nor Ben, either. But you've come at last, Abby, you've come at last. Let me take your hand, daughter, for I can't see yet. They don't seem to help me here as you thought they would. And I'm *so hungry*, Abby!—do you think you could manage to get the old man a little something to eat before we start home?"

The woman had grown paler and paler as she listened to these words which the old man poured out in eager haste, like one whose thoughts and feelings long pent within himself for want of a listener now rushed forth pell-mell into speech.

"He does not know me," she whispered—"he does not know me. Well, I will not undeceive him now. He is happy in this delusion,— let him keep it for the present." Then, aloud, she said:

"You are hungry, father? do you not have food enough here?"

"Oh, I have my share, Abby; I have my share. But my appetite's varying, and sometimes when they bring it I can't eat it, and then when I want it most I can't get it. I'm one of many here, and I've been so lonesome, Abby. But then I knew you'd come for me all in good time. And, Ben—how is Ben, Abby? does he want to see his old father again? Ah, Ben was a nice little boy—a nice little boy. But 'Liz'beth wan't no kind of a mother for such a high-strung lad. And then he hadn't oughter married that sickly sort of girl that ran off an' left him. Sakes alive! what a temper she had! It sort of broke Ben down living with her as long as he did. But he remembers his old father at last, don't he? And he wants to have me home to die. Ah, Ben has a good heart after all!"

"I must not tell him; I must not," whispered the woman as she listened. "Bitter to me as his deception is, I must let him remain in it." Then with a sudden bracing of the nerves, and a visible effort, she said:

"Ben is away from home now, father. He will not be there to meet you, but you'll not mind that: I shall make you so comfortable; I want you at home during the holidays."

So he went out from the horror and loneliness and gloom of the Poor House, to the comfortable home which Edith had provided for herself and child in the years since she left Ben. Eva was a precocious little maiden of nine now, wise and womanly beyond her years. So soon as Edith learned of the old man's desolate fate, she resolved to bring him home. Eva could attend to his wants during the day, while she was in the school-room, and the interrupted studies could be pursued in the evening. Or she could hire assistance if he were as troublesome as report had said. He had been a harsh old man, and had helped to widen the breach between her and Ben. But he was the father of the man she had married, and she could not let him die in the Poor House. So she brought him home.

"Don't I hear a child's voice?" he asked, as Eva came dancing out to greet them. "Who is it, Abby?"

"Why, it's your own little granddaughter Eva," cried the child, clasping his withered hand in her two soft palms. "Don't you remember me? Mamma says you used to love me."

Edith's heart stood still. Surely now he would understand. And would he be angry and harsh with her?

The old man's face lighted.

"Ah, I see, I see," he said musingly, "Abby and Ben have taken the little one home. It must be Edith is dead. She was such a puny

~ 257 ~

thing." Then turning his face to the woman who was guiding his faltering footsteps, he asked:

"And is Edith dead?"

"Yes," she answered quietly, "Edith is dead." And added "to *you*," in a whisper.

"He must never be undeceived," she thought. "It would be too severe a blow; the truth might kill him." And to Eva she said a little later:

"Dear, your grandfather is very ill, and not quite right in his mind. He thinks my name is Abby, and you must not correct him or dispute any strange thing he may say."

The journey left the old man very weak indeed, but he talked almost constantly.

"It was so good of you, Abby, to take the little girl home," he would say. "But I knowed you had a good heart, and Ben too. He was fond of his old father, spite of his rough ways. It was pooty lonesome—pooty lonesome, off there at that place—that Institute where you sent me. Some folks said it was the Poor House, but I knew better—I knew better. Ben and you would never send me there. I s'pose it was a good place, but they had too many patients. Sometimes I was cold and hungry and all alone for hours and hours. Oh, it's good to be back home with you—you, Abby—but why don't Ben come?"

"Ben is away, father."

"Oh, yes, yes. Business, I suppose. Ben'll turn out all right at last. I always thought so. After he sort o' outgrows 'Liz'beth's trainin'. But I hope he'll get back for Christmas. Somehow I've been thinkin' lately 'bout the Christmas days when Ben was a little boy. We allus put something in his stockin' that night, no matter if twan't no more'n a sweet cake. Sakes alive! how he prized things he found in his stockin' Christmas mornin's! I got to thinkin' 'bout it all last Christmas out at that there Institute, and I just[Pg 237] laid an' bawled like a baby, I was so home-sick like. Seemed to me if I could just *see* Ben's face again, I'd ask nothin' more of Heaven. And now I think if I can just hear his voice again, it'll be enough. Do you think he'll git home for Christmas, Abby?"

"I hope so, dear father, but I cannot tell." Edith answered softly, her heart seeming to break in her breast as she listened.

She knew very well that Ben would not go across the street to see the father he had deserted, and that she could never send for him to come to *her* house, to pay even a last visit of mercy.

"What will I do—how can I explain to him, when Christmas comes and Ben does not appear?" she thought.

But the way was shown her by that great Peace-Maker who helps us out of all difficulties at last.

Christmas Eve, the old man's constant chatter grew flighty and incoherent. He talked of people and things unknown to Edith, and spoke his mother's name many times. Then he fell asleep. In the morning he seemed very weak, and his voice was fainter.

"Such a strange dream as I have had, 'Lis'beth," he said, as Edith put her hand on his brow, and smoothed back the thin, white hair.

"Such a strange dream, I thought Ben had grown into a man, and had left me alone—all alone to die. I'm so glad to be awake and find it isn't true. How dark it is, and how long the night seems! To-morrow is Christmas. Did you put something in Ben's stockings, 'Lis'beth? I have forgotten."

~ 259 ~

"Yes," answered Edith, in a choked voice.

"And it's gettin' colder, 'Lis'beth. Hadn't you better look after Ben a little? See if he's covered up well in his crib. You're so careless, 'Lis'beth, the boy'll take his death o' cold yet. And he's all I've got. He'll make a fine man, a fine man if you don't spoil him, 'Lis'beth. But you hain't no real sense for trainin' a boy, somehow. Is he covered up? It's bitter, bitter cold."

"He is well covered," Edith answered. The old man seemed to doze again. Then he roused a little.

"It's dawn," he said. "I see the light breaking. Little Ben'll be crawling out for his stockin' pooty quick: I oughter had the fire made afore this, to warm his little toes. Strange you couldn't a' waked me, 'Liz'beth! You don't never seem to have no foresight."

Then the old man fell back on Edith's arm, dead.

THE CHRISTMAS GOBLINS.

BY CHARLES DICKENS.

In an old abbey town, a long, long while ago there officiated as sexton and gravedigger in the churchyard one Gabriel Grubb. He was an ill conditioned cross-grained, surly fellow, who consorted with nobody but himself and an old wicker-bottle which fitted into his large, deep waistcoat pocket.

A little before twilight one Christmas Eve, Gabriel shouldered his spade, lighted his lantern, and betook himself toward the old churchyard, for he had a grave to finish by next morning, and feeling very low, he thought it might raise his spirits, perhaps, if he went on with his work at once.

He strode along until he turned into the dark lane which led to the churchyard—a nice, gloomy, mournful place into which the towns-people did not care to go except in broad daylight, consequently he was not a little indignant to hear a young urchin roaring out some jolly song about a Merry Christmas. Gabriel waited until the boy came up, then rapped him over the head with his lantern five or six times to teach him to modulate his voice. And as the boy hurried away, with his hand to his head, Gabriel Grubb chuckled to himself and entered the churchyard, locking the gate behind him.

He took off his coat, put down his lantern, and getting into an unfinished grave, worked at it for an hour or so with right good will. But the earth was hardened with the frost, and it was no easy matter to break it up and shovel it out. At any other time this would have made Gabriel very miserable, but he was so pleased at having stopped the small boy's singing that he took little heed of the scanty progress he had made when he had finished work for the night, and looked down into the grave with grim satisfaction, murmuring as he gathered up his things:

"Brave lodgings for one, brave lodgings for one,

A few feet of cold earth when life is done."

"Ho! ho!" he laughed, as he set himself down on a flat tombstone, which was a favorite resting-place of his, and drew forth his wicker-bottle. "A coffin at Christmas! A Christmas box. Ho! ho! ho!"

"Ho! ho! ho!" repeated a voice close beside him.

"It was the echoes," said he, raising the bottle to his lips again.

"It was not," said a deep voice.

Gabriel started up and stood rooted to the spot with terror, for his eyes rested on a form that made his blood run cold.

Seated on an upright tombstone close to him was a strange, unearthly figure. He was sitting perfectly still, grinning at Gabriel Grubb with such a grin as only a goblin could call up.

"What do you here on Christmas Eve?" said the goblin, sternly.

"I came to dig a grave, sir," stammered Gabriel.

"What man wanders among graves on such a night as this?" cried the goblin.

"Gabriel Grubb! Gabriel Grubb!" screamed a wild chorus of voices that seemed to fill the churchyard.

"What have you got in that bottle?" said the goblin.

"Hollands, sir," replied the sexton, trembling more than ever, for he had bought it of the smugglers, and he thought his questioner might be in the excise department of the goblins.

"Who drinks Hollands alone, and in a churchyard on such a night as this?"

"Gabriel Grubb! Gabriel Grubb!" exclaimed the wild voices again.

"And who, then, is our lawful prize?" exclaimed the goblin, raising his voice.

The invisible chorus replied, "Gabriel Grubb! Gabriel Grubb!"

"Well, Gabriel, what do you say to this?" said the goblin, as he grinned a broader grin than before.

The sexton gasped for breath.

"What do you think of this, Gabriel?"

"It's—it's very curious, sir, very curious, sir, and very pretty," replied the sexton, half-dead with fright. "But I think I'll go back and finish my work, sir, if you please."

"Work!" said the goblin, "what work?"

"The grave, sir."

"Oh! the grave, eh? Who makes graves at a time when other men are merry, and takes a pleasure in it?"

Again the voices replied, "Gabriel Grubb! Gabriel Grubb!"

"I'm afraid my friends want you, Gabriel," said the goblin.

"Under favor, sir," replied the horror-stricken sexton, "I don't think they can; they don't know me, sir; I don't think the gentlemen have ever seen me."

"Oh! yes, they have. We know the man who struck the boy in the envious malice of his heart because the boy could be merry and he could not."

Here the goblin gave a loud, shrill laugh which the echoes returned twenty-fold.

"I—I am afraid I must leave you, sir," said the sexton, making an effort to move.

"Leave us!" said the goblin; "ho! ho! ho!"

As the goblin laughed he suddenly darted toward Gabriel, laid his hand upon his collar, and sank with him through the earth. And when he had had time to fetch his breath he found himself in what appeared to be a large cavern, surrounded on all sides by goblins ugly and grim.

"And now," said the king of the goblins, seated in the centre of the room on an elevated seat—his friend of the churchyard—"show the man of misery and gloom a few of the pictures from our great storehouses."

As the goblin said this a cloud rolled gradually away and disclosed a small and scantily furnished but neat apartment. Little children were gathered round a bright fire, clinging to their mother's gown, or gamboling round her chair. A frugal meal was spread upon the table and an elbow-chair was placed near the fire. Soon the father entered and the children ran to meet him. As he sat down to his meal the mother sat by his side and all seemed happiness and comfort.

"What do you think of that?" said the goblin.

Gabriel murmured something about its being very pretty.

"Show him some more," said the goblin.

Many a time the cloud went and came, and many a lesson it taught to Gabriel Grubb. He saw that men who worked hard and earned their scanty bread were cheerful and happy. And he came to the conclusion it was a very respectable sort of a world after all. No sooner had he formed it than the cloud closed over the last picture seemed to settle on his senses and lull him to repose. One by one the goblins faded from his sight, and as the last one disappeared he sank to sleep.

The day had broken when he awoke, and found himself lying on the flat gravestone, with the wicker-bottle empty by his side. He got on his feet as well as he could, and brushing the frost off his coat, turned his face toward the town.

But he was an altered man, he had learned lessons of gentleness and good-nature by his strange adventures in the goblin's cavern.

THE SONG OF THE STAR.

BY REV. C. H. MEAD.

"Oh, boys; you can count me out on that—all I can get goes to my mother and sisters for Christmas."

The speaker was a manly little newsboy, with good features, a clean face and bright eyes. His clothes looked neat, though they were adorned with numerous patches.

"But see here, Will. Christmas only comes once a year, and why shouldn't we fellers have our banquet as well as the silk-stockings? What would they know about things going on in the world anyway, if we newsboys didn't supply 'em with papers? All in favor of having a banquet, hold up yer hands!"

Up went a score of hands—some dirty, some clean and some speckled, but Will's hand remained down. "See here, Will, what's the reason you won't stay by us?"

The boy hesitated a moment and then said: "Boys, it's mighty close times up at our house; fried chicken and pound cake don't come our way, turkeys roost too high for us, and, and—well, boys, if you must know it, about the only good thing we kids have up there is our mother's love. See these patches! My mother put them on. See these stockings! My mother has been mending this same pair of stockings for more than a year, and she washes and irons them after I've gone to bed at night. Every stitch of mother's needle and thread is a stitch of love, and one night not long ago, I opened my eyes and saw my mother's tears dropping on the sleeve of my coat at the same time she was putting the patch on this elbow. I tell you, boys, the best thing I've got in the world is my mother, and the best Christmas gift I ever had is my mother's love. If I had a million dollars, I'd give them all to my mother in return for her love. No, no, boys; no banquet for me, as long as I know my mother is starving herself that we children may have more to eat."

"Well," replied one of the boys, "if I had a mother like that, maybe I'd feel the same way; but all we get at our house is a good licking from a drunken mother, and I'm going in for a square meal at Christmas, if I never has another."

The boys, gathered on the sidewalk by one of the parks, were suddenly startled by a cry "Look out there!" and the next moment a runaway horse dashed into their midst; little Will was knocked over, and was soon carried into a neighboring drug store, all unconscious of what had happened. It was soon discovered that his arm was broken, and his body bruised in a number of places. The moment he regained consciousness and found what had occurred, he said:

"Take me to my mother; she will take care of me somehow, though this isn't exactly the kind of a Christmas gift I meant she should have. Say, boys, one of you go up to our house, and tell her easy about this; don't burst in sudden and scare her, but tell her it isn't dangerous, and—well, just tell her I love her."

The boys wiped their eyes and one of them said, "This busts up our banquet, fellers; I'll go and tell Will's mother, and, say, fellers, shan't I tell her we will give our banquet money to help her out at Christmas?"

A hearty "You bet we will," was the response, as big Tom sped away to carry the news to Will's mother, while kind hands helped carry the injured boy to his home. It was a poor home into which he was borne, but everything was as neat and tidy as could be. A woman stood at the door, and it needed but one glance to know that she was the mother of Will. Poverty and hunger had failed to rob her of her beauty, and there was an air of refinement about her that told of better days and happier surroundings.

"Christmas hasn't come yet, mother," said Will, "but I have. Don't you worry; I'll come out of this all right, and we will have a good Christmas yet."

The mother kissed him tenderly as she said, "No, I will not worry, so long as I have God, and you, and Josie, and Maggie, and Tot. When Christmas comes round, Will, it will be a good day whatever it brings."

"It will bring yer heaps of things, Mrs. Sandford," blurted out big Tom, "for we fellers has given up havin' a banquet, and are going to bring yer something that Will can't bring now. Don't yer worry a bit," and here the rough fellow burst into tears, and rushed out of the house.

A few more days, and then Christmas Eve came round, and a bright night it was. Will lay sleeping on the bed, his mother near by, pretending to read, but in reality using the dear old Bible as a shield to hide the tears that trickled down her cheeks. The mother was thinking, and thinking fast, too. It was only a little over thirteen years since her father had closed the door in her face and told her never to return. The man she loved was not the fashionable fop her father had selected for her as a husband, and secretly she had given her hand to the man to whom long before she had given her heart. All went well, until three years ago, when her husband died suddenly, and she found herself with no means and four children to take care of. Too proud to apply to her father for help, she struggled on as best she could, leaning hard on the God whom her mother had taught her to love.

Her children were a comfort to her, for they had inherited the natural goodness of both their parents. Her tears now fell fast, for as she thought, she also listened to the voices of her two youngest children who were standing over by the window together.

"Say, Maggie, does yer see dat bright star up dere? I wonder if dat is de star what de shepherds seen! If it is, it seems to be looking right down at us. Maybe Jesus is in dat star, and if He is, He won't forget us, will He?"

And Tot looked at Maggie as the latter said: "Jesus loved little children, Tot, when He was on the earth, and I guess He loves them yet. That's a very bright star—it must be the one that was seen by the shepherds at Bethlehem."

"I think so, too," said Tot, "and may be Josie will hear some of dem 'good tidings' while she is out. Oh! Maggie, Jesus must love mother; she is so good, and I think He has sent that star to tell us to look out for good news."

And where was Josie all this time? The mother thought she had gone into a neighbor's, where she frequently went, and so felt no anxiety.

Out in the streets of the big city, side by side walked plenty and poverty, wealth and wretchedness, happiness and hunger, gladness and grief. Some carried bundles in their arms, while others carried burdens in their hearts. Over all, the good God watched, and down upon all the bright star shone. But what is that? Suddenly on one of the streets the people stopped and listened. On the steps of a stoop leading up to a lighted mansion stood a little girl who looked like a bright angel from heaven. Far above, overhead, shone the bright star that Maggie and Tot had seen; it was their star and it was her star, for Josie, too, had discovered it, and somehow felt that the star that had brought "good tidings of great joy" to the shepherds on Bethlehem's plains, had come again and to bring once more "good tidings." She had mounted the steps to get nearer the star, and then all unconscious of the people, in a rich, sweet voice, she sang:—

I think, when I read that sweet story of old,

When Jesus was here among men;

How He called little children, as lambs to His fold;

I should like to have been with Him then.

I wish that His hands had been placed on my head,

hat His arms had been thrown around me;

That I might have seen His kind look, when He said,

"Let the little ones come unto Me."

As she sang, her gaze was fixed on the star, and even her hands were lifted toward it. The people looked at her; an angel had appeared in their midst—her face, her voice, her upturned eyes, her uplifted hands, held them spell-bound, until some one looking up in the direction she pointed, cried out: "See that star!" Heavenward went the gaze of the multitude, and once more there seemed to come to them a voice, saying: "Fear not, for behold I bring you good tidings of great joy, which shall be to all people." The face of Josie was illumined and even the multitude that had gathered, failed to alarm her. The star with its "good tidings" was over her head and in her heart as well. "Who are you, my child?" said a gentleman who had come up on the steps where she stood. "Please, sir, I am Josie Sandford." The gentleman gave a start and said, "Sandford, Josie Sandford? Pray where do you live, Josie?" She told him, and in response to other questions, told of mother, brother and sisters.

"Oh, sir; do you see the star? I am sure it has some 'good tidings' for us at our house, and I must hurry home and tell mother all about it. Good-bye."

Away sped the child until she reached her home, and then entering the room quietly, she went up to her mother and said: "Have you seen the star, mother?" Maggie and Tot cried out, "We've seen it; come, mother, and look quick." The mother went quietly to the window, and there beheld a star of wonderful brightness, and as she gazed, her face took on a new light and into her heart came a great peace. The sleeping boy was awakened by the voices, and he, too, made his way to the window and looked at the star. "At evening time it shall be light."

It had come, and—something else had come, too, for steps were heard on the stairs, followed by a knock on the door, on opening which, in came a company of newsboys headed by big Tom. They bore bundles and baskets, provisions and poultry, sunshine and sugar, toys and turnips, good-will and grapes, cheer and celery, and things that no one but those who had lacked for them, would ever have thought of. Big Tom was the spokesman for the happy company.

"If yer please, Mrs. Sandford," he said, "there's our banquet. We wasn't going to come until to-morrow morning, but when we got the things all together, we just couldn't wait any longer, so we've brought 'em to-night, and if it isn't too soon, ma'am, we wishes you, and Will, and Josie, and Maggie, and Tot a 'Merry Christmas,' doesn't we, boys?"

"Indeed we does!" responded the boys. The faces of that mother and her children were a sight to behold. Smiles and tears greeted the boys, and the mother and her three girls had a kiss for each of them. Then Tot said: "I knowed it. I knowed it! De star had Jesus in it, and I knowed He see Maggie and me looking up at it."

"Well, boys," said Mrs. Sandford, "you shall have your banquet, for I want you all to take Christmas dinner with us to-morrow."

"Yes, boys, you shall all take dinner with Mrs. Sandford and her children to-morrow, but it must be at the home of her parents and not here," said a gentleman who had not been noticed as he stood in the hallway.

Mrs. Sandford started as the owner of the voice entered the room, and little Josie sprang toward him at the same moment. She resembled her mother and was her namesake as well. The gentleman stretched out his arms toward Mrs. Sandford as he said to her:

"Josie, can you forgive me for the harshness with which I drove you years ago from my door? God only knows how I have suffered, and for years I have hunted high and low for you, and have advertised time and again. But all was in vain, until to-night I saw your face and heard your voice once more, as my grandchild, Josie, stood singing on the steps and gazing at the star. In her I found you again, and oh, how your mother and I have prayed for this time to come."

Long before he had finished, the daughter was in her father's arms once more, and the children were clinging to their new-found grandparent. The newsboys looked on in wonder, and suddenly little Tot ran to the window and then cried out—"Oh, grandpa, the star is here yet, and it shines brighter than before," and she threw a kiss up to the star.

Christmas morning came and found them all in a home of plenty. A chair that had long stood vacant at that table, was once more filled, and near it were four other chairs for the new-found grand-children. Was it a "Merry Christmas," did you inquire? Just ask those newsboys who came at two o'clock if they ever had such a banquet before or since, or whether they ever saw a home in which the "Star of Bethlehem" shone with greater splendor. And over the earth the star still shines, and will continue to shine until all mankind shall yet have a "Merry Christmas."

INDIAN PETE'S CHRISTMAS GIFT.

BY HERBERT W. COLLINGWOOD.

The moon was just peeping over the pines as Pete Shivershee slunk down the road from the lumber camp into the forest. Pete did not present a surpassingly dignified appearance as he skulked through the clearing, but he was not a very dignified person even at his best.

Most persons would have said, I think, that Pete's method of departure was hardly appropriate for one who had been selected by the citizens of Carter's Camp to go on an important mission. But Pete had his own reasons for his actions. He crept along behind the stumps and logs till he reached the forest. Then, as if the shadow gave him fresh courage and dignity, he drew himself upright, and started at a sharp trot down the road toward the village.

We have said that Pete had reasons for his conduct. They were good ones. In the first place, he was an Indian. Not a "noble son of the forest," such as Cooper loved to picture, but a mean, dirty, yellow-faced "*Injun*." Lazy and worthless, picking up a living about the lumber camps, working as little as he could, and eating and drinking as much as possible: such was the messenger. The mission was worse yet.

It was Christmas Eve. The snow covered the ground, and the ice had stilled for the time the mouth of the roaring river. It was Saturday night as well; and for some time past the lumbermen had been considering the advisability of keeping the good old holiday with some form of celebration suited to the occasion.

The citizens of Carter's Camp were not remarkably fastidious. They knew but one form of celebration, and they had no thought of hunting out new ones. The one thing needful to make a

celebration completely successful was—liquor. This they must
have in order to do justice to the day.

The temperance laws of Carter's were very strict. Not that the
moral sentiment of the place was particularly high, but it had
been noticed that the amounts of labor and whisky were in inverse
proportion. The more whisky, the less labor. It was a pure question
of political economy. The foreman had often stated that he would
prosecute to the fullest extent of the law the first man caught
bringing whisky into camp. The foreman did not attempt,
perhaps, to deny that his knowledge of the law was somewhat
crude. He had forcibly stated, however, that should a case be
brought before him, he would himself act as judge and jury, while
his fist and foot would take the place of witness and counsel.
There was something so terrible in this statement, coming as it
did from the largest man in camp, that very little whisky had
thus far been brought in.

Christmas had come, and the drinking element in Carter's Camp
proposed that Pete Shivershee—the "Injun"—be sent to town for a
quantity of the liquid poison, that the drinkers might "enjoy"
themselves.

Bill Gammon found Pete curled up by the stove. He took him out
of doors and explained the business in hand. Bill prided himself
somewhat on his ability to "git work out of Injuns." Pete muttered
only "all right." He took the money Bill gave him, and then slunk
away down the road for the forest, as we have seen him.

*   *   *   *   *

Bill felt so confident of the success of his experiment that he did
not hesitate to inform the boys that Pete was "dead sure" to return.
He would stake his reputation upon it.

~ 275 ~

Pete was in a hard position. If he loved anything in this world, it was whisky. If there was anything he feared, it was Bill's fist. The two were sure to go together. The money jingling in his pocket suggested unlimited pleasures, but over every one hung Bill's hard fist. He ran several miles through the forest, till, turning a corner of the road, he came upon a little clearing, in which stood a small log house. Pete knew the place well. Here lived Jeff Hunt with his wife, a French woman, and their troop of children.

Jeff was a person of little importance by the side of his wife, though, like all "lords of creation," he considered himself the legal and proper head of the family, as well as one of the mainstays of society. His part of the family government consisted, for the most part, in keeping the house supplied with wood and water, and in smoking his comfortable pipe in the corner, while his wife bent over her tub.

Mrs. Hunt was the only woman near the camp, and so all the laundry work fell to her. Laundry work in the pine woods implies mending and darning, as well as washing and ironing, and the poor little woman had her hands full of work surely. It was rub, rub, rub, day after day, over the steaming tub, with the children running about like little wolves, and Jeff kindly giving his advice from his comfortable corner. And even after the children were in bed at night, she must sit up and mend the clean clothes.

What a pack of children there were! How rough and strong they seemed, running about all day, all but poor little Marie, the oldest. She had never been strong, and now at last she was dying of consumption. She could not sit up at all, but lay all day on the little bed in the corner, watching her mother with sad, beautiful eyes.

The brave little Frenchwoman's heart almost failed her at times, as she saw how day by day the little form grew thinner, the eyes more beautiful, the cheeks more flushed. She knew the signs too well, but there was nothing she could do.

Pete was a regular visitor at Jeff's and always a welcome one. His work was to carry the washing to and from camp. He came nearer to feeling like a man at Jeff's house than at any other place he knew of. Everyone but Mrs. Hunt and little Marie called him only "Injun," but they always said "Mr. Shivershee." The "Meester Shivershee" of the little Frenchwoman was the nearest claim to respectability that Pete felt able to make. One night while carrying home the clothes, he dropped them in the mud. He never minded the whipping Bill Gammon gave him half as much as he did poor Mrs. Hunt's tears, to think how her work had gone for nothing.

As Pete came trotting down the road, Jeff stood in front of his house chopping stove-wood from a great log. A lantern, hung on a stump, provided light for his purpose. Pete stopped from sheer force of habit in front of the house, and Jeff, glad of any chance to interrupt his work, paused to talk with him.

"Walk in, Injun," said Jeff, hospitably. "Yer clo'es ain't quite ready, but the woman will hev 'em all up soon—walk in."

It suddenly came over Pete that this was his night for taking the clothes home, but his present errand was of far more importance than mere laundry work.

"Me no stop. I goin' ter town. Great work. Large bizness." By which vague hints he meant no doubt to impress Jeff with a sense of the dignity of his mission, and yet cunningly to keep its object concealed.

"Goin' to town, be ye? Great doin's ter camp ter-morrer, I s'pose. I'll be round ef I kin git away, but walk in, Injun, an' git yer supper, an' see the wimmin," and Jeff opened the door for Pete to pass in.

The thought of supper was too much for Pete and he slunk in after Jeff and stood in the corner by the door. The room was hardly an inviting one, and yet if Pete had been a white man some thoughts of "home, sweet home," must have passed through his mind. But he was only a despised "Injun."

A rough board table was laid for supper at one side of the room. In the corner little Marie lay with the firelight falling over her poor thin face. Pete must have felt, as he looked at her, like some hopeless convict gazing through his prison bars upon some fair saint passing before him. She seemed to be in another world than his; there seemed between them a gulf that could not be bridged. Three of the larger children were sobbing in the corner, while the rest formed a sorrowful group about an old box in which were two or three simple plants frozen and yellow. Mrs. Hunt was frying pork over the hot stove. As she looked up at Pete, he noticed that she had been crying.

Jeff was the very prince of hosts. He made haste to make Pete feel at home.

"Set by, Injun. So the boys is goin' ter kinder cellybrate ter-morrer, be they?"

But Pete felt that his mission must not be disclosed. "What matter is with kids?" he asked, to change the subject.

"Oh, they're jest a-yellin' about them flowers," explained Jeff. "Ye see they hev been a-trainin' some posies indoors against ter-morrer, ye know. Ter-morrer's Christmas, ye see, an' them kids they hed an idee they'd hev some flowers fer ter dekerate thet corner

~ 278 ~

where the little gal is. Little gals, when they ain't well, like sech things, ye know."

Pete nodded. He was not aware of this love of diminutive females, but it would not show very good breeding to appear ignorant.

"Wall, ye see," continued Jeff, "they kep the flowers away from the little gal, meanin' ter s'prise her like. But jest this afternoon they gut ketched by the frost, an' now there they be stiffer'n stakes. It is kinder bad, ain't it—'specially ez it's Christmas, too?"

"What Crissmus?" put in Pete.

"Oh, Christmas? Wall, it's a sorter *day* like. It's somethin' like other days, an' yet it ain't. But then, Injun, I don't s'pose ye would understand ef I wuz ter tell ye." And Jeff concealed his own ignorance, as many wiser and better men have done, by assuming a tone too lofty for his audience.

But Mrs. Hunt could explain, even if Jeff could not. She paused on the way to the stove with a dish of pork in her hand.

"It eez the day of the good Lord, Meester Shivershee. It eez the day when the good Lord He was born, and when all people should be glad." But the little woman belied her own creed as she thought of little Marie and the dead flowers.

I hardly think Pete gained a very clear idea of the day, even from Mrs. Hunt's explanation. It was, I fear, all Greek to him.

"What flowers fer?" he asked, as, in response to Jeff's polite invitation, he "sat by" and began supper.

"Wall, it's a sorter idee of the wimmin," explained Jeff. "Looks kinder pooty to see flowers round; ye see, kinder slicks up a room

~ 279 ~

like. All these things hez ter come inter keepin' house, ye see, Injun." With which broad explanation Jeff helped himself to a piece of pork.

But Mrs. Hunt was bound to explain too. Her explanation was certainly more poetic.

"It eez the way we show our love for the good Lord, Meester Shivershee. What is more beautiful than the flowers? We take the flowers, and with much love we place them upon the walls, and we make others happy with them, and the good Lord, who loves us all, He is pleased,"—but here, seeing the sobbing children and the frozen plants, she could not help wiping her eyes upon her apron.

The little sufferer on the bed saw this action. Her voice was almost gone. "Never mind, mamma," she whispered; but the beautiful eyes were filled with tears, for she knew that mamma *would* mind— that she could not help it.

Pete listened to all this attentively. "Injun" that he was, of course he could not understand it all, and yet he could hardly help seeing something of the sorrow that the loss of the flowers had brought upon the family. He finished his supper, and then slunk out at the door again. Jeff followed him out.

"Little gal ever git well?" asked Pete.

"No; I don't s'pose she will," answered Jeff. "There ain't no hopes held out fer her. Makes it kinder bad, ye see. Nice, clever little gal as ever lived, too. Stop in an' git yer clo'es when ye come back, will ye?"

"All right," muttered Pete, as he trotted away toward the town.

*   *   *   *   *

I wonder what Pete was thinking about as he ran through the forest. An "Injun's" thoughts on any ordinary subject cannot be very deep, yet when one comes from such a scene as Pete had just witnessed, and when such sad eyes as Marie's haunt one all along a lonely road, even an "Injun's" thoughts must be worth noticing. Let us imagine what Pete's thoughts were as he shuffled mile after mile through the snow. The scene he had just left rose before his dulled "Injun" mind. How kind Mrs. Hunt had always been to him! She was the only one that called him "Mister." How queer it was that the children should cry because the flowers were killed! How little Marie had looked at him! Somehow Pete could not drive those sad eyes away. They seemed to be looking at him from every stump, from every tree. They were filled with tears now—could it be because the flowers were frozen?

It is no wonder that when at last the few lingering village lights came into view, Pete was wondering how he could help matters out.

It was quite late, and most of the shops were closed. Only here and there some late worker showed a light. The bar-rooms were open full blast, and as Pete glided down the sawdust street it needed all the remembrance of Bill's fist to keep him from parting with a portion of the jingling money for an equal amount of good cheer. But the fist had the best of it, and he went straight on to the last bar-room. Surely Bill was right. Nothing but a miracle could stop him.

But the miracle was performed, and when Pete least expected it.

Pete knew better than to go into the front door of the bar-room. He knew how well he and all his race are protected by the government. It had been decided that no one should be allowed to sell liquor to an "Injun"—at least at the regular bar. If an "Injun," however, could so far lose sight of his personal dignity as to come sneaking in at the back door, and pay an extra price for his liquor, whose business was it?

~ 281 ~

Pete knew the way of bar-tenders. He had been in the business before. He did not go in at the front door where the higher-bred white men were made welcome, but slunk down an alley by the side of the building, meaning to go in the back way.

There was no light in the store next the bar-room. It was a milliner's store and had been closed for some hours. But in the back room two women were working away anxious to finish a hat, evidently intended for some village belle's Christmas. Pete stopped in the dark alley for a moment to watch them.

A man sat asleep in a chair by the stove, but the women worked on with tireless fingers. The hat was growing more and more brilliant under their quick touches. By their side stood a basket of artificial flowers and bright ribbons. It seemed to Pete that he had never before seen anything so beautiful. Here were flowers—why could he not get some for the little sick girl?

It was a severe struggle for the poor "Injun," out there in the dark alley. The thought of the thrashing he would receive on the one hand, and the sad eyes of Marie on the other. What could he do? But even an "Injun" can remember a kindness. It may have been a miracle, or it may have been just the out-cropping of the desire to repay a kindness which even an "Injun" is said to possess. At any rate the eyes conquered and Pete braved the fist of Bill. For fear that he should lose courage, he pushed against the door of the room, and entered without ceremony.

There was a great commotion, I can assure you. The idea of an "Injun" pushing his way into the back parlor of a milliner's shop was too much of a revolutionary proceeding to pass unnoticed. The women dropped their work with a little scream, while the man started from his chair with most violent intent upon poor Pete.

"What be ye after here, Injun?" he growled. "Hump yerself outer here—git a-goin'!"

But Pete pulled out his money, at the sight of which the standing army of the milliner's store paused. Money has smoothed over many an outrage. It might perhaps excuse even such an action on the part of an "Injun."

"I want flowers," Pete said, pointing to the basket. "Give me flowers—I pay."

"Oh, ye wanter buy sum of them artyficial flowers, do ye? This is a pooty time o' night ter come flower huntin,' ain't it? Jest pick out yer flowers, an' then climb out!"—and he held the basket out at arm's length for Pete to select.

Pete took a great red rose, and a white flower. There was not very much of a stock to select from, but Pete, with "Injun" instinct, selected the largest and gaudiest.

"Them is wurth about ten shillins," figured up the merchant, taking the money from Pete's hand.

Pete carefully placed the flowers in the pocket of his ragged coat, and started for the door. The milliner's man, rendered affable by the most surprising bargain he had just made, naturally wished to retain the patronage of such a model customer.

"Want anything in our line, Injun, jest call round an' we'll please ye. Only come a little afore bed-time when ye come again." But Pete slunk out at the door and did not hear him.

Pete's money was nearly gone, but he had a scheme in his head. He slunk in at the back door of the bar-room, and obtained his jug, and what whiskey he could buy with the rest of his money.

~ 283 ~

Then up the street he ran again, out of town, stopping only once at the pump to fill the jug to the top with water. Resolutely fastening in the stopper, and not even raising the jug to his mouth, he started for camp at his long, swinging trot, with the jug in his hand. Mile after mile was passed over, yet Pete did not stop till Jeff Hunt's cabin came in sight. Hiding his jug behind a log, he crept up to the window and looked in.

The light was burning on the table, while Mrs. Hunt sat nodding over her work. She had been mending the clothes so that Pete could take them back with him. Tired out, she had fallen asleep. The box of frozen plants still stood by the table. Pete grinned as he saw them, thinking of the great flowers in his pocket. Marie was asleep. Over her head were hung long clusters of moss, with masses of ground pine and red berries.

Pete stole to the door and went in. Mrs. Hunt woke with a start, but at sight of Pete smiled in her weary way. Pete made up his bundle of clothes, and then pulled out the great red rose and the white flower. He laid them on the table with—"Flowers fer little gal. Sick. Make her think Crissmus. Good flowers. All color. No fade. No smell. No wear out." Then, catching up his bundle, he slunk away without waiting for Mrs. Hunt's thanks.

*   *   *   *   *

When Bill Gammon woke in the morning, he found the jug at the foot of his bunk. But Pete was nowhere to be seen. He had left the jug and fled.

The Christmas celebration at Carter's was a very tame affair. Many were the curses showered upon Pete, and had that worthy been present, I doubt if even the thought of the famous miracle would have sustained him in the beating he would have received. But if Pete's conduct produced such a sad effect upon the

~ 284 ~

festivities at Carter's, the joy it caused at Jeff Hunt's cabin made matters even. The glad Christmas sun, glad with the promise of the "old, old story," came dancing and sparkling over the trees, and looked down in wonderful tenderness upon the humble cabin. The first bright beams fell upon the bed where little Marie waslying. They showed her the rose and the white flower nestling in the evergreens. The children came and stood in wonder before the rude flowers. How wonderful they were! Where could they have come from?

The face of the little girl was more patient than before. The eyes seemed more tender, and yet not so sad. Perhaps the glad sun, the same good sun that had looked upon that far-away tomb from which the stone had rolled, whispered to her, as it played about her face, how soon the stone would roll from her life; how soon she would forget all her care and trouble, and enter the land of sunshine and flowers. It may be that the good old Christmas sun even hunted out poor despised Pete, and told him something of its happiness. I am sure he deserved it. Let us hope so at any rate.

MY CHRISTMAS DINNER.

It was on the twentieth of December last that I received an invitation from my friend, Mr. Phiggins, to dine with him in Mark Lane, on Christmas Day. I had several reasons for declining this proposition. The first was that Mr. P. makes it a rule, at all these festivals, to empty the entire contents of his counting-house into his little dining parlor; and you consequently sit down to dinner with six white-waistcoated clerks, let loose upon a turkey. The second was that I am not sufficiently well read in cotton and sugar, to enter with any spirit into the subject of conversation. And the third was, and is, that I never drink Cape wine. But by far the most prevailing reason remains to be told. I had been anticipating for some days, and was hourly in the hope of receiving, an invitation to spend my Christmas Day in a most irresistible quarter. I was expecting, indeed, the felicity of eating plum-pudding with an angel; and, on the strength of my imaginary engagement, I returned a polite note to Mr. P., reducing him to the necessity of advertising for another candidate for Cape and turkey.

The twenty-first came. Another invitation—to dine with a regiment of roast-beef eaters, at Clapham. I declined this also, for the above reason, and for one other, viz., that, on dining there ten Christmas Days ago, it was discovered, on sitting down, that one little accompaniment of the roast beef had been entirely overlooked. Would it be believed!—but I will not stay to mystify—I merely mention the fact. They had forgotten the horseradish.

The next day arrived, and with it a neat epistle, sealed with violet-colored wax, from Upper Brook street. "Dine with the ladies—at home on Christmas Day." Very tempting, it is true; but not exactly the letter I was longing for. I began, however, to debate within myself upon the policy of securing this bird in hand, instead of waiting for the two that were still hopping about the bush, when the consultation was suddenly brought to a close, by a prophetic view of the portfolio of drawings fresh from boarding-school—moths and roses on embossed paper;—to say nothing of the album, in which I stood engaged to write an elegy on a Java sparrow, that had been the favorite in the family for three days. I rung for gilt-edged, pleaded a world of polite regret, and again declined.

The twenty-third dawned; time was getting on rather rapidly; but no card came. I began to despair of any more invitations, and to repent of my refusals. Breakfast was hardly over, however, when the servant brought up—not a letter—but an aunt and a brace of cousins from Bayswater. They would listen to no excuse; consanguinity required me, and Christmas was not my own. Now my cousins kept no albums; they are really as pretty as cousins can be; and when violent hands, with white kid gloves, are laid on one, it is sometimes difficult to effect an escape with becoming elegance. I could not, however, give up my darling hope of a pleasanter prospect. They fought with me in fifty engagements—that I pretended to have made. I showed them the Court Guide, with ten names obliterated—being those of persons who had *not* asked me to mince-meat and mistletoe; and I ultimately gained my cause by quartering the remains of an infectious fever on the sensitive fears of my aunt, and by dividing a rheumatism and a sprained ankle between my sympathetic cousins.

As soon as they were gone, I walked out, sauntering involuntarily in the direction of the only house in which I felt I could spend a "happy" Christmas. As I approached, a porter brought a large hamper to the door. "A present from the country," thought I, "yes, they *do* dine at home; they must ask me; they know that I am in town." Immediately afterward a servant issued with a letter; he took the nearest way to my lodgings, and I hurried back by another street to receive the so-much-wished-for invitation. I was in a state of delirious delight.

I arrived—but there was no letter. I sat down to wait, in a spirit of calmer enjoyment than I had experienced for some days; and in less than half an hour a note was brought to me. At length, the desired despatch had come; it seemed written on the leaf of a lily with a pen dipped in dew. I opened it—and had nearly fainted with disappointment. It was from a stock-broker, who begins an anecdote of Mr. Rothschild before dinner, and finishes it with the fourth bottle—and who makes his eight children stay up to supper and snap-dragon. In macadamizing a stray stone in one of his periodical puddings, I once lost a tooth, and with it an heiress of some reputation. I wrote a most irritable apology, and despatched my warmest regards in a whirlwind.

December the twenty-fourth—I began to count the hours, and uttered many poetical things about the wings of Time. Alack! no letter came;—yes, I received a note from a distinguished dramatist, requesting the honor, etc. But I was too cunning for this, and practiced wisdom for once. I happened to reflect that his pantomime was to make its appearance on the night after, and that his object was to perpetrate the whole programme upon me. Regret that I could not have the pleasure of meeting Mr. Paulo, and the rest of the *literati* to be then and there assembled, was of course immediately expressed.

My mind became restless and agitated. I felt, amidst all these invitations, cruelly neglected. They served, indeed, but to increase my uneasiness, as they opened prospects of happiness in which I could take no share. They discovered a most tempting dessert, composed of forbidden fruit. I took down "Childe Harold," and read myself into a sublime contempt of mankind. I began to perceive that merriment is only malice in disguise, and that the chief cardinal virtue is misanthropy.

I sat "nursing my wrath," till it scorched me; when the arrival of another epistle suddenly charmed me from this state of delicious melancholy and delightful endurance of wrong. I sickened as I surveyed, and trembled as I opened it. It was dated——, but no matter; it was not *the* letter. In such a frenzy as mine, raging to behold the object of my admiration condescend, not to *eat* a custard, but to render it invisible—to be invited perhaps to a tart fabricated by her own ethereal fingers; with such possibilities before me, how could I think of joining a "friendly party,"—where I should inevitably sit next to a deaf lady, who had been, when a little girl, patted on the head by Wilkes, or my Lord North, she could not recollect which—had taken tea with the author of "Junius," but had forgotten his name—and who once asked me "whether Mr. Munden's monument was in Westminster Abbey or St. Paul's?"—I seized a pen, and presented my compliments. I hesitated—for the peril of precariousness of my situation flashed on my mind; but hope had still left me a straw to catch at, and I at length succeeded in resisting this late and terrible temptation.

After the first burst of excitement, I sunk into still deeper despondency. My spirit became a prey to anxiety and remorse. I could not eat; dinner was removed with unlifted covers. I went out. The world seemed to have acquired a new face; nothing was to be seen but raisins and rounds of beef. I wandered about like Lear—I had given up all! I felt myself grated against the world like a nutmeg. It grew dark—I sustained a still gloomier shock. Every chance seemed to have expired, and everybody seemed to have a delightful engagement for the next day. I alone was disengaged—I felt like the Last Man! To-morrow appeared to have already commenced its career; mankind had anticipated the future; "and coming mince pies cast their shadows before."

In this state of desolation and dismay, I called—I could not help it—at the house to which I had so fondly anticipated an invitation, and a welcome. My protest must here however be recorded, that though I called in the hope of being asked, it was my fixed determination not to avail myself of so protracted a piece of politeness. No: my triumph would have been to have annihilated them with an engagement made in September, payable three months after date. With these feelings, I gave an agitated knock—they were stoning the plums, and did not immediately attend. I rung—how unlike a dinner bell it sounded! A girl at length made her appearance, and, with a mouthful of citron, informed me that the family had gone to spend their Christmas Eve in Portland Place. I rushed down the steps, I hardly knew whither. My first impulse was to go to some wharf and inquire what vessels were starting for America. But it was a cold night—I went home and threw myself on my miserable couch. In other words, I went to bed.

I dozed and dreamed away the hours till day-break. Sometimes I fancied myself seated in a roaring circle, roasting chestnuts at a blazing log: at others, that I had fallen into the Serpentine while skating, and that the Humane Society were piling upon me a Pelion, or rather a Vesuvius of blankets. I awoke a little refreshed. Alas! it was the twenty-fifth of the month—It was Christmas Day! Let the reader, if he possess the imagination of Milton, conceive my sensations.

I swallowed an atom of dry toast—nothing could calm the fever of my soul. I stirred the fire and read Zimmermann alternately. Even reason—the last remedy one has recourse to in such cases—came at length to my relief: I argued myself into a philosophic fit. But, unluckily, just as the Lethean tide within me was at its height, my landlady broke in upon my lethargy, and chased away by a single word all the little sprites and pleasures that were acting as my physicians, and prescribing balm for my wounds.

She paid me the usual compliment, and then—"Do you dine at home to-day, sir?" abruptly inquired she. Here was a question. No Spanish inquisitor ever inflicted such complete dismay in so short a sentence. Had she given me a Sphynx to expound, a Gordian tangle to untwist; had she set me a lesson in algebra, or asked me the way to Brobdingnag; had she desired me to show her the North Pole, or the meaning of a melodrama:—any or all of these I might have accomplished. But to request me to define my dinner—to inquire into its latitude—to compel me to fathom that sea of appetite which I now felt rushing through my frame—to ask me to dive into futurity, and become the prophet of pies and preserves!—My heart died within me at the impossibility of a reply.

She had repeated the question before I could collect my senses around me. Then, for the first time it occurred to me that, in the event of my having no engagement abroad, my landlady meant to invite me! "There will at least be the two daughters," I whispered to myself; "and after all, Lucy Matthews is a charming girl, and touches the harp divinely. She has a very small, pretty hand, I recollect; only her fingers are so punctured by the needle—and I rather think she bites her nails. No, I will not even now give up my hope. It was yesterday but a straw—to-day it is but the thistledown; but I will cling to it to the last moment. There are still four hours left; they will not dine till six. One desperate struggle, and the peril is past; let me not be seduced by this last golden apple, and I may yet win my race." The struggle was made—"I should not dine at home." This was the only phrase left me, for I could not say that "I should dine out." Alas! that an event should be at the same time so doubtful and so desirable. I only begged that if any letter arrived, it might be brought to me immediately.

The last plank, the last splinter, had now given way beneath me. I was floating about with no hope but the chance of something almost impossible. They had "left me alone," not with my glory, but with an appetite that resembled an avalanche seeking whom it might devour. I had passed one dinnerless day, and half of another; yet the promised land was as far from sight as ever. I recounted the chances I had missed. The dinners I might have enjoyed, passed in a dioramic view before my eyes. Mr. Phiggins and his six clerks—the Clapham beef-eaters—the charms of Upper Brook street—my pretty cousins, and the pantomime writer—the stock broker, whose stories one forgets, and the elderly lady who forgets her stories—they all marched by me, a procession of apparitions. Even my landlady's invitation, though unborn, was not forgotten in summing up my sacrifices. And for what?

Four o'clock. Hope was perfectly ridiculous. I had been walking upon the hair-bridge over a gulf, and could not get into Elysium after all. I had been catching moonbeams, and running after notes of music. Despair was my only convenient refuge; no chance remained, unless something should drop from the clouds. In this last particular I was not disappointed; for, on looking up, I perceived a heavy shower of snow, yet I was obliged to venture forth; for being supposed to dine out, I could not of course remain at home. Where to go I knew not: I was like my first father—"the world was all before me." I flung my coat round me, and hurried forth with the feelings of a bandit longing for a stiletto. At the foot of the stairs, I staggered against two or three smiling rascals, priding themselves upon their punctuality. They had just arrived—to make the tour of Turkey. How I hated them!—As I rushed by the parlor, a single glance disclosed to me a blazing fire, with Lucy and several lovely creatures in a semi-circle. Fancy, too, gave me a glimpse of a sprig of mistletoe—I vanished from the house, like a spectre at day-break.

How long I wandered about is doubtful. At last I happened to look through a kitchen window, with an area in front, and saw a villain with a fork in his hand, throwing himself back in his chair choked with ecstasy. Another was feasting with a graver air;

he seemed to be swallowing a bit of Paradise, and criticising its flavor. This was too much for mortality—my appetite fastened upon me like an alligator. I darted from the spot; and only a few yards further discerned a house with rather an elegant exterior, and with some ham in the window that looked perfectly sublime. There was no time for consideration—to hesitate was to perish. I entered; it was indeed "a banquet-hall deserted." The very waiters had gone home to their friends. There, however, I found a fire; and there—to sum up all my folly and felicity in a single word—
I DINED.

THE POOR TRAVELER.

BY CHARLES DICKENS.

[Dickens' introduction to this story describes his going to Rochester on Christmas Eve and seeing there a quaint old charity, which provided for the entertainment of "six poor travelers who not being rogues or proctors might receive gratis for one night lodging, entertainment and fourpence each." In honor of the day a special meal is provided for the travelers then in the charity. After the meal, when the travelers have gathered around the fire, their entertainer gives them the reason for the unwonted feast as "Christmas Eve, my friends, when the Shepherds, who were poor travelers, too, in their way, heard the Angels sing, 'On earth, peace: Good will toward men.'" Then each traveler was invited to relate a story, and among those told was the following.]

In the year one thousand seven hundred and ninety-nine, a relative of mine came limping down, on foot, to the town of Chatham. He was a poor traveler, with not a farthing in his pocket.

My relative came down to Chatham to enlist in a cavalry regiment, if a cavalry regiment would have him; if not, to take King George's shilling from any corporal or sergeant who would put a bunch of ribbons in his hat. His object was to get shot; but he thought he might as well ride to death as be at the trouble of walking.

My relative's Christian name was Richard, but he was better known as Dick. He dropped his own surname on the road down, and took up that of Doubledick. He was passed as Richard Doubledick; age, twenty-two; height, five foot ten; native place, Exmouth, which he had never been near in his life. There was no cavalry in Chatham when he limped over the bridge with half a shoe to his dusty feet, so he enlisted into a regiment of the line, and was glad to get drunk and forget all about it.

You are to know that this relative of mine had gone wrong, and run wild. His heart was in the right place, but it was sealed up. He had been betrothed to a good and beautiful girl, whom he had loved better than she—or perhaps even he—believed; but in an evil hour he had given her cause to say to him solemnly, "Richard, I will never marry any other man. I will live single for your sake, but Mary Marshall's lips"—her name was Mary Marshall—"never address another word to you on earth. Go, Richard! Heaven forgive you!" This finished him. This brought him down to Chatham. This made him Private Richard Doubledick, with a determination to be shot.

There was not a more dissipated and reckless soldier in Chatham barracks, in the year one thousand seven hundred and ninety-nine, than Private Richard Doubledick. He associated with the dregs of every regiment; he was as seldom sober as he could be, and was constantly under punishment. It became clear to the whole barracks that Private Richard Doubledick would very soon be flogged.

Now the Captain of Richard Doubledick's company was a young gentleman not above five years his senior, whose eyes had an expression in them which affected Private Richard Doubledick in a very remarkable way. They were bright, handsome, dark eyes,—what are called laughing eyes generally, and, when serious, rather steady than severe,—but they were the only eyes now left in his narrowed world that Private Richard Doubledick could not stand. Unabashed by evil report and punishment, defiant of everything else and everybody else, he had but to know that those eyes looked at him for a moment, and he felt ashamed. He could not so much as salute Captain Taunton in the street like any other officer. He was reproached and confused,—troubled by the mere possibility of the Captain's looking at him. In his worst moments, he would rather turn back, and go any distance out of his way, than encounter those two handsome, dark, bright eyes.

One day, when Private Richard Doubledick came out of the Black hole, where he had been passing the last eight and forty hours, and in which retreat he spent a good deal of his time, he was ordered to betake himself to Captain Taunton's quarters. In the stale and squalid state of a man just out of the Black hole, he had less fancy than ever for being seen by the Captain; but he was not so mad yet as to disobey orders, and consequently went up to the terrace overlooking the parade-ground, where the officers' quarters were; twisting and breaking in his hands, as he went along, a bit of the straw that had formed the decorative furniture of the Black hole.

"Come in!" cried the Captain, when he knocked with his knuckles at the door. Private Richard Doubledick pulled off his cap, took a stride forward, and felt very conscious that he stood in the light of the dark, bright eyes.

There was a slight pause. Private Richard Doubledick had put the straw in his mouth, and was gradually doubling it up into his windpipe and choking himself.

"Doubledick," said the Captain, "do you know where you are going to?"

"To the devil, sir," faltered Doubledick.

"Yes," returned the Captain. "And very fast."

Private Richard Doubledick turned the straw of the Black hole in his mouth, and made a miserable salute of acquiescence.

"Doubledick," said the Captain, "since I entered his Majesty's service, a boy of seventeen, I have been pained to see many men of promise going that road; but I have never been so pained to see a man determined to make the shameful journey as I have been, ever since you joined the regiment, to see you."

Private Richard Doubledick began to find a film stealing over the floor at which he looked; also to find the legs of the Captain's breakfast-table turning crooked, as if he saw them through water.

"I am only a common soldier, sir," said he. "It signifies very little what such a poor brute comes to."

"You are a man," returned the Captain, with grave indignation, "of education and superior advantages; and if you say that, meaning what you say, you have sunk lower than I had believed. How low that must be, I leave you to consider, knowing what I know of your disgrace, and seeing what I see."

"I hope to get shot soon, sir," said Private Richard Doubledick; "and then the regiment and the world together will be rid of me."

The legs of the table were becoming very crooked. Doubledick, looking up to steady his vision, met the eyes that had so strong an influence over him. He put his hand before his own eyes, and the breast of his disgrace-jacket swelled as if it would fly asunder.

"I would rather," said the young Captain, "see this in you, Doubledick, than I would see five thousand guineas counted out upon this table for a gift to my good mother. Have you a mother?"

"I am thankful to say she is dead, sir."

"If your praises," returned the Captain, "were sounded from mouth to mouth through the whole regiment, through the whole army, through the whole country, you would wish she had lived to say, with pride and joy, 'He is my son!'"

"Spare me, sir," said Doubledick. "She would never have heard any good of me. She would never have had any pride and joy in owning herself my mother. Love and compassion she might have had, and would have always had, I know; but not—Spare me, sir! I am a broken wretch, quite at your mercy!" And he turned his face to the wall, and stretched out his imploring hand.

"My friend—" began the Captain.

"God bless you, sir!" sobbed Private Richard Doubledick.

I have heard from Private Richard Doubledick's own lips, that he dropped down upon his knee, kissed that officer's hand, arose, and went out of the light of the dark, bright eyes, an altered man.

In that year, one thousand seven hundred and ninety-nine, the French were in Egypt, in Italy, in Germany, where not? Napoleon Bonaparte had likewise begun to stir against England in India, and most men could read the signs of the great troubles that were coming on. In the very next year, when we formed an alliance with Austria against him. Captain Taunton's regiment was on service in India. And there was not a finer non-commissioned officer in it,—no, nor in the whole line,—than Corporal Richard Doubledick.

In eighteen hundred and one, the Indian army were on the coast of Egypt. Next year was the year of the proclamation of the short peace, and they were recalled. It had then become well known to thousands of men, that wherever Captain Taunton, with the dark, bright eyes, led, there, close to him, ever at his side, firm as a rock,

true as the sun, and brave as Mars, would be certain to be found,
while life beat in their hearts, that famous
soldier, *Sergeant Richard Doubledick.*

Eighteen hundred and five, besides being the great year of
Trafalgar, was a year of hard fighting in India. That year saw
such wonders done by a Sergeant-Major, who cut his way single-
handed through a solid mass of men, recovered the colors of his
regiment, which had been seized from the hand of a poor boy shot
through the heart, and rescued his wounded Captain, who was
down, and in a very jungle of horses' hoofs and sabres,—saw such
wonders done, I say, by this brave Sergeant-Major, that he was
specially made the bearer of the colors he had won;
and *Ensign Richard Doubledick* had risen from the ranks.

Sorely cut up in every battle, but always reinforced by the bravest
of men,—for the fame of following the old colors, shot through and
through, which Ensign Richard Doubledick had saved, inspired
all breasts,—this regiment fought its way through the Peninsular
war, up to the investment of Badajos in eighteen hundred and
twelve. Again and again it had been cheered through the British
ranks until the tears had sprung into men's eyes at the mere
hearing of the mighty British voice, so exultant in their valor; and
there was not a drummer boy but knew the legend, that wherever
the two friends, Major Taunton, with the dark, bright eyes, and
Ensign Richard Doubledick, who was devoted to him, were seen to
go, there the boldest spirits in the English army became wild to
follow.

One day, at Badajos,—not in the great storming, but in repelling
a hot sally of the besieged upon our men at work in the trenches,
who had given way,—the two officers found themselves hurrying
forward, face to face, against a party of French infantry, who
made a stand. There was an officer at their head, encouraging his
men,—a courageous, handsome, gallant officer of five-and-thirty,

~ 299 ~

whom Doubledick saw hurriedly, almost momentarily, [Pg 278] but saw well. He particularly noticed this officer waving his sword, and rallying his men with an eager and excited cry, when they fired in obedience to his gesture, and Major Taunton dropped.

It was over in ten minutes more, and Doubledick returned to the spot where he had laid the best friend man ever had, on a coat spread upon the wet clay. Major Taunton's uniform was opened at the breast, and on his shirt were three little spots of blood.

"Dear Doubledick," said he, "I am dying."

"For the love of Heaven, no!" exclaimed the other, kneeling down beside him, and passing his arm round his neck to raise his head. "Taunton! My preserver, my guardian angel, my witness! Dearest, truest, kindest of human beings! Taunton! For God's sake!"

The bright, dark eyes—so very, very dark, now, in the pale face—smiled upon him; and the hand he had kissed thirteen years ago laid itself fondly on his breast.

"Write to my mother. You will see home again. Tell her how we became friends. It will comfort her, as it comforts me."

He spoke no more, but faintly signed for a moment toward his hair as it fluttered in the wind. The Ensign understood him. He smiled again when he saw that, and, gently turning his face over on the supporting arm as if for rest, died, with his hand upon the breast in which he had revived a soul.

No dry eye looked on Ensign Richard Doubledick that melancholy day. He buried his friend on the field, and became a lone, bereaved man. Beyond his duty he appeared to have but two remaining cares in life,—one, to preserve the little packet of hair he was to give to Taunton's mother; the other, to encounter that French officer who had rallied the men under whose fire Taunton fell. [Pg 279] A new legend now began to circulate among our troops; and it was, that when he and the French officer came face to face once more, there would be weeping in France.

The war went on—and through it went the exact picture of the French officer on the one side, and the bodily reality upon the other—until the battle of Toulouse was fought. In the returns sent home appeared these words: "Severely wounded, but not dangerously, *Lieutenant* Richard Doubledick."

At midsummer-time, in the year eighteen hundred and fourteen, Lieutenant Richard Doubledick, now a browned soldier, seven-and-thirty years of age, came home to England invalided. He brought the hair with him, near his heart. Many a French officer had he seen since that day; many a dreadful night, in searching with men and lanterns for his wounded, had he relieved French officers lying disabled; but the mental picture and the reality had never come together.

Though he was weak and suffered pain, he lost not an hour in getting down to Frome in Somersetshire, where Taunton's mother lived. In the sweet, compassionate words that naturally present themselves to the mind to-night, "he was the only son of his mother, and she was a widow."

It was a Sunday evening, and the lady sat at her quiet garden-window, reading the Bible; reading to herself, in a trembling voice, that very passage in it, as I have heard him tell. He heard the words: "Young man, I say unto thee, arise!"

He had to pass the window; and the bright, dark eyes of his debased time seemed to look at him. Her heart told her who he was; she came to the door quickly, and fell upon his neck.

"He saved me from ruin, made me a human creature, won me from infamy and shame. O God, forever bless him! As He will, He will!"

"He will!" the lady answered. "I know he is in heaven!" Then she piteously cried, "But O my darling boy, my darling boy!"

Never from the hour when Private Richard Doubledick enlisted at Chatham had the Private, Corporal, Sergeant, Sergeant-Major, Ensign, or Lieutenant breathed his right name, or the name of Mary Marshall, or a word of the story of his life, into any ear except his reclaimer's. That previous scene in his existence was closed. He had firmly resolved that his expiation should be to live unknown; to disturb no more the peace that had long grown over his old offences; to let it be revealed, when he was dead, that he had striven and suffered, and had never forgotten; and then, if they could forgive him and believe him—well, it would be time enough—time enough!

But that night, remembering the words he had cherished for two years, "Tell her how we became friends. It will comfort her, as it comforts me," he related everything. It gradually seemed to him as if in his maturity he had recovered a mother; it gradually seemed to her as if in her bereavement she had found a son. During his stay in England, the quiet garden into which he had slowly and painfully crept, a stranger, became the boundary of his home; when he was able to rejoin his regiment in the spring, he left the garden, thinking was this indeed the first time he had ever turned his face toward the old colors with a woman's blessing!

He followed them—so ragged, so scarred and pierced now, that they would scarcely hold together—to Quatre Bras and Ligny. He stood beside them, in an awful stillness of many men, shadowy through the mist and drizzle of a wet June forenoon, on the field of

~ 302 ~

Waterloo. And down to that hour the picture in his mind of the French officer had never been compared with the reality.

The famous regiment was in action early in the battle, and received its first check in many an eventful year, when he was seen to fall. But it swept on to avenge him, and left behind it no such creature in the world of consciousness as Lieutenant Richard Doubledick.

Through pits of mire and pools of rain; along deep ditches, once roads, that were pounded and ploughed to pieces by artillery, heavy wagons, tramp of men and horses, and the struggle of every wheeled thing that could carry wounded soldiers; jolted among the dying and the dead, so disfigured by blood and mud as to be hardly recognizable for humanity; dead, as to any sentient life that was in it, and yet alive,—the form that had been Lieutenant Richard Doubledick, with whose praises England rang, was conveyed to Brussels. There it was tenderly laid down in hospital; and there it lay, week after week, through the long, bright summer days, until the harvest, spared by war, had ripened and was gathered in.

Slowly laboring, at last, through a long, heavy dream of confused time and place, presenting faint glimpses of army surgeons whom he knew, and of faces that had been familiar to his youth,—dearest and kindest among them, Mary Marshall's, with a solicitude upon it more like reality than anything he could discern,—Lieutenant Richard Doubledick came back to life. To the beautiful life of a calm autumn evening sunset, to the peaceful life of a fresh, quiet room with a large window standing open; a balcony beyond, in which were moving leaves and sweet-smelling flowers; beyond, again, the clear sky, with the sun full in his sight, pouring its golden radiance on his bed.

It was so tranquil and so lovely that he thought he had passed into another world. And he said in a faint voice, "Taunton, are you near me?"

A face bent over him. Not his, his mother's.

"I came to nurse you. We have nursed you many weeks. You were moved here long ago. Do you remember nothing?"

"Nothing."

The lady kissed his cheek, and held his hand, soothing him.

"Where is the regiment? What has happened? Let me call you mother. What has happened, mother?"

"A great victory, dear. The war is over, and the regiment was the bravest in the field."

His eyes kindled, his lips trembled, he sobbed, and the tears ran down his face. He was very weak, too weak to move his hand.

From that time, he recovered. Slowly, for he had been desperately wounded in the head, and had been shot in the body, but making some little advance every day. When he had gained sufficient strength to converse as he lay in bed, he soon began to remark that Mrs. Taunton always brought him back to his own history. Then he recalled his preserver's dying words, and thought, "It comforts her."

One day he awoke out of a sleep, refreshed, and asked her to read to him. But the curtain of the bed, softening the light, which she always drew back when he awoke, that she might see him from her table at the bedside where she sat at work, was held undrawn; and a woman's voice spoke, which was not hers.

"Can you bear to see a stranger?" it said softly. "Will you like to see a stranger?"

"Stranger!" he repeated. The voice awoke old memories, before the days of Private Richard Doubledick.

"A stranger now, but not a stranger once," it said in tones that thrilled him. "Richard, dear Richard, lost through so many years, my name—"

He cried out her name "Mary," and she held him in her arms, and his head lay on her bosom.

*　　*　　*　　*　　*

Well! They were happy. It was a long recovery, but they were happy through it all. The snow had melted on the ground, and the birds were singing in the leafless thickets of the early spring, when those three were first able to ride out together, and when people flocked about the open carriage to cheer and congratulate *Captain* Richard Doubledick.

But even then it became necessary for the Captain, instead of returning to England, to complete his recovery in the climate of Southern France. They found a spot upon the Rhône, within a ride of the old town of Avignon, and within view of its broken bridge, which was all they could desire; they lived there, together, six months; then returned to England. Mrs. Taunton, growing old after three years—though not so old as that her bright, dark eyes were dimmed—and remembering that her strength had been benefited by the change, resolved to go back for a year to those parts. So she went with a faithful servant, who had often carried her son in his arms; and she was to be rejoined and escorted home, at the year's end, by Captain Richard Doubledick.

She wrote regularly to her children (as she called them now), and they to her. She went to the neighborhood of Aix; and there, in their own château near the farmer's house she rented, she grew into intimacy with a family belonging to that part of France. The intimacy began in her often meeting among the vineyards a pretty child, a girl with a most compassionate heart, who was never tired of listening to the solitary English lady's stories of her poor son and the cruel wars. The family were as gentle as the child, and at length she came to know them so well that she accepted their invitation to pass the last month of her residence abroad under their roof. All this intelligence she wrote home, piecemeal as it came about, from time to time; and at last enclosed a polite note, from the head of the château, soliciting, on the occasion of his approaching mission to that neighborhood, the honor of the company of that man so justly celebrated, Captain Richard Doubledick.

Captain Doubledick, now a hardy, handsome man in the full vigor of life, broader across the chest and shoulders than he had ever been before, dispatched a courteous reply, and followed it in person. Traveling through all that extent of country after three years of peace, he blessed the better days on which the world had fallen. The corn was golden, not drenched in unnatural red; was bound in sheaves for food, not trodden underfoot by men in mortal fight. The smoke rose up from peaceful hearths, not blazing ruins. The carts were laden with the fair fruits of the earth, not with wounds and death. To him who had so often seen the terrible reverse, these things were beautiful indeed; and they brought him in a softened spirit to the old château near Aix upon a deep blue evening.

It was a large château of the genuine old ghostly kind, with round towers, and extinguishers, and a high leaden roof, and more windows than Aladdin's palace. The entrance doors stood open, as doors often do in that country when the heat of the day is past; and the Captain saw no bell or knocker, and walked in.

He walked into a lofty stone hall, refreshingly cool and gloomy after the glare of a Southern day's travel. Extending along the four sides of this hall was a gallery, leading to suites of rooms; and it was lighted from the top. Still no bell was to be seen.

"Faith," said the Captain, halting, ashamed of the clanking of his boots, "this is a ghostly beginning!"

He started back, and felt his face turn white. In the gallery, looking down at him, stood the French officer—the officer whose picture he had carried in his mind so long and so far. Compared with the original, at last—in every lineament how like it was!

He moved and disappeared, and Captain Richard Doubledick heard his steps coming quickly down into the hall. He entered through an archway. There was a bright, sudden look upon his face, much such a look as it had worn in that fatal moment.

Monsieur le Capitaine Richard Doubledick? Enchanted to receive him!

"He has not remembered me, as I have remembered him; he did not take such a note of my face, that day, as I took of his," thought Captain Richard Doubledick. "How shall I tell him?"

"You were at Waterloo," said the French officer.

"I was," said Captain Richard Doubledick. "And at Badajos."

Left alone with the sound of his own stern voice in his ears, he sat down to consider. What shall I do, and how shall I tell him? At that time, unhappily, many deplorable duels had been fought between English and French officers arising out of the recent war; and these duels, and how to avoid this officer's hospitality, were the uppermost thought in Captain Richard Doubledick's mind.

"His mother, above all," the Captain thought. "How shall I tell *her*?"

"Spirit of my departed friend," said he, "is it through thee these better thoughts are rising in my mind? Is it thou who hast shown me, all the way I have drawn to meet this man, the blessings of the altered time? Is it thou who hast sent thy [Pg 286] stricken mother to me, to stay my angry hand? Is it from thee the whisper comes, that this man did his duty as thou didst,—and as I did, through thy guidance, which has wholly saved me here on earth,—and that he did no more?"

He sat down, with his head buried in his hands, and, when he rose up, made the second strong resolution in his life,—that neither to the French officer, nor to the mother of his departed friend, nor to any soul, while either of the two was living, would he breathe what only he knew. And when he touched that French officer's glass with his own, that day at dinner, he secretly forgave him in the name of the Divine Forgiver of Injuries.

THE LEGEND OF THE CHRISTMAS TREE.

Most children have seen a Christmas tree, and many know that the pretty and pleasant custom of hanging gifts on its boughs comes from Germany; but perhaps few have heard or read the story that is told to little German children, respecting the origin of this custom. The story is called "The Little Stranger," and runs thus:

In a small cottage on the borders of a forest lived a poor laborer, who gained a scanty living by cutting wood. He had a wife and two children who helped him in his work. The boy's name was Valentine, and the girl was called Mary. They were obedient, good children, and a great comfort to their parents. One winter evening, this happy little family were sitting quietly round the hearth, the snow and the wind raging outside, while they ate their supper of dry bread, when a gentle tap was heard on the window, and a childish voice cried from without: "Oh, let me in, pray! I am a poor little child, with nothing to eat, and no home to go to, and I shall die of cold and hunger unless you let me in."

Valentine and Mary jumped up from the table and ran to open the door, saying: "Come in, poor little child! We have not much to give you, but whatever we have we will share with you."

The stranger-child came in and warmed his frozen hands and feet at the fire, and the children gave him the best they had to eat, saying: "You must be tired, too, poor child! Lie down on our bed; we can sleep on the bench for one night."

Then said the little stranger-child: "Thank God for all your kindness to me!"

So they took their little guest into their sleeping-room, laid him on the bed, covered him over, and said to each other: "How thankful we ought to be! We have warm rooms and a cozy bed, while this poor child has only heaven for his roof and the cold earth for his sleeping-place."

When their father and mother went to bed, Mary and Valentine lay quite contentedly on the bench near the fire, saying, before they fell asleep: "The stranger-child will be so happy to-night in his warm bed!"

These kind children had not slept many hours before Mary awoke and softly whispered to her brother: "Valentine, dear, wake, and listen to the sweet music under the window."

Then Valentine rubbed his eyes and listened. It was sweet music indeed, and sounded like beautiful voices singing to the tones of a harp:

"O holy Child, we greet thee! bringing

Sweet strains of harp to aid our singing.

"Thou, holy Child, in peace art sleeping,

While we our watch without are keeping.

"Blest be the house wherein thou liest.

Happiest on earth, to heaven the highest."

The children listened, while a solemn joy filled their hearts; then they stepped softly to the window to see who might be without.

In the east was a streak of rosy dawn, and in its light they saw a group of children standing before the house, clothed in silver garments, holding golden harps in their hands. Amazed at this sight, the children were still gazing out of the window, when a light tap caused them to turn round. There stood the stranger-child before them clad in a golden dress, with a gleaming radiance round his curling hair. "I am the little Christ-child," he said, "who wanders through the world bringing peace and happiness to good children. You took me in and cared for me when you thought me a poor child, and now you shall have my blessing for what you have done."

A fir tree grew near the house; and from this he broke a twig, which he planted in the ground, saying: "This twig shall become a tree, and shall bring forth fruit year by year for you."

No sooner had he done this than he vanished, and with him the little choir of angels. But the fir-branch grew and became a Christmas tree, and on its branches hung golden apples and silver nuts every Christmas-tide.

Such is the story told to German children concerning their beautiful Christmas trees, though we know that the real little Christ-child can never be wandering, cold and homeless, again in our world, inasmuch as he is safe in heaven by his Father's side; yet we may gather from this story the same truth which the Bible plainly tells us—that any one who helps a Christian child in distress, it will be counted unto him as if he had indeed done it unto Christ himself. "Inasmuch as ye have done it unto the least of these my brethren, ye have done it unto me."

THE PEACE EGG.

BY JULIANA HORATIA EWING.

Every one ought to be happy at Christmas. But there are many things which ought to be, and yet are not; and people are sometimes sad even in the Christmas holidays.

The Captain and his wife were sad, though it was Christmas Eve. Sad, though they were in the prime of life, blessed with good health, devoted to each other and to their children, with competent means, a comfortable house on a little freehold property of their own, and, one might say, everything that heart could desire. Sad, though they were good people, whose peace of mind had a firmer foundation than their earthly goods alone; contented people, too, with plenty of occupation for mind and body. Sad—and in the nursery this was held to be past all reason—though the children were performing that ancient and most entertaining play or Christmas mystery, known as "The Peace Egg," for their benefit and behoof alone.

The play was none the worse that most of the actors were too young to learn parts, so that there was very little of the rather tedious dialogue, only plenty of dress and ribbons, and of fighting with the wooden swords. But though Robert, the eldest of the five children, looked bonny enough to warm any father's heart, as he marched up and down with an air learned by watching many a parade in barrack-square and drill ground, and though Nicholas did not cry in spite of falling hard, and Dora, who took the part of the Doctor, treading accidentally on his little finger in picking him up, still the Captain and his wife sighed nearly as often as they smiled, and the mother dropped tears as well as pennies into the cap which Tom, as the King of Egypt, brought round after the performance.

II.

Many, many years back the Captain's wife had been a child herself, and had laughed to see the village mummers act "The Peace Egg," and had been quite happy on Christmas Eve. Happy, though she had no mother. Happy, though her father was a stern man, very fond of his only child, but with an obstinate will that not even she dared thwart. She had lived to thwart it, and he had never forgiven her. It was when she married the Captain. The old man had a prejudice against soldiers, which was quite reason enough, in his opinion, for his daughter to sacrifice the happiness of her future life by giving up the soldier she loved. At last he gave her her choice between the Captain and his own favor and money. She chose the Captain, and was disowned and disinherited.

The Captain bore a high character, and was a good and clever officer, but that went for nothing against the old man's whim. He made a very good husband too; but even this did not move his father-in-law, who had never held any intercourse with him or his wife since the day of their marriage, and who had never seen his own grand-children.

Amid the ups and downs of their wanderings, the discomforts of shipboard and of stations in the colonies, bad servants, and unwonted sicknesses, the Captain's tenderness never failed. If the life was rough the Captain was ready. He had been, by turns, in one strait or another, sick-nurse, doctor, carpenter, nursemaid and cook to his family, and had, moreover, an idea that nobody filled these offices quite so well as himself. Withal, his very profession kept him neat, well-dressed, and active. In the roughest of their ever-changing quarters he was a smart man, and never changed his manner from that of the lover of his wife's young days.

As years went and children came, the Captain and his wife grew tired of traveling. New scenes were small comfort when they heard of the death of old friends. One foot of the dear, old, dull home sky was dearer, after all, than miles of the unclouded heavens of the South. The grey hills and over-grown lanes of her old home haunted the Captain's wife by night and day, and home-sickness (that weariest of all sicknesses) began to take the light out of her eyes before their time. It preyed upon the Captain too. Now and then he would say, fretfully, "I *should* like a resting-place in our own country, however small, before *everybody* is dead! But the children's prospects have to be considered." The continued estrangement from the old man was an abiding sorrow also, and they had hopes that, if only they could get home, he might be persuaded to peace and charity this time.

At last they were sent home. But the hard old father still would not relent. He returned their letters unopened. This bitter disappointment made the Captain's wife so ill that she almost died, and in one month the Captain's hair became iron gray. He reproached himself for having ever taken the daughter from her father, "to kill her at last," as he said. And (thinking of his own children) he even reproached himself for having robbed the old widower of his only child. After two years at home his regiment was ordered again on foreign duty. He failed to effect an exchange, and they prepared to move once more—from Chatham to Calcutta. Never before had the packing to which she was so well accustomed, been so bitter a task to the Captain's wife.

It was at the darkest hour of this gloomy time that the Captain came in, waving above his head a letter which changed all their plans.

Now close by the old home of the Captain's wife there had lived a man, much older than herself, who yet had loved her with a devotion as great as that of the young Captain. She never knew it, for when he saw that she had given her heart to his younger rival, he kept silence, and he never asked for what he knew he might have had—the old man's authority in his favor. So generous was the affection which he could never conquer, that he constantly tried to reconcile the father to his children whilst he lived, and, when he died, he bequeathed his house and small estate to the woman he had loved.

"It will be a legacy of peace," he thought, on his death bed. "The old man cannot hold out when she and her children are constantly in sight. And it may please God that I shall know of the reunion I have not been permitted to see with my eyes."

And thus it came about that the Captain's regiment went to India without him, and that the Captain's wife and her father lived on opposite sides of the same road.

III.

The eldest of the Captain's children was a boy. He was named Robert, after his grandfather, and seemed to have inherited a good deal of the old gentleman's character, mixed with gentler traits. He was a fair, fine boy, tall and stout for his age, with the Captain's regular features, and (he flattered himself) the Captain's firm step and martial bearing. He was apt—like his grandfather—to hold his own will to be other people's law, and (happily for the peace of the nursery) this opinion was devoutly shared by his brother Nicholas. Though the Captain had left the army, Robin continued to command an irregular force of volunteers in the nursery, and never was colonel more despotic. His brothers and sisters were by turn infantry, cavalry, engineers, and artillery, according to his whim.

The Captain alone was a match for his strong-willed son.

"If you please, sir," said Sarah, one morning, flouncing in upon the Captain, just as he was about to start for the neighboring town,—"If you please, sir, I wish you'd speak to Master Robert. He's past my powers."

"I've no doubt of it," thought the Captain, but he only said, "Well, what's the matter?"

"Night after night do I put him to bed," said Sarah, "and night after night does he get up as soon as I'm out of the room, and says he's orderly officer for the evening, and goes about in his night-shirt and his feet as bare as boards."

The Captain fingered his heavy moustache to hide a smile, but he listened patiently to Sarah's complaints.

"It ain't so much *him* I should mind, sir," she continued, "but he goes round the beds and wakes up the other young gentlemen and Miss Dora, one after another, and when I speak to him, he gives me all the sauce he can lay his tongue to, and says he's going round the guards. The other night I tried to put him back in his bed, but he got away and ran all over the house, me hunting him everywhere, and not a sign of him, till he jumps out on me from the garret stairs and nearly knocks me down. 'I've visited the outposts, Sarah,' says he; 'all's well.' And off he goes to bed as bold as brass."

"Have you spoken to your mistress?" asked the Captain.

"Yes, sir," said Sarah. "And missis spoke to him, and he promised not to go round the guards again."

"Has he broken his promise?" asked the Captain, with a look of anger, and also of surprise.

"When I opened the door last night, sir," continued Sarah, in her shrill treble, "what should I see in the dark but Master Robert a-walking up and down with the carpet-brush stuck in his arm. 'Who goes there?' says he. 'You awdacious boy!' says I, 'Didn't you promise your ma you'd leave off them tricks?' 'I'm not going round the guards,' says he; 'I promised not. But I'm for sentry-duty to-night.' And say what I would to him, all he had for me was, 'You mustn't speak to a sentry on duty.' So I says, 'As sure as I live till morning, I'll go to your pa,' for he pays no more attention to his ma than to me, nor to any one else."

"Please to see that the bed is taken out of my dressing-room," said the Captain. "I will attend to Master Robert."

With this Sarah had to content herself, and she went back to the nursery. Robert was nowhere to be seen, and made no reply to her summons. On this the unwary nursemaid flounced into the bed-room to look for him, when Robert, who was hidden beneath a table, darted forth, and promptly locked her in.

"You're under arrest," he shouted, through the keyhole.

"Let me out!" shrieked Sarah.

"I'll send a file of the guard to fetch you to the orderly-room, by-and-by," said Robert, "for 'preferring frivolous complaints.'" And he departed to the farmyard to look at the ducks.

That night, when Robert went up to bed, the Captain quietly locked him into his dressing-room, from which the bed had been removed.

"You're for sentry duty, to-night," said the Captain. "The carpet-brush is in the corner. Good-evening."

As his father anticipated, Robert was soon tired of the sentry game in these new circumstances, and long before the night had half worn away he wished himself safely undressed and in his own comfortable bed. At half-past twelve o'clock he felt as if he could bear it no longer, and knocked at the Captain's door.

"Who goes there?" said the Captain.

"Mayn't I go to bed, please?" whined poor Robert.

"Certainly not," said the Captain. "You're on duty."

And on duty poor Robert had to remain, for the Captain had a will as well as his son. So he rolled himself up in his father's railway rug, and slept on the floor.

The next night he was very glad to go quietly to bed, and remain there.

IV.

The Captain's children sat at breakfast in a large, bright nursery.
It was the room where the old bachelor had died, and
now *her* children made it merry. This was just what he would have
wished.

They all sat round the table, for it was breakfast-time. There were
five of them, and five bowls of boiled bread-and-milk smoked
before them. Sarah (a foolish, gossiping girl, who acted as nurse
till better could be found) was waiting on them, and by the table
sat Darkie, the black retriever, his long, curly back swaying
slightly from the difficulty of holding himself up, and his
solemn hazel eyes fixed very intently on each and all of the
breakfast bowls. He was as silent and sagacious as Sarah was
talkative and empty-headed. Though large, he was unassuming.
Pax, the pug, on the contrary, who came up to the first joint of
Darkie's leg, stood defiantly on his dignity (and his short
stumps). He always placed himself in front of the bigger dog, and
made a point of hustling him in doorways and of going first
downstairs.

Robert's tongue was seldom idle, even at meals. "Sarah, who is
that tall old gentleman at church, in the seat near the pulpit?" he
asked. "He wears a cloak like what the Blues wear, only all blue,
and is tall enough for a Life-guardsman. He stood when we were
kneeling down, and said, *Almighty and most merciful Father*,
louder than anybody."

Sarah knew who the old gentleman was, and knew also that the
children did not know, and that their parents did not see fit to tell
them as yet. But she had a passion for telling and hearing news,
and would rather gossip with a child than not gossip at all. "Never
you mind, Master Robin," she said, nodding sagaciously. "Little
boys aren't to know everything."

"Ah, then, I know you don't know," replied Robert; "if you did, you'd tell."

"I do," said Sarah.

"You don't," said Robin.

"Your ma's forbid you to contradict, Master Robin," said Sarah; "and if you do I shall tell her. I know well enough who the old gentleman is, and perhaps I might tell you, only you'd go straight off and tell again."

"No, no, I wouldn't!" shouted Robin. "I can keep a secret, indeed I can! Pinch my little finger, and try. Do, do tell me, Sarah, there's a dear Sarah, and then I shall know you know." And he danced round her, catching at her skirts.

To keep a secret was beyond Sarah's powers.

"Do let my dress be, Master Robin," she said, "you're ripping out all the gathers, and listen while I whisper. As sure as you're a living boy, that gentleman's your own grandpapa."

Robin lost his hold on Sarah's dress; his arms fell by his side, and he stood with his brows knit for some minutes, thinking. Then he said, emphatically, "What lies you do tell, Sarah!"

"Oh, Robin!" cried Nicholas, who had drawn near, his thick curls standing stark with curiosity, "Mamma said 'lies' wasn't a proper word, and you promised not to say it again."

"I forgot," said Robin, "I didn't mean to break my promise. But she does tell—ahem!—*you know what.*"

~ 321 ~

"You wicked boy!" cried the enraged Sarah; "how dare you say such a thing, and everybody in the place knows he's your ma's own pa."

"I'll go and ask her," said Robin, and he was at the door in a moment; but Sarah, alarmed by the thought of getting into a scrape herself, caught him by the arm.

"Don't you go, love; it'll only make your ma angry. There; it was all my nonsense."

"Then it's not true?" said Robin, indignantly. "What did you tell me so for?"

"It was all my jokes and nonsense," said the unscrupulous Sarah, "But your ma wouldn't like to know I've said such a thing. And Master Robert wouldn't be so mean as to tell tales, would he, love?"

"I'm not mean," said Robin stoutly; "and I don't tell tales; but you do, and you tell *you know what*, besides. However, I won't go this time; but I'll tell you what—if you tell tales of me to papa any more, I'll tell him what you said about the old gentleman in the blue cloak." With which parting threat Robin strode off to join his brothers and sisters.

V.

After Robert left the nursery he strolled out of doors, and, peeping through the gate at the end of the drive, he saw a party of boys going through what looked like a military exercise with sticks and a good deal of stamping; but, instead of mere words of command, they all spoke by turns, as in a play. Not being at all shy, he joined them, and asked so many questions that he soon got to know all about it. They were practicing a Christmas mumming-play, called "The Peace Egg." Why it was called thus they could not tell him, as there was nothing whatever about eggs in it, and so far from being a play of peace, it was made up of a series of battles between certain valiant knights and princes. The rehearsal being over, Robin went with the boys to the sexton's house (he was father to one of the characters called the "King of Egypt") where they showed him the dresses they were to wear. These were made of gay-colored materials, and covered with ribbons, except that of the "Black Prince of Paradine," which was black, as became his title. The boys also showed him the book from which they learned their parts, and which was to be bought at the post-office store.

"Then are you the mummers who come round at Christmas, and act in people's kitchens, and people give them money, that mamma used to tell us about?" said Robin.

The boy hesitated a moment and then said, "Well, I suppose we are."

"And do you go out in the snow from one house to another at night; and oh, don't you enjoy it?" cried Robin.

"We like it well enough," the lad admitted.

Robin bought a copy of "The Peace Egg." He was resolved to have a nursery performance, and to take the chief part himself. The others were willing for what he wished, but there were difficulties. In the first place, there are eight characters in the play, and there were only five children. They decided among themselves to leave out the "Fool," and Mamma said that another character was not to be acted by any of them, or indeed mentioned; "the little one who comes in at the end," Robin explained. Mamma had her reasons, and these were always good. She had not been altogether pleased that Robin had bought the play. It was a very old thing, she said, and very queer; not adapted for a child's play. If Mamma thought the parts not quite fit for the children to learn, they found them much too long: so in the end she picked out some bits for each, which they learned easily, and which, with a good deal of fighting, made quite as good a story of it as if they had done the whole. What may have been wanting otherwise was made up for by the dresses, which were charming.

Robin was St. George, Nicholas the valiant Slasher, Dora the Doctor, and the other two Hector and the King of Egypt. "And now we've no Black Prince!" cried Robin in dismay.

"Let Darkie be the Black Prince," said Nicholas.

"When you wave your stick he'll jump for it, and then you can pretend to fight with him."

"It's not a stick, it's a sword," said Robin.

"However, Darkie may be the Black Prince."

"And what's Pax to be?" asked Dora; "for you know he will come if Darkie does, and he'll run in before everybody else too."

"Then he must be the Fool," said Robin, "and it will do very well, for the Fool comes in before the rest, and Pax can have his red coat on, and the collar with the little bells."

———————

VI.

Robin thought that Christmas would never come. To the Captain and his wife it seemed to come too fast. They had hoped it might bring reconciliation with the old man, but it seemed they had hoped in vain.

There were times now when the Captain almost regretted the old bachelor's bequest. The familiar scenes of her old home sharpened his wife's grief. To see her father every Sunday in church, with marks of age and infirmity upon him, but with not a look of tenderness for his only child, this tried her sorely.

"She felt it less abroad," thought the Captain. "A home in which she frets herself to death, is after all, no great boon."

Christmas Eve came.

"I'm sure it's quite Christmas enough now," said Robin. "We'll have 'The Peace Egg' to-night."

So as the Captain and his wife sat sadly over their fire, the door opened, and Pax ran in shaking his bells, and followed by the nursery mummers. The performance was most successful. It was by no means pathetic, and yet, as has been said, the Captain's wife shed tears.

"What is the matter, mamma?" said Robert, abruptly dropping his sword and running up to her.

"Don't tease mamma with questions," said the Captain; "she is not very well, and rather sad. We must all be very kind and good to poor dear mamma;" and the Captain raised his wife's hand to his lips as he spoke. Robin seized the other hand and kissed it tenderly. He was very fond of his mother. At this moment Pax took a little run, and jumped on to mamma's lap, where, sitting facing the company, he opened his black mouth and yawned, with a ludicrous inappropriateness worthy of any clown. It made everybody laugh.

"And now we'll go and act in the kitchen," said Nicholas.

"Supper at nine o'clock, remember," shouted the Captain. "And we are going to have real frumenty and Yule cakes, such as mamma used to tell us of when we were abroad."

"Hurray!" shouted the mummers, and they ran off, Pax leaping from his seat just in time to hustle the Black Prince in the doorway. When the dining-room door was shut, Robert raised his hand, and said "Hush!"

The mummers pricked their ears, but there was only a distant harsh and scraping sound, as of stones rubbed together.

"They're cleaning the passages," Robert went on, "and Sarah told me they meant to finish the mistletoe, and have everything cleaned up by supper-time. They don't want us, I know. Look here, we'll go *real mumming* instead. That *will* be fun!"

Nicholas grinned with delight.

"But will mamma let us?" he enquired.

"Oh, it will be all right if we're back by supper-time," said Robert, hastily. "Only of course we must take care not to catch cold. Come and help me to get some wraps."

The old oak chest in which spare shawls, rugs, and coats were kept was soon ransacked, and the mummers' gay dresses hidden by motley wrappers. But no sooner did Darkie and Pax behold the

coats, etc., than they at once began to leap and bark, as it was
their custom to do when they saw any one dressing to go out.
Robin was sorely afraid that this would betray them; but though
the Captain and his wife heard the barking they did not guess the
cause.

So the front door being very gently opened and closed, the
nursery mummers stole away.

VII.

It was a very fine night. The snow was well-trodden on the drive, so that it did not wet their feet, but on the trees and shrubs it hung soft and white.

"It's much jollier being out at night than in the daytime," said Robin.

"Much," responded Nicholas, with intense feeling.

"We'll go a wassailing next week," said Robin. "I know all about it, and perhaps we shall get a good lot of money, and then we'll buy tin swords with scabbards for next year. I don't like these sticks. Oh, dear, I wish it wasn't so long between one Christmas and another."

"Where shall we go first?" asked Nicholas, as they turned into the high road.

"This is the first house," he said. "We'll act here;" and all pressed in as quickly as possible. Once safe within the grounds, they shouldered their sticks, and marched with composure.

"You're going to the front door," said Nicholas. "Mummers ought to go to the back."

"We don't know where it is," said Robin, and he rang the front-door bell. There was a pause. Then lights shone, steps were heard, and at last a sound of much unbarring, unbolting, and unlocking. It might have been a prison. Then the door was opened by an elderly, timid-looking woman, who held a tallow candle above her head.

"Who's there?" she said, "at this time of night."

"We're Christmas mummers," said Robin, stoutly; "we didn't know the way to the back door, but——"

"And don't you know better than to come here?" said the woman. "Be off with you, as fast as you can."

"You're only the servant," said Robin. "Go and ask your master and mistress if they wouldn't like to see us act. We do it very well."

"You impudent boy, be off with you!" repeated the woman. "Master'd no more let you nor any other such rubbish set foot in this house——"

"Woman!" shouted a voice close behind her, which made her start as if she had been shot, "who authorizes you to say what your master will or will not do, before you've asked him? The boy is right. You *are* the servant, and it is not your business to choose for me whom I shall or shall not see."

"I meant no harm, sir, I'm sure," said the housekeeper; "but I thought you'd never——"

"My good woman," said her master, "if I had wanted somebody to think for me, you're the last person I should have employed. I hire you to obey orders, not to think."

"I'm sure, sir," said the housekeeper, whose only form of argument was reiteration, "I never thought you would have seen them——"

"Then you were wrong," shouted her master. "I will see them. Bring them in."

He was a tall, gaunt old man, and Robin stared at him for some minutes, wondering where he could have seen somebody very like him. At last he remembered. It was the old gentleman of the blue cloak.

The children threw off their wraps, the housekeeper helping them, and chattering ceaselessly, from sheer nervousness.

"Well, to be sure," said she, "their dresses are pretty, too. And they seem quite a better sort of children, they talk quite genteel. I might ha' knowed they weren't like common mummers, but I was so flusterated hearing the bell go so late, and——"

"Are they ready?" said the old man, who had[Pg 305] stood like a ghost in the dim light of the flaring tallow candle, grimly watching the proceedings.

"Yes, sir. Shall I take them to the kitchen, sir?"

"——for you and the other idle hussies to gape and grin at? No. Bring them to the library," he snapped, and then stalked off, leading the way.

The housekeeper accordingly led them to the library, and then withdrew, nearly falling on her face as she left the room by stumbling over Darkie, who slipped in last like a black shadow.

The old man was seated in a carved oak chair by the fire.

"I never said the dogs were to come in," he said.

"But we can't do without them, please," said Robin, boldly. "You see there are eight people in 'The Peace Egg,' and there are only five of us; and so Darkie has to be the Black Prince, and Pax has to be the Fool, and so we have to have them."

~ 331 ~

"Five and two make seven," said the old man, with a grim smile; "what do you do for the eighth?"

"Oh, that's the little one at the end," said Robin, confidently. "Mamma said we weren't to mention him, but I think that's because we're children.—You're grown up, you know, so I'll show you the book, and you can see for yourself," he went on, drawing "The Peace Egg" from his pocket: "there, that's the picture of him, on the last page; black, with horns and a tail."

The old man's stern face relaxed into a broad smile as he examined the grotesque woodcut; but when he turned to the first page the smile vanished in a deep frown, and his eyes shone like hot coals with anger. He had seen Robin's name.

"Who sent you here?" he asked, in a hoarse voice. "Speak, and speak the truth! Did your mother send you here?"

Robin thought the old man was angry with them for playing truant. He said, slowly, "N—no. She didn't exactly send us; but I don't think she'll mind our having come if we get back in time for supper. Mamma never *forbid* our going mumming, you know."

"I don't suppose she ever thought of it," Nicholas said candidly, wagging his curly head from side to side.

"She knows we're mummers," said Robin, "for she helped us. When we were abroad, you know, she used to tell us about the mummers acting at Christmas, when she was a little girl; and so we thought we'd be mummers, and so we acted to papa and mamma, and so we thought we'd act to the maids, but they were cleaning the passages, and so we thought we'd really go mumming; and we've got several other houses to go to before supper-time; we'd better begin, I think," said Robin; and without more ado he began to march round and round, raising his sword, and the performance went off quite as creditably as before.

As the children acted the old man's anger wore off. He watched them with an interest he could not repress. When Nicholas took some hard thwacks from Robert without flinching, the old man clapped his hands; and after the encounter was over, he said he would not have had the dogs excluded on any consideration. It was just at the end, when they were all marching round and round, holding on by each other's swords "over the shoulder," and singing "A mumming we will go, etc.," that Nicholas suddenly brought the circle to a stand-still by stopping dead short, and staring up at the wall before him.

"What *are* you stopping for?" said Robert, turning indignantly around.

"Look there!" cried Nicholas, pointing to a little painting which hung above the old man's head.

Robin looked, and said abruptly, "It's Dora."

"Which is Dora?" asked the old man in a strange, sharp tone.

"Here she is," said Robin and Nicholas in one breath, as they dragged her forward.

"She's the Doctor," said Robin, "and you can't see her face for her things. Dor, take off your cap and pull back that hood. There! Oh, it *is* like her!"

It was the portrait of her mother as a child; but of this the nursery mummers knew nothing. The old man looked as the peaked cap and hood fell away from Dora's face and fair curls, and then he uttered a sharp cry, and buried his head upon his hands. The boys stood stupefied, but Dora ran up to him, and putting her little hands on his arms, said, in childish pitying tones, "Oh, I am so sorry! Have you got a headache? May Robin put the shovel in the fire for you? Mamma has hot shovels for her headaches." And though the old man did not speak or move, she went on coaxing him, and stroking his head, on which the hair was white. At this moment Pax took one of his unexpected runs, and jumped on to the old man's knee, in his own particular fashion, and then yawned at the company. The old man was startled, and lifted his face suddenly. It was wet with tears.

"Why, you're crying!" exclaimed the children with one breath.

"It's very odd," said Robin, fretfully. "I can't think what's the matter to-night. Mamma was crying too when we were acting, and papa said we weren't to tease her with questions, and he kissed her hand, and I kissed her hand too. And papa said we must all be very good and kind to poor dear mamma, and so I mean to be, she's so good. And I think we'd better go home, or perhaps she'll be frightened," Robin added.

"She's so good, is she?" asked the old man. He had put Pax off his knee, and taken Dora on to it.

"Oh, isn't she!" said Nicholas, swaying his curly head from side to side as usual.

"She's always good," said Robin, emphatically; "and so's papa. But I'm always doing something I oughtn't to," he added, slowly. "But then, you know, I don't pretend to obey Sarah. I don't care a fig for Sarah; and I won't obey any woman but mamma."

"Who's Sarah?" asked the grandfather.

"She's our nurse," said Robin, "and she tells—I mustn't say what she tells—but it's not the truth. She told one about *you* the other day," he added.

"About me?" said the old man.

"She said you were our grandpapa. So then I knew she was telling *you know what.*"

"How did you know it wasn't true?" the old man asked.

"Why, of course," said Robin, "if you were our mamma's father, you'd know her, and be very fond of her, and come to see her. And then you'd be our grandfather, too, and you'd have us to see you, and perhaps give us Christmas-boxes. I wish you were," Robin added with a sigh. "It would be very nice."

"Would *you* like it?" asked the old man of Dora.

And Dora, who was half asleep and very comfortable, put her little arms about his neck as she was wont to put them around the Captain's, and said, "Very much."

He put her down at last, very tenderly, almost unwillingly, and left the children alone. By-and-by he returned, dressed in the blue cloak, and took Dora up again.

"I will see you home," he said.

The children had not been missed. The clock had only just struck nine when there came a knock[Pg 309] on the door of the dining-room, where the Captain and his wife still sat by the Yule log. She said "Come in," wearily, thinking it was the frumenty and the Christmas cakes.

But it was her father, with her child in his arms!

———————————

VIII.

The Captain had many friends who knew of the sad estrangement between his wife and her father. Some of them were in church the next day, which was Christmas Day, when the Captain's wife came in. They would have hid their faces, but for the startling sight that met the gaze of the congregation. The old grandfather walked into church abreast of the Captain.

"They've met in the porch," whispered one under the shelter of his hat.

"They can't quarrel publicly in a place of worship," said another, turning pale.

"She's gone into his seat," cried a girl in a shrill whisper.

"And the children after her," added her sister, incautiously aloud.

There was now no doubt about the matter. The old man in his blue cloak stood for a few moments politely disputing the question of precedence with his handsome son-in-law. Then the Captain bowed and passed in, and the old man followed him.

By the time that the service was ended everybody knew of the happy peacemaking, and was glad. One old friend after another came up with blessings and good wishes. This was a proper Christmas, indeed, they said. There was a general rejoicing.

But only the grandfather and his children knew that it was hatched from "The Peace Egg."

End of the book.